Banking and Securities Regulation
in the Netherlands

Dutch Business Law

The series Dutch Business Law is a continuous publication in loose-leaf form under the editorial supervision of Steven R. Schuit, a former partner of Allen & Overy and professor of law at Utrecht University and at Nyenrode Business University.

This current publication is a bound edition of the series previously published in loose-leaf form.

The purpose of Dutch Business Law is to provide a good understanding of the practical implications of the relevant areas in Dutch law under consideration. The authors are seasoned practitioners, experienced in representing international clients in the Dutch legal arena.

This series makes no pretence at being a survey of the entire Dutch business law – either in scope or in substance. It contains generalisations and simplifications and cannot be regarded as presenting complete and in depth advice in the areas covered.

KLUWER LAW INTERNATIONAL

Banking and Securities Regulation in the Netherlands

By

Bas Jennen and Niels van de Vijver

Wolters Kluwer
Law & Business

AUSTIN   BOSTON   CHICAGO   NEW YORK   THE NETHERLANDS

Published by:
Kluwer Law International
P.O. Box 85889
2508 CN The Hague
The Netherlands
E-mail: sales@kluwerlaw.com
Website: http://www.kluwerlaw.com

Sold and distributed in North, Central and South America by:
Aspen Publishers, Inc.
7201 McKinney Circle
Frederick, MD 21704
USA
E-mail: customer.service@aspenpublishers.com

Sold and distributed in all other countries by:
Extenza-Turpin Distribution Services
Stratton Business Park
Pegasus Drive
Biggleswade
Bedfordshire SG18 8TQ
United Kingdom
E-mail: sales@kluwer.com

Printed on acid-free paper.

ISBN 978-90-411-2863-8

Foreword

This book was written in turbulent times. In many ways, writing it was the natural consequence of the introduction of the Dutch Financial Supervision Act in 2007. This Act aimed to consolidate and modernise previously existing legislation in the areas of banking, insurance, capital markets and consumer finance. The idea of the Act was to abandon, at least from a regulatory point of view, the sectoral approach that the regulators had previously adopted with respect to the various players in the financial markets, and to formulate, to the extent practically feasible, principle-based (rather than rule-based) rules which would apply across the board. The implementing regulations were designed to provide more detailed rules, fine-tuned to deal with the specific characteristics of the markets and their participants. The result has been that this Act and its implementing regulations now provide a modern, highly sophisticated and rather complex regulatory framework, within which the implementing provisions of the various European Directives should relatively easily be able to find their place. There are now some 20 EU Directives relevant to the Dutch financial regulatory climate, so that it may be more accurate by and large to state that the Act is a "vehicle" for implementing EU Directives rather than being Dutch legislation per se.

At the time of the introduction of the Act, the hope and expectation was that this huge legislative exercise would be the beginning of a period of relative calm on the regulatory front. It was of course recognised that there were still a few European directives, notably MiFID and the Transparency Directive, that needed to be implemented in Holland, and that in reality regulation of the financial markets is a neverending task. But the seismic subsequent events, both on a global scale and locally in the Netherlands, proved this hope and expectation to be groundless. The Netherlands was relatively more vulnerable to these events because of the disproportionately large size and international reach of its financial institutions. The takeover of ABN AMRO Bank by the RBS, Santander and Fortis consortium was the first of these events. This takeover has led to some serious soul-searching as to the powers of government and supervisory authorities in ensuring that the interests of all stakeholders are properly protected. This dramatic transaction was soon followed by the near-collapse of Fortis Bank Nederland and the ensuing takeover of this bank by the Dutch State. The credit crisis was by then raging and nearing its peak, and the ensuing support that the Dutch government felt should be provided to ING, Aegon, ABN AMRO Bank and SNS had dramatically changed the Dutch financial landscape. The EU rules and requirements on the consequences of this State support are now substantially contributing to this dramatic change, as is the now apparently general perception that the "bancassurance" model that Dutch institutions in the past embraced with some enthusiasm seems no longer effectively workable or in any event out of favour. There is as yet much uncertainty, both in Brussels and in Holland, as to what the ideal regulatory requirements are for financial institutions in terms of structure, solvency and liquidity. On top of all this, the collapse of two small banks, first Van Der Hoop and more recently DSB, as well as the effect in Holland of the demise of the Icelandic banks, raised serious questions as to the efficacy of Dutch (and indeed European) bank insolvency rules and the efficiency of the supervisory authorities in applying these rules.

All these developments have led to much uncertainty, and will undoubtedly lead to further changes in the regulatory environment, largely prompted by Brussels. But the sophisticated framework of the Act and its implementing regulations will remain in place. This book is the first attempt in the Netherlands to provide an in-depth overview of the rules governing the banking and the securities sector in the Netherlands. It accordingly provides a unique insight into the Dutch regulatory system. The two authors are experts in this field and have been actively and directly involved, as practitioners, in the events described above, and this naturally has substantively contributed to the quality and usability of this book. Of course, as their colleague, I am biased. But I genuinely believe this book to be a very useful addition indeed to the scarce literature on this topic.

The Act and its implementing regulations provide a complex set of rules, which, perhaps inevitably, is not very accessible or user-friendly. I would hope and expect that this book will help the reader not only in understanding the system, but also in finding his or her way in this vast but fascinating maze.

Prof. Mr Victor de Serière

Table of Contents

Chapter 2
Securities Regulation   **107**

Preface

In the past two decades, Netherlands financial regulation has been one of the fastest changing areas of the law, with supervisory authorities such as the Ministry of Finance, the Authority for the Financial Markets (AFM) and the Dutch Central Bank (DNB) having to constantly adjust the regulatory environment to bring it in line with the latest market developments. In addition, an impressive amount of new legislation has been and is still being produced at EU level and this requires continuing local implementation. The recent financial crisis is expected to lead to yet another wave of EU and international legislation which may mean that this publication can be expected to become out of date relatively quickly. The reader should therefore be aware that the law in this area is still constantly changing and that this work reflects the laws and regulations as stated at the time of writing.

This publication contains a summary of the most important Netherlands banking and securities laws and regulations and does not pretend to give an exhaustive and detailed overview thereof. Its primary aim is to give the non-Dutch reader an insight into the basic structure and concepts of this abstract and sometimes complicated area of the law. Only few English language publications have appeared on the issues dealt with herein and hopefully this work can be a small contribution to a better comprehension of Netherlands financial law.

This publication is a joint effort of two lawyers of the Amsterdam office of Allen & Overy LLP. Bas Jennen, a senior associate specialising in Financial Regulation in the Litigation Department, is responsible for Chapter 1 and Niels van de Vijver, a partner and head of the office's International Capital Markets team, is responsible for Chapter 2. We would like to thank our colleagues who have assisted with the drafting and review of this book. In particular, we would like to thank Victor de Serière and Ali Anakhrouch for their help with Chapter 1 and Ellen Cramer-De Jong and Joost Elsenburg for their help with Chapter 2.

We have stated the law as at 1 June 2010, although coverage is included of a limited number of provisions not yet in force at that date.

Niels van de Vijver
Bas Jennen
Amsterdam, July 2010

Chapter 1
Banking Regulation

1.   GENERAL INTRODUCTION

1.1   The Dutch Regulatory Framework

The Dutch banking regulation is included in the Financial Supervision Act (*Wet op het financieel toezicht* or **WFT**). The WFT came into force on 1 January 2007, replacing seven then existing financial supervision acts. This completed the reform of the financial supervision legislation in the Netherlands. The intention behind the WFT was to anchor the new cross-sectoral functional approach within the Dutch supervisory system. This functional approach has replaced the traditional sectoral approach. Until 1 January 2007, the Credit Supervision Act 1992 (*Wet toezicht kredietwezen 1992*) formed the legal basis for banking supervision in the Netherlands. The supervision of financial institutions pursuant to the WFT rests with the Dutch Central Bank (*De Nederlandsche Bank* or **DNB**) and the Netherlands Authority for the Financial Markets (*Autoriteit Financiële Markten* or **AFM**). DNB is responsible for prudential supervision and the AFM has been allocated the task of supervision of the conduct of business of financial undertakings. The purpose of prudential supervision is to ensure the solidity of financial undertakings and contribute to the stability of the financial sector.[1] The AFM's conduct of business supervision focuses on ensuring orderly and transparent financial market processes, integrity in relations between market parties and due care in the provision of services to clients.[2] With regard to banks, DNB is the authorising regulator, and

---

1.   Art. 1:24(1) WFT.
2.   Art. 1:25(1) WFT.

therefore the main bank regulator (or supervisor) in the Netherlands. As central bank, DNB is also responsible for systemic supervision.

This chapter starts with a description of the Dutch banking sector and the financial regulators. Subsequently, the WFT will be introduced. The remainder of the chapter focuses on the regulation of banks in the Netherlands and the supervision that is exercised over them. This will include market access, prudential supervision, conduct of business supervision, as well as regulatory approval and notification obligations. Following this, supervisory powers and enforcement will be explained. Finally, several other regulatory issues will be addressed, including the deposit guarantee scheme, the prohibition on receiving repayable funds and the relevant Anti-Money Laundering and Terrorist Financing legislation.

1.2   The Banking Environment in the Netherlands

In the WFT a "bank" is defined as an undertaking whose business is to receive repayable funds from others than professional market parties beyond a restricted circle and to grant credits for its own account. The term "credit institution" (*kredietinstelling*) in the WFT includes a "bank" as well as an "electronic money institution" (*electronischgeldinstelling*). This chapter will mainly address banks. In the Dutch context they include such institutions as universal banks (that are engaged in both commercial and investment banking activities), savings banks, mortgage banks and securities institutions that have a bank status (so-called "security credit institutions" (*effectenkredietinstellingen*)). Larger, internationally operating banking groups that are based in the Netherlands include (in alphabetical order) ABN AMRO Bank, ING and Rabobank. The latter two also have large insurance businesses,[3] as does SNS, a medium-sized banking and insurance group. On 3 October 2008, the State of the Netherlands acquired the Dutch banking operations of ABN AMRO and Fortis Bank and ABN AMRO Bank and Fortis Bank Nederland legally merged as of 1 July 2010. Rabobank has a structure which is different from the others in that it is a cooperative bank. The main bank is Rabobank Nederland (officially called Coöperatieve Centrale Raiffeisen-Boerenleenbank B.A.) which has its head office in Utrecht. The many Rabobanks in the Netherlands are also cooperatives. They are separate legal entities, rather than branches of Rabobank Nederland. This means that they all have a banking licence in their own right. Examples of smaller Dutch banks are Friesland Bank and F. van Lanschot Bankiers.

---

3. However, on 26 October 2009, ING announced that it will move towards a complete separation of its banking and insurance operations. This will be achieved over the next four years by a divestment of all insurance and asset management activities.

Each has a strong basis in a particular region of the Netherlands, Friesland Bank in the north and Van Lanschot in the south (established in 1737 in 's-Hertogenbosch and still having its head office there). Another Dutch bank, with a history dating back to 1720, was MeesPierson. This bank no longer exists as a separate legal entity, however, since after its takeover by Fortis it was merged into Fortis Bank Nederland and as of 1 July 2010 into ABN AMRO Bank. Finally, various foreign banks are present in the Netherlands, including Deutsche Bank and BNP Paribas, either through a subsidiary and/or a branch.

1.3   DNB

In 1814, in the wake of the Napoleonic era, the Netherlands regained independence and became a kingdom. King William I established DNB that very same year. The introduction of the EMU made it necessary to amend the Bank Act, the act on which DNB is based. The new Bank Act 1998 (*Bankwet 1998*)[4] replaced the Bank Act that had been in place since 1948. Under the Bank Act 1948, the position of DNB could be characterised as independent, albeit under the responsibility of the Minister of Finance. Since the introduction of the Bank Act 1998, and revocation of the instruction right of the Minister of Finance, DNB is not only *de facto* independent but also *de iure*.

Today, DNB is a public limited company (*naamloze vennootschap*) that is governed by an Executive Board, consisting of a President and up to five Executive Directors (*Directie*), and a Supervisory Board (*Raad van Commissarissen*). In addition, there is an advisory body called the Bank Council (*Bankraad*).

On a public-law level, DNB has a dual function, being both part of the European System of Central Banks (**ESCB**) and an autonomous administrative authority (*zelfstandig bestuursorgaan*). As a part of the ESCB, DNB is co-responsible for the determination and implementation of the monetary policy for the Economic Monetary Union (the euro zone (**EMU**)), besides its task to exercise oversight of payment systems to ensure safe and reliable payment processing. As an autonomous administrative authority, DNB exercises prudential supervision of financial institutions. In addition to these responsibilities, DNB has certain other tasks assigned to it under the Bank Act 1998. These include the collection of statistical data and the compiling of certain statistics on the basis thereof.

In 1952 the role of DNB as the supervisor of the banking system was formalised. Step by step, in the years that followed, this supervisory role was expanded to include all financial institutions. Financial supervision underwent a transformation

---

4.   Bank Act 1998 (*Bankwet 1998*), Bulletin of Acts and Decrees (*Staatsblad*) 1998, 200.

in 2002, when DNB was given responsibility for prudential supervision of financial institutions and the soundness of the financial system. At the same time, the supervision of conduct of business was entrusted to the AFM. In 2004, DNB merged with the Pensions and Insurance Supervisor (*Pensioen- en Verzekeringskamer* or **PVK**).

1.4 The AFM

The Securities Board of the Netherlands (*Stichting Toezicht Effectenverkeer* or **STE**), the predecessor of the AFM, was founded in 1988 and commenced supervising the Dutch securities exchanges in early 1989. The STE has been designated the "watchdog" of the Dutch securities markets. The AFM was set up on 1 March 2002 as the successor to the STE. Since the coming into force of the WFT on 1 January 2007, the AFM is formally responsible for the supervision of conduct of business and the disclosure of information by all financial market participants in the Netherlands (savings, lending, investment and insurance). The conduct of business supervision focuses on ensuring orderly and transparent financial market processes, integrity in relations between market parties and due care in the provision of services to clients. In that role, the AFM supervises the various securities exchanges and the off-exchange market and grants licences to and supervises, *inter alia*, investment firms (broker-dealers, portfolio managers).

The AFM is a an autonomous administrative authority. In that capacity, the AFM has independent responsibility for the fulfilment of its supervisory function. The AFM is a foundation (*stichting*) and is governed by a three to five member Executive Board (*Bestuur*) and a Supervisory Council (*Raad van Toezicht*). The day-to-day supervisory functions for which the AFM is responsible are delegated to staff, of which there are a growing number in the AFM's Amsterdam office.

1.5 Cooperation between Supervisors

The cooperation between DNB and the AFM is described in the WFT. In addition, the AFM and DNB have concluded a covenant[5] regarding the cooperation and coordination of supervision and other related tasks. The covenant contains further agreements to avoid potential overlap and to ensure that the supervision is carried out efficiently and effectively. Where possible and worthwhile, the supervisors thus make use of the information and expertise available to them (taking account

---

5. *Convenant Stichting Autoriteit Financiële Markten en De Nederlandsche Bank N.V.*, Government Gazette (*Staatscourant*) 10 juli 2007, no. 130, p.20.

of the relevant statutory provisions on confidentiality) and of the infrastructure available to them for requesting information and data from supervised financial undertakings. DNB and the AFM also cooperate in relation to the formulation of regulations and policy.

In cases involving financial undertakings operating internationally, DNB and the AFM also cooperate with the supervisory authorities in the other countries where the undertaking is active.

2.   THE FINANCIAL SUPERVISION ACT (WFT)

2.1   Introduction to the WFT

The WFT entered into force on 1 January 2007, to replace the Credit Supervision Act 1992 and six other existing financial supervision acts. The WFT includes all rules and conditions that apply to the financial markets and the supervision of the market parties. The WFT also implemented the Basel 2 Capital Accord.[6] The WFT currently consists of the following five parts:

- Part 1 General Provisions;
- Part 2 Market access of financial undertakings;
- Part 3 Prudential supervision of financial undertakings;
- Part 4 Conduct of business supervision of financial undertakings; and
- Part 5 Market conduct supervision.

The tasks and responsibilities of DNB and the AFM are set out in Part 1, together with their supervisory powers and the rules on their cooperation. Part 2 includes all requirements in relation to authorisations for financial undertakings wishing to pursue their business in the Netherlands. Part 3 sets out the prudential standards which must be met by financial undertakings in the Netherlands. The conduct of business requirements applicable to financial undertakings are set out in Part 4. Part 5 contains market conduct rules applicable to all parties operating in the financial markets.

Additional rules have been laid down in a number of orders in council (*Algemene Maatregel van Bestuur*) as well as in a various ministerial regulations (*ministeriële regeling*). The AFM and DNB have also drawn up a variety of supervisory rules and policy rules.

---

6.   See further paragraph 2.2.3.

2.2   The European Basis of the WFT

The WFT is to a large extent based on EU directives. Unlike EU regulations, directives have no direct effect in the Member States. They are addressed to the Member States, requiring them to implement the requirements set by the directives in their own legislation and/or regulations. The basis for the directives is the Treaty establishing the European Economic Union (**EEC Treaty**), in particular Article 57 thereof, which prohibits discriminatory treatment with regard to the establishment and provision of services based on nationality or the fact that an undertaking is established in another Member State.

    A fair number of EU directives have shaped Dutch bank regulations over the years. The following EU directives were consolidated into the Recast Banking Directive and the Recast Capital Adequacy Directive in 2006, and, therefore, are no longer in force:

- The 1973 Directive;[7]
- The First Banking Directive;[8]
- The First Consolidated Supervision Directive;[9]
- The Own Funds Directive;[10]
- The Second Banking Directive;[11]
- The Solvency Ratio Directive;[12]
- The Second Consolidated Supervision Directive;[13]
- The Large Exposures Directive;[14]

---

7. Council Directive on the abolition of restrictions on freedom of establishment and freedom to provide services in respect of self-employed activities of banks and other financial institutions No. 73/183 O.J. EUR. COMM. (No. L 194) 1 (1973).
8. First Council Directive 77/780/EEC of 12 December 1977 on the coordination of the laws, regulations and administrative provisions relating to the taking up and pursuit of the business of credit institutions.
9. Council Directive 83/350/EEC of 13 June 1983 on the supervision of credit institutions on a consolidated basis.
10. Council Directive 89/299/EEC of 17 April 1989 on the own funds of credit institutions.
11. Second Council Directive 89/646/EEC of 15 December 1989 on the coordination of laws, regulations and administrative provisions relating to the taking up and pursuit of the business of credit institutions and amending Directive 77/780/EEC.
12. Council Directive 89/647/EEC of 18 December 1989 on a solvency ratio for credit institutions.
13. Council Directive 92/30/EEC of 6 April 1992 on the supervision of credit institutions on a consolidated basis.
14. Council Directive 92/121/EEC of 21 December 1992 on the monitoring and control of large exposures of credit institutions.

- The Consolidated Banking Directive;[15]
- The Capital Adequacy Directive.[16]

The most relevant directives that are still in force are:

2.2.1 *The Deposit Guarantee Scheme Directive*[17]

This directive was adopted to address the situation in which deposits made with a credit institution that has branches in another Member State, become unavailable. It was considered that in the event of the closure of an insolvent credit institution, the depositors at any host Member State branch must be protected by the same guarantee scheme as the depositors in the home Member State of the bank. This is also in line with the system under the Recast Banking Directive where branches are permitted to be active in the other Member States on the basis of a licence issued in the Member State of origin and are initially subject to supervision in the home state regulator. The aim is a harmonised minimum level of deposit protection wherever deposits are located in the EU.

2.2.2 *The Financial Conglomerates Directive*[18]

This directive recognises that, while EU directives provided for rules on the supervision of credit institutions, insurance undertakings and investment firms, both on a stand alone basis and as part of homogeneous financial groups, no rules were provided for financial conglomerates (i.e. financial groups that provide services and products in different sectors of the financial markets, those of banking or investments and insurance). In particular, there was no prudential supervision on a group-wide basis of financial conglomerates, covering such aspects as solvency and risk concentration. The supplementary supervision rules are to apply to financial conglomerates with significant cross-sectoral activities. According to the rules, the competent authorities are to assess the financial situation of credit institu-

---

15. Directive 2000/12/EC of the European Parliament and of the Council of 20 March 2000 relating to the taking up and pursuit of the business of credit institutions.
16. Council Directive 93/6/EEC of 15 March 1993 on the capital adequacy of investments firms and credit institutions.
17. Directive 94/19/EC of the European Parliament and the Council of 30 May 1994 on deposit-guarantee schemes.
18. Directive 2002/87/EC of the European Parliament and of the Council of 16 December 2002 on the supplementary supervision of credit institutions, insurance undertakings and investment firms in a financial conglomerate and amending Council Directives 73/239/EEC, 79/267/EEC, 92/49/EEC, 92/96/EEC, 93/6/EEC and 93/22/EEC, and Directives 98/78/EC and 2000/12/EC of the European Parliament and of the Council.

tions, insurance undertakings and investment firms in a financial conglomerate at a group-wide level, in particular as regards solvency and risk concentration.

2.2.3 *The Recast Banking Directive[19] and the Recast Capital Adequacy Directive[20]*

The Recast Banking Directive and the Recast Capital Adequacy Directive (together also referred to as the Capital Requirements Directive or **CRD**) are the translation of the Basel framework agreement for prudential supervision of credit institutions and investment firms (**Basel 2**) into European legislation.[21] The directives and its annexes have been implemented in the WFT and its underlying regulations. The Basel 2 Framework represented a fundamental change in banking supervision. It describes a more comprehensive measure and minimum standard for capital adequacy. It sought to improve on the existing rules (Basel Capital Accord 1988 or **Basel 1**) by aligning regulatory capital requirements more closely to the underlying risks that banks face. Basel 2 uses a "three pillars" concept:

- Pillar 1: the minimum capital requirements per risk type: credit risk, market risk and operational risk;
- Pillar 2: the internal processes for risk management and for the calculation of the internal capital requirements and efforts by supervisors to review the bank's assessments. All material risks faced by the bank should be addressed in the capital assessment;
- Pillar 3: requirements for the disclosure of the bank's key financial data.

In September 2009, a Directive[22] amending the CRD was adopted (together

---

19. Directive 2006/48/EC of the European Parliament and of the Council of 14 June 2006 relating to the taking up and pursuit of the business of credit institutions (recast).
20. Directive 2006/49/EC of the European Parliament and of the Council of 14 June 2006 on the capital adequacy of investment firms and credit institutions (recast).
21. The Bank for International Settlements (**BIS**) in Basel, Switzerland, acts as a central banker for central banks. It also promotes international cooperation in relation to, inter alia, prudential supervision, providing the secretariat for the so-called Basel Committee on Banking Supervision (**Basel Committee**). The Basel Committee consists of representatives of the central banks and other regulators of the G10 countries and Luxembourg, and aims to promote international consistency of supervision standards. In 1988, the Basel Committee agreed the Basel Capital Accord (**Basel 1**).
22. Directive 2009/111/EC of the European Parliament and of the Council of 16 September 2009 amending Directives 2006/48/EC, 2006/49/EC and 2007/64/EC as regards banks affiliated to central institutions, certain own funds items, large exposures, supervisory arrangements, and crisis management.

with two implementing directives[23] referred to as **CRD 2**). Amendments include measures to:

- make technical changes to the capital requirements for the trading book, including Credit Risk Mitigation for counterparty credit risk;
- revise rules on the large exposures regime;
- establish rules on the treatment of hybrid capital instruments within original own funds;
- revise the rules related to capital requirements for securitisation positions; and
- clarify the supervisory framework for crisis management and establish colleges of supervisors to enhance both the efficiency and the effectiveness of supervision;
- effect an extension of the waiver for cooperative banks;
- further elaborate on the rules on liquidity risk management;
- make certain other technical changes.

The amendments to the CRD have to be transposed into domestic law by 31 October 2010 and will then be applied from 31 December 2010. Moreover, the European Commission has adopted a proposal to further amend the CRD (**CRD 3**). The proposed amendments address capital requirements for the trading book and re-securitisations, disclosure of securitisation exposures, and remuneration policies. It has also indicated their intention to adopt a proposal for a third set of amendments (**CRD 4**).[24]

3.   MARKET ACCESS OF BANKS

3.1   The Concept of "Bank"

The WFT contains licensing obligations and requirements for credit institutions. A "credit institution" includes a "bank" as well as an "electronic money institution".[25]

---

23. Commission Directive 2009/27/EC of 7 April 2009 amending certain Annexes to Directive 2006/49/EC of the European Parliament and of the Council as regards technical provisions concerning risk management and Commission Directive 2009/83/ECof 27 July 2009 amending certain Annexes to Directive 2006/48/EC of the European Parliament and of the Council as regards technical provisions concerning risk management.
24. http://ec.europa.eu/internal_market/bank/regcapital/index_en.htm.
25. Art. 1:1 WFT (definition of "credit institution"). Under Directive 2000/46/EC on the taking up, pursuit of and prudential supervision of the business of electronic money institutions (the

An "electronic money institution" is defined as a party, not being a bank, whose business it is to obtain funds in exchange for which electronic money is issued with which payments can be made, also to parties other than the party issuing the electronic money.[26] The WFT defines "electronic money" (*elektronisch geld*) simply as a monetary value stored on an electronic device or stored on-distance in a central accounting record.[27] Electronic money institutions established in the Netherlands require a licence from DNB. The WFT provides for mutual recognition of the authorisation to receive funds in exchange for electronic money.[28] Hereafter, we will merely focus on banks.

The WFT defines a "bank" as an undertaking whose business is to receive repayable funds from others than professional market parties beyond a restricted circle and to grant credits for its own account.[29] This definition differs from that in the EU Directives. The Recast Banking Directive defines a credit institution (other than an electronic money institution) as an undertaking whose business is to receive deposits or other repayable funds "from the public" and to grant credits for its own account. The restrictive criterion "from the public" is not included in the definition in the WFT. This criterion is implemented in the WFT by inserting the elements "others than professional market parties" and "beyond a restricted circle". The reasoning behind this is that the element "public" in common parlance has a broad meaning.

3.1.1 Business

The element "business" is an essential element of various definitions in the WFT. It follows from the Explanatory Memorandum to the WFT that a party shall be deemed to conduct activities as its business if they are (i) separately identifiable activities of the company and (ii) not conducted solely to support the main activities of the company.[30] Criteria for a separately identifiable activity are, for example, the presence of a separate treasury and separate bookkeeping for the activity

---

E-money Directive), electronic money institutions are not (or not necessarily) credit institutions.

26. Art. 1:1 WFT (definition of "electronic money institution").

27. Art. 1:1 WFT (definition of "electronic money").

28. An exemption from the prohibition to issue electronic money unless a licence has been obtained, is available to issuers of electronic money with a maximum monetary value of EUR 150 per electronic storage device, provided the total liabilities of the issuer related to the issue of the electronic money never exceed EUR 6 million and certain other conditions are met (Art. 1:5 WFT).

29. Art. 1:1 WFT (definition of "bank"). It is important to realise that a bank is defined by its activities, rather than by its legal form.

30. Parliamentary Papers (*Kamerstukken*) II 2004–2005, 29 708, no. 10, p.168.

concerned. Supporting the main activities includes, for example, cash management or the providing of finance by an industrial, a holding or an intermediate holding company solely to facilitate its own industrial activities or those of its subsidiaries. The purpose of the financing activities is decisive. If the purpose of the financing activities is confined to the (non-financial) main activities of the company or the business activities of its (non-financial) operating companies, then it will not qualify as "making a business" and does therefore not constitute a bank. If, however, the purpose of the financing activities is to make a profit, then the conclusion will be the opposite. Many industrial and holding companies that borrow and use the proceeds thereof to fund their subsidiaries in the form of either equity or shareholder loans stay clear of the WFT on the basis of this interpretation.

3.1.2 Repayable Funds

Repayable funds are funds that must be repaid at some point, for whatever reason, and where it is clear beforehand which nominal sum must be repaid.[31]

3.1.3 Professional Market Party

A professional market party is:[32]

    (a) a qualified investor;
    (b) a subsidiary of a qualified investor that is included in the supervision of the qualified investor on a consolidated basis;
    (c) any other persons or companies designated by the Decree on Definitions (*Besluit definitiebepalingen Wft*) as professional market parties.[33] This concerns (legal) persons or companies (in short): (i) whose balance sheet total amounts to EUR 500 million or more; (ii) whose net own funds amounts to EUR 10 million or more and which have been regularly active in the financial markets;[34] (iii) which have been rated by a competent (in DNB's opinion) credit rating agency, or which have issued securities or have taken out loan facilities that have been rated by such credit rating agency;

---

31. Art. 1:1 WFT (definition of "repayable funds"). The Explanatory Memorandum to the WFT refers to the element "deposits or other repayable funds" in the definition of "credit institution" in Art. 4(1)(a) Recast Banking Directive (Parliamentary Papers II 2004–2005, 29 708, no. 19, p.374-375).
32. Art. 1:1 WFT (definition of "professional market party").
33. Art. 3 Decree on Definitions.
34. During a minimum period of two consecutive years before the redeemable funds are made available, on two occasions a month on average.

(iv) which are special purpose vehicles (SPVs).[35] In addition, the following parties are deemed professional market parties (in short): persons or companies from which repayable funds are received if the nominal value of the initial receivable is at least EUR 50,000; or the initial receivable has been obtained for a consideration of at least EUR 50,000. If receivables are "packaged", this package must represent a nominal value or consideration of at least EUR 50,000.

A qualified investor is defined as:[36]

(a) a legal person or company that holds a licence or is otherwise regulated to be active on the financial markets;

(b) a legal person or company that does not hold a licence or is not otherwise regulated to be active on the financial markets and whose only corporate object is to invest in securities;

(c) a national or regional government body, central bank, international or supranational financial organisation or other similar international institution;

(d) a legal person or company having its registered office in the Netherlands that: (i) is classified as a small enterprise under rules to be laid down by Decree;[37] and (ii) is registered by the AFM as a qualified investor at its own request;

(e) a legal person or company, not being a legal person or company as referred to in d. above;

(f) a natural person residing in the Netherlands who satisfies the criteria to be laid down by Decree[38] and who is registered by the AFM as a qualified investor at his own request; or

---

35. SPVs are defined as (in summary) legal persons or companies that were set up especially to conduct certain transactions as referred to in Art. 3(1)(d) Decree on Definitions, including transactions to acquire receivables that will serve as collateral for securities; transactions to invest in sub-participating interests or derivative instruments for transferring credit risks, again to serve as collateral for securities; or to extend credit for the exclusive benefit of one or more other professional market parties.

36. Art. 1:1 WFT (definition of "qualified investor").

37. Pursuant to Art. 4(1) Decree on Definitions small enterprises are, legal persons or companies, which, according to the most recent annual accounts or consolidated accounts, fulfil at least two of the following three criteria are designated as a small enterprise:
    (a) the average number of employees during the financial year is less than 250;
    (b) the balance sheet total is no more than EUR 43 million;
    (c) the annual net turnover is no more than EUR 50 million.

38. Pursuant to Art. 4(2) Decree on Definitions, such natural persons are natural persons who fulfil at least two of the following three criteria:

(g) a natural person or enterprise classified as a qualified investor in another Member State as referred to in Article 2(1)(e)(iv) and (v) respectively of the Prospectus Directive.[39]

3.1.4   A Restricted Circle

A restricted circle is deemed a circle composed of persons or companies from which a person or company obtains the disposal of repayable funds, provided that:

(a) the circle is accurately defined;
(b) the criteria for access are predetermined and verifiable and do not facilitate easy access; and
(c) the lenders already have a legal relationship with the borrower, based on which they reasonably can be aware of the borrower's financial position.[40]

The rationale of the exemption is that, in view of the specific relationship within the closed circle, it is thought that the lenders are themselves sufficiently capable of assessing the solidity of the borrower and, therefore, supervision on the borrower is not required. This concept is explained in more detail in the Explanatory Memorandum to the WFT.[41] It is explained that the restricted circle should be present during the entire period that the repayable funds are outstanding and that the legal relationship must have existed before there was an intention to invite funds. A restricted circle may not be 'construed' for the purpose of raising funds.

3.1.5   Grant Credits for its own Account

The granting of credit is understood to be the granting of nominally repayable funds to another party in order to make a profit. The benefits to the lender or a

---

(a) the natural person has carried out at least 10 transactions of a significant size on the securities markets, per quarter, over the previous four quarters;
(b) the size of the natural person's securities portfolio exceeds EUR 500,000;
(c) the natural person works or has worked for at least one year in the financial sector in a professional position which requires knowledge of securities investment.
39. Directive 2003/71/EC of the European Parliament and of the Council of 4 November 2003 on the prospectus to be published when securities are offered to the public or admitted to trading. This provision means that certain natural persons and small and medium-sized enterprises (SME's) that are considered qualified investors in another Member State, are also considered qualified investors in the Netherlands.
40. Art. 1:1 WFT (definition "restricted circle").
41. Parliamentary Papers II 2004–2005, 29 708, no. 10, p.170-173, and Parliamentary Papers II 2004–2005, 29 708, no. 19, p.364.

related party must be 'in money's worth'. A party is deemed to be acting 'for its own account' if it bears the financial risk of granting those credits. A party that receives a profit or loss related compensation for the granting of credits, also acts 'for its own account'.

3.1.6   *Finance Companies*

For tax and other reasons, many groups, both Dutch and non-Dutch, have a Dutch finance company (*financieringsmaatschappij*) in the form of a subsidiary which they use for group financing activities. The typical group finance company raises repayable funds in the international financial markets, usually under a parent guarantee, and on-lends the proceeds of its borrowings to its parent or other group companies. The repayable funds may be raised by borrowing under loans or by issuing bonds. These finance companies will not be considered "banks" because they attract funds only from professional market parties (see above). A second type of finance company includes Dutch orphan companies that may be used as SPVs e.g. for securitisations or repackagings. These SPVs will also not be considered "banks" because they issue securities only to professional market parties.

3.1.7   *Exemption for Group Finance Companies*

The prohibition to conduct the business of a bank without authorisation does not apply to a 'group finance company' which raises repayable funds, even when they obtain repayable funds from others than professional market parties beyond a restricted circle, provided:

- the repayable funds are obtained by means of the issuing of securities in accordance with the relevant provisions of the WFT and regulations pursuant thereto;[42]
- the group finance company holds a guarantee from an authorised bank or its parent company in respect of the full amount of repayable funds; and
- the group finance company grants at least 95% of its balance sheet total as credit within the group of which it forms part. A group means the legal person and its subsidiaries collectively.[43]

On application, DNB may grant dispensation from the above requirements, if the applicant demonstrates that it cannot reasonably comply with these provisions

---

42. Chapter 5.1 of the WFT on rules on offering securities.
43. Art. 3:2 WFT in conjunction with Art. 2:11(3) WFT.

and that the objectives which these requirements seek to achieve are achieved in other ways.[44]

4. CREDIT INSTITUTIONS ESTABLISHED IN THE NETHER-LANDS

4.1 Licence Application

An enterprise or institution established in the Netherlands that wishes to take up the banking business must apply to DNB for a licence.[45]

The licence application[46] must contain the following information:[47]

(a) a statement of the name, address, telephone and fax number of the bank;
(b) a statement of its legal form;
(c) if the bank is a legal person, a statement of the registered office, the name according to the articles of association and the trade name or names;
(d) if the bank is listed in the Trade Register, a statement of the registration number;
(e) if available, a certified copy of the articles of association;
(f) a business plan, in which it must be specified which activities the bank wants to carry out;
(g) details enabling DNB to assess the expertise of the persons determining the day-to-day policy of the bank;[48]
(h) details enabling DNB to assess the trustworthiness of the persons who determine or co-determine policy or belong to a supervisory body;[49]

---

44. Art. 3:2(3) WFT.
45. Art. 2:11 WFT.
46. DNB has drawn up various Application Forms for this purpose.
47. Art. 8 Financial Enterprises Market Access Decree (*Besluit Markttoegang financiële onderne-mingen Wft*) in conjunction with Art. 2:12(5) WFT.
48. Pursuant to Art. 8(2) Financial Enterprises Market Access Decree these details include: (a) a statement of the name, date of birth, place of birth, nationality, private address, telephone and fax number and position of the person in question; (b) a curriculum vitae; (c) a list of the relevant diplomas; (d) a copy of a valid identity document; and (e) a list of referees.
49. Pursuant to Art. 8(3) Financial Enterprises Market Access Decree these details include: (a) a statement of the name, date of birth, place of birth, nationality, private address, telephone and fax number and position of the person in question; (b) a copy of a valid identity document; (c) details with regard to the designated antecedents; and (d) a list of referees. DNB, in cooperation with the AFM, has drawn up Integrity Test Forms for this purpose. This requirement shall not apply if the integrity of the person concerned has already been tested by DNB or the AFM (Art. 8 (4) Financial Enterprises Market Access Decree).

  (i) a description of the proposed policy with regard to the conduct of business in a controlled and sound manner;

  (j) a description of the control structure;

 (k) description of the operational structure with regard to the controlled and sound conduct of business;

  (l) if applicable, a description of the consolidated supervision;

(m) documents from which the minimum amount of own funds, the expected minimum amount of own funds, the expected solvency and the liquidity are apparent;

 (n) if applicable:

      1°. a statement of the size of a qualifying holding;[50]

      2°. details based upon which DNB can assess the trustworthiness of the applicant or holder of a declaration of no objection who could determine or co-determine, or would determine or co-determine, the policy of the bank based on being the holder of a qualifying holding;[51] and

      3°. documents from which the financial position and the legal group structure of the applicant or holder of the declaration of no objection are apparent; and

 (o) if the bank is a subsidiary of a credit institution with a registered office in another state: a statement from the supervisory authority of the state in which the credit institution has its registered office, from which it is apparent that this supervisory authority has approved the aforementioned credit institution having a subsidiary that intends to conduct the business of a credit institution in the Netherlands.

If a bank intends to also provide investment services[52] or perform investment

---

50. As referred to in Art. 3:95 WFT. See paragraph 7.1.1.

51. As referred to in Art. 3:99 WFT.

52. Pursuant to Art. 1:1 WFT, to "provide an investment service" is defined as:

    (a) to receive and forward, in the pursuit of a profession or business, client orders with regard to financial instruments;

    (b) to execute, in the pursuit of a profession or business, orders with regard to financial instruments for the account of those clients;

    (c) asset management;

    (d) to provide advice with regard to financial instruments in the pursuit of a profession or business;

    (e) in the context of an offering, to underwrite or place financial instruments on a fully underwritten basis, in the pursuit of a profession or business;

    (f) in the context of an offering, to place financial instruments on a non-guaranteed basis, in the pursuit of a profession or business.

activities[53] in the Netherlands, the licence application must also contain a description of:[54]

(a) the operational structure with regard to orderly and transparent financial market processes, integrity in relations between market parties and due care in the provision of services to clients and unit holders;[55]
(b) the measures taken to protect clients' rights;[56] and
(c) the proposed policy with regard to preventing and managing conflicts of interest between itself and its clients and among its clients.[57]

4.2　　　　　Licence Requirements

Before granting the licence, DNB will assess whether the applicant complies with the following authorisation requirements.[58]

4.2.1　　　　　*Management*[59]

The day-to-day policy of a bank must be determined by at least two natural persons (the so-called "four eyes principle").[60] These persons shall perform their activities in this respect from the Netherlands (i.e. it is not an absolute requirement that the Management Board members are Dutch residents, but the managers in charge must perform their functions in the Netherlands rather than from abroad).[61] Persons determining the day-to-day policy, under normal circumstances, are the members of the bank's executive board. However, *de facto* directors determining the day-to-day policy are also included. The executive board members are supposed to have sufficient expertise in relation to the business and operations of the financial undertaking.[62] No guidelines are available as to how expertise is being interpreted by

---

53. Pursuant to Art. 1:1 WFT, to "perform an investment activity" is defined as:
    (a) to trade for one's own account in the pursuit of a profession or business;
    (b) to operate a multilateral trading facility in the pursuit of a profession or business.
54. Art. 9 Financial Enterprises Market Access Decree in conjunction with Art. 2:13(2) WFT.
55. As referred to in Art. 4:14 WFT.
56. Art. 4:87 WFT.
57. Art. 4:88 WFT.
58. Art. 2:12 WFT. These requirements are described in further detail in the Prudential Supervision Decree (*Besluit prudentiële regels Wft*).
59. Art. 2:12 (1)(a), (b),(d) en (g) WFT.
60. Art. 3:15(1) WFT.
61. Art. 3:15(2) WFT.
62. Art. 3:8 WFT.

DNB.[63] DNB will assess a managing director's expertise by the following means: his curriculum vitae and – if necessary – a personal interview and/or an interview with his referees. In addition, the managing directors' fit and proper qualities are supposed to be beyond doubt. The application documents must include Integrity Test Forms, drawn up by DNB, containing information on criminal antecedents, private financial antecedents, business-related financial antecedents, supervisory antecedents, tax administrative antecedents and other antecedents. DNB will also consult various public and non-public sources. On the basis of this information DNB will form an opinion of the person's integrity.[64] If the person's integrity has been assessed before, by either DNB or the AFM, no new assessment will be carried out, unless a change in the relevant facts or circumstances has given reasonable cause for a reassessment.[65] In addition to a management board that determines its day-to-day policy, the bank must have a supervisory board (or a comparable body) of at least three members.[66] DNB will usually insist that at least one member of the supervisory board is a Dutch citizen with ample experience in the banking field and generally with respect to the business environment in the Netherlands. The fit and proper qualities of the supervisory board members must be beyond doubt.[67] The fit and proper qualities of supervisory directors are assessed as described above. On 6 November 2009, consultations were started for a draft legislative proposal to, *inter alia*, introduce requirements regarding the expertise of supervisory board members.[68] The intended effective date is 1 July 2011.[69]

---

63. However, the Minister of Finance has announced that DNB is in the process of developing a system of standards regarding expertise testing.
64. Art. 3:9 WFT and Arts. 5-9 Prudential Supervision Decree.
65. Art. 3:9(2) WFT.
66. Pursuant to Art. 3:19(1) WFT a bank that is a public limited company (*naamloze vennootschap*) or a private limited liability company (*besloten vennootschap*) must have a supervisory board, as referred to in Arts. 2:140 and 2:250 respectively of the Civil Code (*Burgerlijk Wetboek*), composed of at least three members. The second subsection prescribes that a bank that has not such legal form, must have a body composed of at least three members whose duties shall be equivalent to those of a supervisory board.
67. Art. 3:9 WFT and Arts. 5-9 Prudential Supervision Decree.
68. Amendment Act Financial Markets 2011 (*Wijzigingswet financiële marken 2011*).
69. It is also worth mentioning in this respect that the persons determining the day-to-day policy (i.e. the members of the executive board) of a mixed financial holding company, a financial holding company or an insurance holding company having its registered office in the Netherlands must be expert in conducting the business operations of the regulated entities concerned (Art. 3:271 WFT). In addition, the integrity of these persons and the persons determining the policy (including the supervisory board members) must be beyond doubt (Art. 3:272 WFT).

4.2.2 *Sound Business Operations*[70]

The bank shall pursue adequate policies securing sound operations. This concerns, among other things, the prevention of: (a) conflicts of interest; (b) any involvement in criminal offences and other violations of the law; (c) confidence in the institution or in the financial markets being affected on account of its clients; and (d) performing any acts that are so contrary to generally accepted standards that they seriously affect the confidence in the institution or in the financial markets.[71]

4.2.3 *Control Structure*[72]

The bank shall not be affiliated to persons in a formal or actual control structure which is so lacking in transparency that it constitutes or may constitute an impediment to the adequate exercise of supervision.[73]

4.2.4 *Controlled Business Operations*[74]

The bank shall organise its operations in such a way as to safeguard controlled and sound business operations. This concerns, among other things, the control of business processes and business risks, integrity risks and financial risks.[75]

4.2.5 *Consolidated Supervision*[76]

A bank that is a subsidiary of a credit institution established in a non-Member State, shall be under sufficient consolidated supervision in the state where the latter credit institution has its registered office.[77]

---

70. Art. 2:12(1)(c) WFT.
71. As referred to in Art. 3:10(1) WFT, further described in Arts. 10-16 Prudential Supervision Decree. See paragraph 5.6.1.
72. Art. 2:12(1)(e) WFT.
73. Art. 3:16 WFT.
74. Art. 2:12(1)(f) WFT.
75. Art. 3:17(1) and (2) WFT and Arts. 17-26 Prudential Supervision Decree.
76. Art. 2:12(1)(h) WFT.
77. Art. 3:31 WFT. See paragraph 5.3.

4.2.6   Own Funds[78]

The minimum amount of own funds shall be at least EUR 5 million.[79] The minimum capital is to a certain extent less relevant, since solvency requirements will (except perhaps for smaller banks) usually dictate that much higher capital requirements are adhered to.

4.2.7   Solvency[80]

The solvency requirement aims to ensure that banks hold sufficient own funds in relation to the size of their liabilities and the nature and extent of their business risks. Its purpose is to maintain sufficient buffers to absorb any potential losses. The level of actual solvency is expressed as a percentage of the risk-weighted assets.[81]

4.2.8   Liquidity[82]

The liquidity requirements mean that credit institutions must be able to fulfil their short-term payment obligations.[83]

On application, DNB may grant a full or partial dispensation from certain of the requirements above, if the applicant demonstrates that it cannot reasonably comply and that the objectives which these requirements seek to achieve are achieved in other ways.[84]

4.2.9   Other Licence Requirements

Furthermore, if the application relates to a bank in which a qualified shareholding[85] is owned, DNB shall only grant a licence if the owner of the qualified shareholding

---

78. Art. 2:12(1)(i) WFT.
79. Art. 48 Prudential Supervision Decree in conjunction with Art. 3:53(1) and (3) WFT. See paragraph 5.1.
80. Art. 2:12(1)(j) WFT.
81. Art. 3:57(1) and (2) WFT. See paragraph 5.2.
82. Art. 2:12(1)(k) WFT.
83. Art. 3:63(1) and (2) WFT. See paragraph 5.5.
84. Art. 2:12(6) WFT.
85. Art. 1:1 WFT defines a qualified shareholding as a direct or indirect holding representing 10% or more of an enterprise's issued capital or the right to exercise, directly or indirectly, 10% or more of the voting rights in an enterprise, or the right to exercise, directly or indirectly, equivalent control over an enterprise, whereby in determining the number of voting rights of

has applied for a declaration of no objection and DNB is of the opinion that the relevant provisions are complied with.[86]

If a bank intends to also provide investment services or perform investment activities, DNB will only grant a banking licence if the applicant demonstrates that it will also comply with the provisions regarding:[87]

(a) the operational structure with regard to orderly and transparent financial market processes, integrity in relations between market parties and due care in the provision of services to clients and unit holders;[88]

(b) the measures taken to protect clients' rights;[89] and

(c) the rules applicable to the trading process and the settlement of transactions in a multilateral trading facility, if the applicant intends to operate a multilateral trading facility.[90]

DNB shall consult the regulator of the Member State involved before granting a licence to a bank which:

(a) is a subsidiary of a credit institution that has been licensed in another Member State;

(b) is a subsidiary of a parent company of such credit institution;

(c) is controlled by a person that also exercises control over such credit institution.[91]

4.3   Licensing Procedure

When applying for a banking licence, the applicant must use the standard Licence Application Forms drawn up by DNB. The application form and the details to be provided shall be submitted as one single copy.[92] DNB must decide on the application within 13 weeks of the date of receipt thereof.[93] However, if DNB requests more data or information as a supplement to the application, this period

---

a party in an enterprise, the voting rights shall also include the voting rights which it has or is deemed to have under Art. 5:45.

86. Art. 2:12(2) and (3) WFT. See paragraph 7.1.
87. Art. 2:13(1) WFT.
88. As referred to in Art. 4:14(2)(c) under 1° to 6° WFT.
89. Art. 4:87 WFT.
90. Art. 4:91a WFT.
91. Art. 1:60(3) WFT.
92. Art. 2 Financial Enterprises Market Access Decree in conjunction with Art. 1:102(1) WFT.
93. Art. 1:102(3) WFT.

shall be extended until DNB has received the information requested.[94] If no or insufficient supplementary information is received within the period it specified, DNB may decide not to consider the application.[95] The licence may be subject to conditions and limitations with a view to the interests which the respective part seeks to protect.[96] After a licence is granted, the bank will be registered in the public register maintained by DNB. The register states which banking activities the bank is allowed to carry out.[97]

A licensed bank may perform at least the activities listed in Annex I to the Recast Banking Directive, unless the licence expressly provides otherwise.[98] These activities are:

1. acceptance of deposits and other repayable funds;
2. lending including, *inter alia*: consumer credit, mortgage credit, factoring, with or without recourse, financing of commercial transactions (including forfeiting);
3. financial leasing;
4. money transmission services;
5. issuing and administering means of payment (e.g. credit cards, travellers' cheques and bankers' drafts);
6. guarantees and commitments;
7. trading for own account or for account of customers in:
    (a) money market instruments (cheques, bills, certificates of deposit, etc.);
    (b) foreign exchange;
    (c) financial futures and options;
    (d) exchange and interest-rate instruments; or
    (e) transferable securities;
8. participation in securities issues and the provision of services related to such issues;
9. advice to undertakings on capital structure, industrial strategy and related questions and advice as well as services relating to mergers and acquisitions;
10. money broking;
11. portfolio management and advice;
12. safekeeping and administration of securities;
13. credit reference services;
14. safe custody services.

---

94. Art. 4:15 General Administrative Law Act (*Algemene wet bestuursrecht* or **AWB**).
95. Art. 4:5 AWB.
96. Art. 1:102(2) WFT.
97. Art. 1:107 WFT.
98. Art. 3:32 WFT.

4.4   Modification, Withdrawal or Limitation of a Licence

DNB may modify, withdraw or limit a licence, either fully or in part, or attach further conditions to the licence, if:[99]

(a) the licence holder has filed an application to that end;

(b) the licence holder, as subsequently becomes apparent, supplied incorrect or incomplete data when applying for the licence, and knowledge of the correct and complete data would have resulted in a different decision;

(c) the licence holder suppressed circumstances or facts on the grounds of which, if they had occurred or been known by the time when the licence was granted, the licence would have been refused;

(d) the licence holder no longer complies with the rules laid down by or pursuant to the WFT, or no longer complies with the conditions or limitations attached to the licence;

(e) the licence holder did not make use of the licence within 12 months of having been granted the licence;

(f) the licence holder has terminated the activity for which the licence was required;

(g) the licence holder has transferred the enterprise for which the licence was granted, either fully or in part;

(h) the licence holder dies (in the case of a natural person) or is dissolved (in the case of a legal person or partnership);

(i) the statement from the auditor[100] regarding the fair presentation of the annual accounts,[101] or the statement of the auditor regarding the fair presentation of the statements submitted by a credit institution[102] does not show that the annual accounts or the statements submitted by the credit institution give a true and fair view of the enterprise's financial position and of its results for the financial year concerned; or

(j) the licence holder has been declared insolvent, or the debt rescheduling arrangement for natural persons has been declared applicable to the licence holder, if a court has appointed an administrator (*onderbewindstelling*)[103] over one or more of the licence holder's assets, or if the licence holder has been placed under guardianship (*ondercuratelestelling*).

---

99. Art. 1:104(1) WFT.
100. Art. 1:1 WFT defines "auditor" as follows: "an auditor as referred to in Art. 2:393(1) Civil Code".
101. That forms part of the other information referred to in Art. 3:71(1) WFT.
102. As referred to in Art. 3:72(7) WFT.
103. As referred to in Arts. 1:380, 1:409 or 1:431 Civil Code.

DNB shall withdraw a licence if:[104]

(a) the emergency regulation (*noodregeling*) is declared by the court and the administrators (*bewindvoerders*) are authorised to wind up the credit institution;[105] or

(b) the emergency regulation is declared by the court and the administrators are authorised to transfer the obligations of the credit institution and to wind up the credit institution.[106]

In the decision to withdraw a licence, DNB may also stipulate that the bank must wind up its business, either fully or in part, within a period to be specified by DNB. During the winding-up, whether or not stipulated by DNB, the bank or its bankruptcy liquidator (*faillissementscurator*) shall be classified as a licensed enterprise.[107]

4.5   European Passport

4.5.1   Branch

A bank established in the Netherlands, licensed by DNB, intending to carry on the banking business[108] through a branch in another Member State,[109] can benefit from the so-called "European passport". The procedure is as follows. For starting its activities through the branch, DNB must have approved this intention.[110] The application for approval must contain the following data:[111]

(a) the Member State where the bank plans to set up the branch;
(b) the address of the branch;
(c) a statement of the activities that the credit institution intends to carry out from the branch;[112]

---

104. Art. 1:104(2) WFT.
105. As referred to in Art. 3:163(1), opening words and under (b), WFT.
106. As referred to in Art. 3:163(1), opening words and under (c), WFT.
107. Art. 1:104(3) WFT.
108. The activities listed in Annex I to the Recast Banking Directive falling within its licence.
109. References to Member States include EU Member States and other states which are part of the European Economic Area (**EEA**) (the latter currently being Norway, Liechtenstein and Iceland).
110. Art. 2:108(1) WFT.
111. Art. 2:108(2) WFT in conjunction with Art. 44 Financial Enterprises Market Access Decree.
112. The activities listed in Annex I to the Recast Banking Directive, as well as the investment services and activities listed in Annex I to the Markets in Financial Instruments Directive

(d) the name and private address of the persons who shall determine the day-to-day policy of the branch, i.e. the branch managers;

(e) a description of the proposed policy with regard to the conduct of business in a controlled and sound manner;[113] and

(f) a description of the operational structure for the controlled and sound conduct of business.[114]

The above details requested by DNB from the bank in support of its passport application follow (more or less) from Article 25 of the Recast Banking Directive. Instead of the details mentioned under (c), (e) and (f) above, Article 25 of the Recast Banking Directive prescribes a programme of operations. Such programme of operations should usually include at least the following information regarding the operations of the branch: business plan, organisational structure, systems and controls, financial information, investment activities (if applicable).[115]

Within three months after receipt of the application and the information required, DNB shall decide on the application. DNB shall approve the intention, unless the credit institution's operations or financial position are inadequate in view of its intention. Within one working day after the decision, DNB shall notify the host regulator. This notification contains also data regarding the size of the own funds and the solvency ratio and, where applicable, information on the deposit guarantee scheme applicable to the commitments of the branch. The credit institution will receive a copy of this notification. Within two months of the notification having been sent to the host regulator, DNB shall inform the credit institution of any conditions which the host regulator attached to the performance of the activities in the Member State concerned.[116]

4.5.2 Cross-border Services

The European passport is also available to a Dutch licensed bank which intends to conduct its business[117] as a cross-border services provider (i.e. not through a branch) to another Member State. The procedure in this case is as follows.[118] Before

---

(Directive 2004/39/EC of the European Parliament and of the Council of 21 April 2004 on markets in financial instruments – **MiFID**) (if applicable).

113. As referred to in Art. 3:10(1) and (2) WFT.
114. As referred to in Art. 3:17(1) WFT.
115. For a more detailed explanation reference is made to Committee of European Banking Supervisors (**CEBS**), Guidelines for passport notifications, 27 August 2009, also including a standard notification form for branch establishment (Annex 2).
116. Art. 2:109 WFT.
117. The activities listed in Annex I to the Recast Banking Directive falling within its licence.
118. Art. 2:110 WFT.

starting the activities, the credit institution must notify DNB in writing of its intention. The notification to DNB must indicate to which Member State the bank intends to provide services and describe the proposed activities. Within one month after receipt of the notification and the information required, DNB will notify the host regulator. DNB sends a copy of the notification to the credit institution.

4.5.3   *Non-compliance*

If a credit institution conducting its business in another Member State, either by the establishment of a branch or by way of the cross-border provision of services, has received an instruction[119] (*aanwijzing*) relating to its operations or its financial situation, and the credit institution has not, or only insufficiently, complied with that instruction, DNB may decide to prevent that credit institution from conducting its business from a branch or through the cross-border provision of services in the other Member State. DNB shall notify the host regulator(s) involved of this decision. From the time of this notification, the credit institution may no longer conduct its business from the branch or as a cross-border service provider in the other Member State.[120]

If a bank which conducts its business from a branch in another Member State fails to comply with the statutory regulations applicable in the host Member State, DNB, having received a notification to that effect from the host state regulator, shall, without delay, issue an instruction to the bank to adhere to the line of conduct set out in the instruction order within a reasonable term specified, in order to put an end to the violation of the statutory regulations applicable in the host Member State. If the bank has not, or only insufficiently, complied with the instruction, DNB, having informed the host state regulator, may prevent the bank from concluding new contracts in the host Member State. DNB shall inform the host state regulator of the measures taken.[121]

If the banking licence of a Dutch bank is withdrawn, DNB must inform the regulators of the Member States in which a the bank has a branch or to which it provides services.[122]

---

119.   As referred to in Art. 1:75 WFT. See further paragraph 9.3.1.
120.   Art. 1:77(1) WFT.
121.   Art. 1:59 WFT.
122.   Art. 1:61(1) WFT.

4.6   The Carrying on of Activities outside the EEA

If a Dutch licensed bank intends to conduct the business of a credit institution from a branch office in a non-Member State, it shall only start doing so after DNB has approved of this intention.[123] The application for approval must indicate:[124]

(a) the Member State where the bank plans to set up the branch;

(b) the address of the branch;

(c) a statement of the activities that the credit institution intends to carry out from the branch, i.e. a business plan;

(d) the name and private address of the persons who shall determine the day-to-day policy of the branch, i.e. the branch managers;

(e) a description of the proposed policy with regard to the conduct of business in a controlled and sound manner;[125] and

(f) a description of the operational structure for the controlled and sound conduct of business.[126]

DNB must make a decision on the application within three months of receipt of the application. DNB shall approve the intention, unless the credit institution's operations or financial position are inadequate in view of its intention. As long as DNB has not given its consent, the bank may not start its activities in the other country.[127]

5.   PRUDENTIAL SUPERVISION

5.1   Own Funds

Before considering the prudential supervision on credit institutions in greater detail, the provisions for credit institutions on own funds will be discussed.

A credit institution is required to have a minimum amount of own funds at its disposal.[128] Rules as regards the size and composition of the minimum amount of own funds have been laid down in the Prudential Supervision Decree. The minimum amount of own funds is:

---

123. Art. 2:111(2) WFT.
124. Art. 2:111(2) WFT in conjunction with Art. 45 Financial Enterprises Market Access Decree.
125. As referred to in Art. 3:10(1) and (2) WFT.
126. As referred to in Art. 3:17(1) WFT.
127. Art. 2:111(3) and (4) WFT.
128. Art. 3:53(1) WFT.

(a) EUR 5 million for a credit institution;
(b) EUR 2.5 million for a credit institution[129] whose business is primarily to provide investment services or perform investment activities in the Netherlands.[130]

The minimum amount of own funds of a credit institution is formed by the value of the following capital components:

(a) for a public limited company (*naamloze vennootschap*) or private limited company (*besloten vennootschap*): the issued and fully paid up share capital, with the exception of cumulative preference shares and preference shares with a fixed term;
(b) for a general partnership (*vennootschap onder firma*): the separated paid up capital components of the managing partners;
(c) for a limited partnership (*commanditaire vennootschap*): the separated paid up capital components of the managing partners as well as the paid up limited partnership capital;
(d) for a cooperative society (*coöperatie*): the capital paid up or contributed by the members;
(e) for a company that has a legal form other than the forms listed above: the positive difference between assets and liabilities;
(f) reserves, with the exception of the revaluation reserves;
(g) positive interim results reviewed by an auditor, less the dividends to be paid out and, in the event that the financial undertaking is an initiator of a securitisation, with the exception of the net profits that have arisen from the capitalisation of future income from the securitised assets and that serve as credit enhancement for the securitisation positions.[131]

These capital components are virtually consistent with the capital components that qualify as core capital. The core capital of a credit institution is one of the key elements in prudential supervision. Solvency supervision and liquidity supervision are jointly referred to as "prudential supervision". Solvency and liquidity supervision are explained below.

---

129. As meant in Art. 2:13 WFT.
130. Art. 48 Prudential Supervision Decree.
131. Art. 50(1) in conjunction with Art. 91(2) Prudential Supervision Decree.

5.2 Solvency Supervision

Pursuant to Article 3:57 WFT a credit institution, having its registered office in the Netherlands, must be sufficiently solvent.[132] The solvency to be maintained is expressed in terms of regulatory capital (*toetsingsvermogen*). A credit institution must also comply with rules as regards maintaining balance sheet items and off-balance sheet items. On application, DNB may, whether or not for a fixed period, grant a full or partial dispensation from the solvency requirements if the applicant demonstrates that it cannot reasonably comply with these requirements and that the objective which these requirements seek to achieve are achieved in other ways.[133]

5.2.1 Regulatory Capital

Credit institutions are required to maintain sufficient capital buffers to absorb possible losses, referred to as regulatory capital. The classification of regulatory capital into categories of components is based on the degree to which the applicable quality criteria are met. The following categories are distinguished.

5.2.1.1 Core Capital

Core capital, also known as Tier 1 capital, is capital of the highest quality, because there is no contractual obligation to repay it (permanence) nor are there impediments to charging any losses to this category of capital. The core capital is formed by the value of the following capital components:

(a) for a public limited company (*naamloze vennootschap*) or private limited company (*besloten vennootschap*): the issued and fully paid up share capital, with the exception of cumulative preference shares and preference shares with a fixed term;

(b) for a general partnership (*vennootschap onder firma*): the separated paid up capital components of the managing partners;

(c) for a limited partnership (*commanditaire vennootschap*): the separated paid up capital components of the managing partners as well as the paid up limited partnership capital;

---

132. The solvency of a credit institution is sufficient under the condition that the regulatory capital to be taken into consideration according to the provisions of the Prudential Supervision Decree at least equals the minimum amount of the regulatory capital. (Art. 59 Prudential Supervision Decree).
133. Art. 3:57(7) WFT.

(d) for a cooperative society (*coöperatie*): the capital paid up or contributed by the members;

(e) for a company that has a legal form other than the forms listed above: the positive difference between assets and liabilities;

(f) reserves, with the exception of the revaluation reserves;

(g) positive interim results reviewed by an auditor, less the dividends to be paid out and, in the event that the financial undertaking is an initiator of a securitisation, with the exception of the net profits that have arisen from the capitalisation of future income from the securitised assets and that serve as credit enhancement for the securitisation positions;

(h) the fund for the coverage of general banking risks;

(i) third party interests;[134]

(j) the negative components of the revaluation reserves, insofar as they have arisen from changes in values of investments in non-interest bearing securities; and

(k) negative interim results.[135]

Hybrid capital instruments, that contain elements of equity and debt, may be recognised as core capital under certain conditions and to a limited degree. The statutory conditions on hybrid capital instruments have been implemented in the Prudential Supervision Decree[136] and the Supervisory Regulation on the Recognition of Hybrid Instruments as Regulatory Capital Components[137] (*Regeling innovatieve financiële instrumenten en immateriële activa*). Hybrid instruments may be issued in either of two ways: directly or indirectly. This distinction is of importance for the manner in which the proceeds from the issue become available to the financial undertaking which includes the hybrid instruments in the calculation of its regulatory capital.

Hybrid instruments are distinguished into innovative and non-innovative financial instruments. This manner of defining and classifying hybrid instruments has been taken over from recent reports from the Committee of European banking Supervisors (**CEBS**) about own funds, in which hybrid instruments are divided into innovative instruments (with an incentive to redeem), non-innovative instruments (without an incentive to redeem) and non-cumulative perpetual preference

---

134. Insofar as it comprises capital components as referred to Art. 91(2) Prudential Supervision Decree.
135. Art. 91(2) Prudential Supervision Decree.
136. Arts. 89-94 Prudential Supervision Decree.
137. Based on Art. 89(2) Prudential Supervision Decree.

shares.[138] Because the Prudential Supervision Decree[139] counts non-cumulative preference shares towards regulatory capital, these shares are not – contrary to the CEBS classification – covered by the definition of hybrid instruments. They are, however, included in the calculation of the limits.

A hybrid instrument may be included up to a maximum of 15% (limit for innovative instruments) or 50% (innovative and non-innovative financial instruments combined), with the proviso that non-cumulative preference shares always count towards these limits. If hybrid instruments are not eligible as core capital, because the aforementioned limit is exceeded, they are automatically eligible as core additional capital.

5.2.1.2   Additional Capital

Additional capital, also known as Tier 2 capital, is divided into two sub-categories: the core additional capital (**upper Tier 2**) and the supplementary additional capital (**lower Tier 2 capital**).[140] Upper Tier 2 capital comprises cumulative preferred shares with no stated maturity, debt instruments with no stated maturity and revaluation reserves.[141] Lower Tier 2 capital consists of long-term subordinated debt.[142] Lower Tier 2 debt with a remaining agreed maturity of less than five years may be included in regulatory capital to a maximum that is reduced over time (under a phasing-out arrangement). Total Tier 2 capital must be smaller than or equal to Tier 1 capital. Lower Tier 2 capital may not exceed 50% of Tier 1 capital.

5.2.1.3   Other Capital

Other capital, also known as Tier 3, is formed by the value of the paid up part of certain short-term subordinated loans.[143] The other capital is taken into account for the calculation of the regulatory capital insofar as it does not amount to more than 250% of the core capital that can be taken into consideration for the coverage of these amounts and requirements.

---

138. CEBS, Report on a quantitative analysis of the characteristics of hybrids in the European Economic Area (EEA), 13 March 2007, section 20 (notably under c). See http://www.cebs.org/Advice/reportonhybrids1303.pdf.pdf.
139. Arts. 91(2) and 95(2) Prudential Supervision Decree.
140. Art. 92(1) Prudential Supervision Decree.
141. Art. 92(2) Prudential Supervision Decree.
142. Art. 92(3) Prudential Supervision Decree.
143. Art. 93 Prudential Supervision Decree.

5.2.2   Minimum Amount of the Regulatory Capital

The minimum amount of the regulatory capital of a credit institution is the total of:

(a) 8% of the total of the amount of the risk-weighted assets and off-balance sheet items for the credit risk, including the counterparty credit risk and dissolution risk, with regard to the whole undertaking, with the exception of trading portfolio and the non-liquid assets of the bank;

(b) the amount for the required solvency in respect of the trading portfolio to cover the position risks, settlement risks, delivery risks, counterparty risks and in event of a limit breach, large exposures;

(c) the amount of the required solvency with regard to the total undertaking to cover currency risks and commodity risks; and

(d) the amount of the required solvency with regard to the whole undertaking to cover operational risk.[144]

The amount of a risk-weighted asset or off-balance sheet item (above under (a)) must be equal to the exposure value multiplied by the risk weights allocated to that asset or off-balance sheet item.[145] In the calculation of the regulatory capital for each individual item the foreseeable amount of the taxes due on this item are taken into account.[146]

A credit institution is allowed to choose between different approaches to risk management and how capital requirements are calculated: simple, standardised approaches and more complex approaches on the basis of internal estimates. The principle applicable to all approaches is: the lower the risk, the lower the capital requirement.

Basel 2[147] consists of three "pillars," which credit institutions must implement as a whole:

– Pillar 1 (minimum capital requirements): the minimum capital requirements per risk type: credit risk, market risk and operational risk
– Pillar 2 (supervisory review): the internal processes for risk management and for the calculation of the internal capital requirements, the economic capital and how the supervisor views these internal processes: supervisory review

---

144. Art. 60(1) Prudential Supervision Decree.
145. Art. 61(1) Prudential Supervision Decree.
146. Art. 89(1) Prudential Supervision Decree.
147. Basel 2 is translated into European legislation via the CRD, as implemented in de WFT. See also paragraph 2.2.3.

– Pillar 3 (market discipline): requirements for the disclosure of key financial data as calculated for pillar 1.

5.2.2.1   Pillar 1

The regulatory capital required as referred to in Section 3:57 WFT is also referred to as the Pillar I capital.

The Regulation on Solvency Requirements for Credit Risk (*Regeling solvabiliteitseisen voor het kredietrisico*) contains rules for calculating the solvency requirement for credit risk that banks must comply with as part of their total actual funds.[148] Two approaches are possible for this calculation: (i) the Standardised Approach; or (ii) the Internal Ratings Based approach.

The Standardised Approach to credit risk is part of Basel 2 and is laid down in the Regulation on Solvency Requirements for Credit Risk.[149] In this sense, the Standardised Approach represents a continuation of Basel 1. The capital requirement for credit risk is fixed at 8% of the aggregate of the risk-weighted items. The risk weighting can be derived from external ratings and/or determined by fixed risk weighting. Basel 1 did not provide for the possibility of using ratings for supervisory purposes. The Standardised Approach makes it possible to use external ratings to determine the risk weighting of claims. External ratings are risk classifications set by external credit rating agencies. A bank may use the ratings of a given rating agency only if the agency is recognised by DNB. For recognised rating agencies DNB also indicates how the ratings should be linked to risk weighting (known as mapping).

The use of external ratings in the Standardised Approach makes it possible to allow for the different degrees of risk inherent in claims. However, a credit institution may be unable or unwilling to use an external rating for certain claims. This may be the case, for example, if no rating is available from a recognised rating agency or the use of external ratings is not considered cost effective. For such cases the Standardised Approach provides fixed risk weighting for all categories of claim (including off-balance sheet items), ranging from 0% for items with a very low credit risk to 150% for high-risk items.

A credit institution may be granted permission to use the Internal Ratings Based (**IRB**) approach to credit risk.[150] In the IRB approach, the capital require-

---

148. The Regulation on Solvency Requirements for Credit Risk contains specific rules on, inter alia, covered bonds and eligible types of credit derivatives, including credit default swaps, total return swaps and credit-linked notes to the extent of their cash funding, and also lays down a securitisation framework.
149. Art. 2:1 et seq. Regulation in Solvency Requirements for Credit Risk.
150. Art. 3:3 Regulation in Solvency Requirements for Credit Risk.

ments are determined on the basis of a prescribed weight function which differs per portfolio. The capital requirements for a credit institution exposure depends on the probability of default, the expected loss at the time of default and the expected exposure at the time of default. Within the IRB approach there are two approaches: (i) the Foundation IRB approach; and (ii) the more sophisticated Advanced IRB Approach. In order to get permission from DNB, the internal models must meet an extensive set of conditions.

The Regulation on Capital Adequacy Requirements for Market Risk (*Regeling solvabiliteitseisen voor het marktrisico*) contains rules for calculating the requisite capital adequacy of credit institutions to cover the market risk on their trading book and the commodity and currency risks in respect of all their business operations. Rules are set out for calculating the requisite capital adequacy to cover:

- the position risks, settlement and counterparty risks and large exposures in respect of their trading book;
- the currency and commodity risks in respect of all their business operations; and
- the other risks that can be regarded as equivalent to the risks referred to above.

The 'trading book' comprises positions in securities and other financial instruments that are held for trading purposes and are exposed mainly to market risk.[151]

The provisions concerning the trading book do not apply to credit institutions that have only a minor trading book. The conditions on this point are contained in the 'de minimis' exemption.[152] In such a case the requisite solvency for the trading book is calculated in accordance with the Regulation on Capital Adequacy Requirements for Credit Risk. The calculation of the position risk, the currency risk and the commodity risk can be calculated in a standardised approach and an IRB approach.[153] The standardised approach lays down uniform rules for calculating the scope of the relevant risks and the required solvency to cover the risks. The internal models approach provides for credit institutions to use their own internal models in calculating the capital adequacy requirements for these risks instead of or in combination with the standardised approach.

The Regulation on Solvency Requirements for Operational Risk (*Regeling Solvabiliteitseisen voor het Operationele Risico*) contains rules for calculating the requisite capital adequacy of credit institutions to cover the operational risk. The

---

151. Art. 2:1 et seq. Regulation on Capital Adequacy Requirements for Market Risk.
152. Art. 1:3 Regulation on Capital Adequacy Requirements for Market Risk.
153. Art. 3:29 Regulation on Capital Adequacy Requirements for Market Risk.

operational risk requirement has, in principle, been set at a level of 12% of the total capital requirement and has been incorporated into the system of capital requirements in such a way that the proportion of the principal existing component, the capital requirement for credit risk, has been reduced by the same percentage, so as to neutralise the effect on the overall regulatory capital requirement.[154]

In the Regulation on Solvency Requirements for Operational Risk three methods are available for calculating the capital requirement for operational risk, marked by increasing complexity and sensitivity:

- – the Basic Indicator Approach;[155]
- – the Standardised Approach;[156] and
- – the Advanced Measurement Approaches.[157]

The Basic Indicator Approach and the Standardised Approach rely on one and eight indicators, respectively. These indicators are three-year averages of observations of net interest income and net non-interest income. On that basis, a capital requirement is calculated using fixed percentages. The Advanced Measurement Approaches rely on internal models. DNB requires credit institutions to use an approach in line with their risk profile.

5.2.2.2 Pillar 2

*Internal Capital Adequacy Assessment Process (**ICAAP**)*

Pursuant to Article 3:17 WFT a credit institution must organise its operations in such a way as to safeguard controlled and sound business operations.[158] This means, *inter alia*, that it must have robust, effective and comprehensive strategies and processes in place which it uses to monitor and ensure on a continuous basis that the size, composition and distribution of its own funds are proportionate to the size and the nature of its current and possible future risks. The bank should verify in a systematic manner that these strategies and procedures are complied with and ensure that any shortcomings or deficiencies are remediated, also referred to as the ICAAP.[159] The scope of application of the ICAAP corresponds with the scope

---

154. Explanatory notes to Chapter 2 and Chapter 3 of the Regulation on Capital Adequacy Requirements for Market Risk.
155. Chapter 2 of the Regulation on Capital Adequacy Requirements for Market Risk.
156. Chapter 3 of the Regulation on Capital Adequacy Requirements for Market Risk.
157. Chapter 4 of the Regulation on Capital Adequacy Requirements for Market Risk.
158. See paragraph 5.6.1.
159. Art. 24a Prudential Supervision Decree.

of application of the Pillar 1 solvency requirements. In other words, the institutions which are subjected to individual or (sub-)consolidated solvency supervision under Pillar 1, must in principle also have an ICAAP in place.

The ICAAP captures all material risks to which a credit institution is exposed. The credit institution must use a risk identification process to demonstrate which risks are incorporated in the ICAAP and which are not. According to DNB the following non-exhaustive list of the risks needs to be assessed by a credit institution:

- – Pillar 1 risks: credit, market and operational risks;
- – risks not sufficiently covered under Pillar 1: securitisation risk, residual risk arising from the application of credit risk mitigation techniques;
- – risks under Pillar 2: interest rate risk in the banking book, concentration risk, reputation risk, pension risk;
- – the impact of external factors: economic environment factors, stress testing results.

The ICAAP must be embedded in the organisational structure, is risk-based, comprehensive and forward-looking. Therefore the ICAAP also need to include an assessment of future capital adequacy.

Stress testing is an essential instrument for the assessment of a credit institution's future capital adequacy and is therefore incorporated in the ICAAP. The institution must be able to show which capital consequences would arise under exceptional but plausible circumstances, and the credit institution will have a contingency plan by which to maintain capital adequacy in these circumstances. Stress testing must be an integral part of the institution's operational management, and the outcome of stress tests is used in formulating strategic objectives.

*Supervisory Review and Evaluation Process (**SREP**)*

The ICAAP is evaluated periodically by DNB. Key to this evaluation, also referred to as the SREP, is the dialogue between the institution and DNB.[160] DNB's evaluation process aims to arrive, through this dialogue with the institution, at a shared view on the size, composition and distribution of the available or ICAAP capital that is appropriate for the size and the nature of its current and possible future risks. Based on the outcome of its evaluation, DNB should decide whether the strategies, procedures and measures and the capital maintained by the bank safeguard proper management and adequately cover the risks. DNB will notify the institution in writing of the outcome of its evaluation.

---

160. The SREP is further implemented in Art. 25a of the Prudential Supervision Decree.

In applying the SREP, DNB takes into account the nature, scale and complexity of the credit institution's business.[161] DNB expects that a large institution whose business is complex will have, in principle, an economic capital model in place, a smaller institution whose business is relatively simple can do with a more basic ICAAP.[162] Whether a credit institution can be designated as a smaller institution depends on DNB's assessment of the nature of the institution's business. Factors influencing this assessment are: the nature of the activities, the complexity of such activities and/or the extent to which the activities are confined to a limited number of types of financial instruments or investment services. The credit institution's market share, its use of internal models and the extent of its cross-border activities also play a role.

If a bank does not satisfy the requirements with regard to the business operations and the regulatory capital, DNB may take special measures, including requiring that the credit institution concerned maintains a higher regulatory capital (SREP capital) than that laid down under Article 3:57 WFT (Pillar 1 capital), or that the credit institution, in connection with solvency requirements, pursues a specific policy with regard to provisions.[163] DNB's power in this regard is without prejudice to the other powers vested in DNB pursuant to the WFT,[164] including the power to give an instruction to an credit institution if it does not comply with the provisions laid down under or pursuant to the WFT, or if DNB detects signs of a development that may jeopardise the own funds, solvency or liquidity of that institution.

5.2.2.3   Pillar 3

A new element of the Basel 2 regime is the disclosure of solvency risks. This disclosure requirement applies to credit institutions, the key data to be disclosed

---

161. DNB bases its assessment of a credit institution's compliance with applicable standards on the guidelines established by the CEBS. The following CEBS guidelines have been taken into account:
    – 'Guidelines on the application of the Supervisory Review Process under Pillar 2' of 25 January 2006;
    – 'Technical aspects of stress testing under the supervisory review process' of 14 December 2006;
    – 'Technical aspects of the management of interest rate risk arising from non-trading activities under the supervisory review process' of 3 October 2006; and
    – 'Technical aspects of the of the management of concentration risk under the supervisory review process' of 14 December 2006.
162. Policy Rule on Principles for the Implementation of Pillar 2 of the Basel 2 Accord (*Beleidsregel uitgangspunten toepassing tweede pijler Kapitaalakkoord Bazel 2*), p.4.
163. Art. 3:111a WFT.
164. See paragraph 9.3.

relate to the credit institution's solvency and related risk profile. In developing the new solvency regime, known as Basel 2, the Basel Committee took the view that making information available to the public, in addition to reporting to the supervisor, has a positive effect on an institution's conduct. The aim is to enhance the quality of risk management within credit institutions.

A credit institution must disclose at least once a year the information referred to in Annex XII, sections 2 and 3, to the Recast Banking Directive that influences or may influence the opinion or decision of any party taking decisions of a financial nature on the basis of that information. The credit institution must disclose some or all of that information with a higher frequency if this should be necessary with a view to the nature of its activities.[165] The credit institution may refrain from disclosing information if such disclosure were to affect its competitive position or reduce the value of its investments, or if the information relates to obligations towards customers or to relations with other counterparties that are subject to a duty of secrecy. In that case, the credit institution must state in the information disclosed that certain information is missing, and why this information is missing. In the place of the missing information, it shall disclose aggregated information in respect of the substance of the missing information.[166]

5.2.3   *Large Exposures*

A special element within the solvency supervision is constituted by the so-called "large-exposure rule". This rule enables DNB to monitor risk categories by a credit institution. Credit institutions should monitor and control their risk concentrations in relation to a single counterparty or group of connected counterparties. The rule does not apply to branches in the Netherlands of a bank established in another member state.

The term 'large exposure' is defined as:

- the non-risk-weighted assets and off-balance sheet items in respect of a counterparty or group of associated counterparties;
- the value of which is at least 10% of the regulatory capital;
- with the exception of the items which a financial undertaking deducts from its regulatory capital and the non-risk-weighted assets and off-balance sheet items which are kept in the normal course of foreign exchange transactions within 48 hours of payment being made and, in the case of

---

165. Art. 3:74a(1) WFT.
166. Art. 3:74a(2) WFT.

securities transactions, within five working days of payment being made or of delivery of the securities, whichever is the earlier.[167]

Large exposures to a single counterparty or group of connected counterparties are subject to a limit of 25% of the regulatory capital, after any netting and after application of a possible inclusion percentage.[168] The total value of large exposures is subject to a limit of 800% of the regulatory capital.[169]

A credit institution must immediately notify DNB when a limit is exceeded. DNB can, upon request, decide that a credit institution is allowed to exceed a limit for a limited period.[170]

Provided that the immediate reporting requirement is complied with, a financial undertaking will be given permission to exceed the limits if it meets the following conditions:

- the entire excess amount occurs within the trading book;
- the credit institution complies with the additional capital requirements in respect of the excess amounts; these additional capital requirements are regulated in the Regulation on Capital Adequacy Requirements for Market Risk;
- the value of the exposures to the relevant counterparty or group of associated counterparties may not exceed 250% of the regulatory capital of the credit institution if not more than ten days have passed since the limit was exceeded;
- the total value of the excess amounts that last for more than ten days may not exceed 300% of the regulatory capital of the credit institution;
- the value of the exposure should be reduced to under the 25% limit within one month from the moment the limit was first exceeded.[171]

Use can be made of this exception only if the credit institution reports to DNB at the end of each quarter all cases in which the limit was exceeded in the previous quarter.[172] Exposures of a credit institution to its parent company, other subsidiaries of the parent company and its own subsidiaries are exempted from the application

---

167. Art. 1 Prudential Supervision Decree.
168. Art. 102(1) Prudential Supervision Decree.
169. Art. 102(2) Prudential Supervision Decree.
170. Art. 102(4) Prudential Supervision Decree.
171. Art. 7:6(1) Regulation on Solvency Requirements for Credit Risk.
172. Art. 7:6(2) Regulation on Solvency Requirements for Credit Risk.

of the limits insofar as such companies have been included in the supervision on a consolidated basis.[173]

5.3 Consolidated Supervision[174]

Consolidated supervision as exercised by DNB focuses primarily on credit institutions which form part of a group and encompasses all elements of Pillar 1 (minimum capital requirement, including large exposures rules), Pillar 2 (SREP) and Pillar 3 (market discipline) of Basel 2 and of the rules on controlled operation.[175] Consolidated supervision means supervision on the basis of the consolidated financial position of the credit institution subject to prudential supervision. Depending on the structure of the group, consolidation may take place at the level of a licensed undertaking or of a financial holding company. From the perspective of the licensed undertaking, there are two consolidation directions:

1.   *Downward consolidation: the licensed credit institution consolidates (financial) subsidiaries*[176]

Financial subsidiaries – that is, credit institutions, investment firms and financial institutions[177] – must be consolidated in full.[178] Excepted from this obligation of full consolidation are financial subsidiaries which are insurance undertakings. The obligation of consolidation does apply to undertakings which provide ancillary services[179] as well as to management companies of undertakings for collective

---

173. Art. 7:8(1) Regulation on Solvency Requirements for Credit Risk.
174. DNB has issued the Policy Rule on Scope of Consolidated and Solo Supervision of Investment Firms and Credit Institutions under the Financial Supervision Act (*Beleidsregel reikwijdte geconsolideerd en solotoezicht op beleggingsondernemingen en kredietinstellingen Wft*) on this subject.
175. As referred to in paragraph 6.1.
176. Art. 276(1) WFT.
177. A financial institution refers to a party, not being a credit institution, that has as its main business the performance of one or more of the activities referred to under 2-12 of Annex I to the Recast Banking Directive, or the acquisition or holding of participating interests in companies (Art. 1:1 WFT).
178. Art. 3:279(1) WFT.
179. Art. 3:268(1), under h, WFT defines an undertaking which provides ancillary services as "an undertaking which carries out activities which have the character of support activities in relation to the main activities of an investment firm or credit institution". An undertaking which provides ancillary services may be an undertaking whose purpose is to hold and administer real estate or to manage data processing services.

investment in transferable securities (UCITS).[180] Proportional consolidation may be permitted in the event that the parent undertaking's capital liability is limited, especially in the case of joint ventures.

DNB may decide not to involve an enterprise in the consolidated supervision if:

(a) the enterprise has its registered office in a non-Member State in which there are statutory impediments to providing the information required for the supervision;
(b) the enterprise to be involved in the supervision is only of negligible importance in light of the objectives of that supervision; or
(c) considering the financial position of that enterprise would be misplaced or misleading in light of the objectives of that supervision.[181]

2.   *Upward consolidation: consolidation is effected at the level of the parent financial holding company of the credit institution*[182]

Consolidated supervision at the level of the non-licensed parent financial holding company of a credit institution is sometimes referred to as "holding company supervision". This form of supervision implies that all prudential supervisory rules, as indicated before, apply to the consolidated financial position of the parent financial holding company.

A financial holding company is a financial institution which, exclusively or mainly, has investment firms, credit institutions or financial institutions as its subsidiaries, including at least one investment firm or credit institution, and which is not a mixed-activity financial holding company[183].[184] The WFT does not provide for a precise quantification of the concept "mainly". DNB relies on the principle that a financial institution qualifies as a financial holding company if it heads a group which, measured in terms of balance sheet total, consists to the extent of more than 80% of financial institutions (subsidiary plus parent undertaking), investment firms (subsidiaries) and credit instructions (subsidiaries).[185]

---

180. Art. 3:279(8) WFT.
181. Art. 3:270 WFT.
182. Art. 3:276(2) WFT.
183. A mixed financial holding company is defined in Art. 3:268(1)(f) WFT) as: a parent enterprise which is not a regulated entity (a credit institution, life insurer, non-life insurer or investment firm) and which, together with its subsidiaries of which at least one is a regulated entity established in a Member State, and with other enterprises, forms a financial conglomerate (as referred to in Art. 3:290).
184. Art. 3:268(1)(d) WFT.
185. DNB's Policy Rule on Scope of Consolidated and Solo Supervision of Investment Firms and Credit Institutions under the Financial Supervision Act, p.7.

If the parent financial holding company of a Dutch licensed credit institution has its registered office in the Netherlands, DNB bears responsibility for holding company supervision. If the parent financial holding company of a Dutch licensed credit institution has its registered office in another Member State, Article 3:275 WFT provides for a number of criteria determining which supervisory authority is responsible for consolidated supervision. Finally, the parent financial holding company of a Dutch licensed undertaking may have its registered office in a third country; in that case the equivalence of the supervision in that country with European consolidated supervision is decisive (if the supervision is not equivalent, the rules regarding EEA consolidated supervision apply *mutatis mutandis*).[186]

5.4 Envisaged Changes to Capital Requirements for Banks

Partly as a result of the financial crisis that erupted in 2007, the CRD has been and is still being adjusted in several respects.[187] The change paths are also referred to as CRD 2 and CRD 3 and CRD 4. The CRD 2 changes have already been published. These changes have to be transposed into domestic law by 31 October 2010 and will be applied from 31 December 2010. The most relevant changes in relation to capital requirements are:

– technical changes to the capital requirements for the trading book, including Credit Risk Mitigation for counterparty credit risk;
– changes to the rules and regulations for large exposures;
– rules on the treatment of hybrid capital instruments within original own funds;
– further elaboration of the rules on liquidity risk management;
– retention of securitisation positions.

5.5 Liquidity Supervision

Unlike the solvency requirements, the liquidity requirements do not find their roots in a European Directive. Under the Prudential Supervision Decree and the Regulation on Liquidity under the WFT (*Regeling liquiditeit Wft*) banks are required to report their liquidity position on a consolidated level to DNB on a monthly basis. The Regulation on Liquidity seeks to ensure, *inter alia*, that banks

---

186. Art. 3:277(1) WFT.
187. See paragraph 2.2.3.

are in a position to cope with an acute short-term liquidity shortage, on the assumption that banks would remain solvent. In principle, the liquidity regulation covers all direct domestic and foreign establishments (subsidiaries/branches), including majority participations.

Pursuant to Article 3:63 WFT, a credit institution must be sufficiently liquid. Rules have been laid down in the Prudential Supervision Decree as regards the minimum level, the composition and the calculation of the liquidity of a credit institution. If a credit institution expects or may reasonably expect that its liquidity does not or will not comply with these rules, it must, without delay, notify the DNB of this.[188]

On application, DNB may, whether or not for a fixed period, grant a full or partial dispensation from the liquidity requirements if the applicant demonstrates that it cannot reasonably comply with those requirements and that the objectives which these requirements seek to achieve are achieved in other ways.[189]

The liquidity of a credit institution is sufficient if the available liquidity at least equals the required liquidity.[190] A credit institution is allowed to:

(a) allocate both the interest received to the present liquidity as well as the interest to be paid to the required liquidity;
(b) not include subsidiaries and branches that each make up less than 1% of the balance sheet total in the liquidity calculations, if at least 95% of the total consolidated balance sheet total is included in the calculation;
(c) not include indirect participations and branches of participations if, in relation to the credit institution as a whole, there is no large liquidity requirement and the liquidity provision is not mainly dependent on the parent company, or the head office respectively, in the liquidity calculations; or
(d) compensate a liquidity shortage in convertible or inconvertible currencies with a surplus in convertible currencies, insofar as the latter originate from a country from which free transfer of liquidity is possible.[191]

The required liquidity of a credit institution is the total of the weighted outgoing cash flows based on the scheduled items, plus the weighted entrusted funds and other items not included in the maturity schedule that can be called up or could lead to a payment obligation during the weekly period or the monthly period

---

188. Art. 3:63(3) WFT.
189. Art. 3:63(4) WFT.
190. Art. 106 Prudential Supervision Decree.
191. Art. 107 Prudential Supervision Decree.

respectively.[192] DNB has laid down rules in the Regulation on Liquidity under the WFT with regard to the aforementioned items and the weighting thereof.

The existing liquidity of a credit institution in the weekly period is formed by the weighted inventory items, the weighted cash inflow of the schedule items during the weekly period and the official stand-by facilities.[193] The credit institution must include in the calculation of the existing liquidity in the weekly period only the assets that are at its disposal in connection with the daily liquidity management in order to be able to provide for the direct liquidity requirement and the incoming cash flows from the core activities, which are taken into account in connection with the daily liquidity management. The following are in any case included:

(a) financial instruments on the basis of which liquid assets can be obtained in a short term by means of selling or lending without incurring more than marginal costs or losses;
(b) inter-bank assets, payable on demand; and
(c) amounts owed by governments and professional money market parties, payable on demand.[194]

The existing liquidity of the credit institution in the monthly period is formed by the weighted inventory items and the weighted cash inflow during the monthly period.[195] The credit institution includes the liquidity surplus of a branch or a subsidiary domiciled outside of the Netherlands in the calculation of the existing liquidity, only insofar as:

(a) the transfer of the liquidity surplus does not lead to a liquidity shortage at the branch or subsidiary according to the local liquidity test;
(b) it concerns a surplus in convertible currencies; and
(c) free and cross-border transfer of liquidity is possible.[196]

In the calculation of the existing liquidity, the credit institution is not allowed to include assets that cannot be transferred unrestrictedly and deposits payable on demand with persons that are not credit institutions or professional money market parties.[197]

---

192. Art. 108 Prudential Supervision Decree.
193. Art. 111(1) Prudential Supervision Decree.
194. Art. 111(2) Prudential Supervision Decree.
195. Art. 111(3) Prudential Supervision Decree.
196. Art. 111(4) Prudential Supervision Decree.
197. Art. 111(5) Prudential Supervision Decree.

5.6 **Supervision of the Administrative Organisation and Internal Controls**

5.6.1 *Controlled and Sound Business Operations*

A bank must have adequate policies to ensure sound operations.[198] This will include the following integrity aspects:

(a) preventing conflicts of interests;
(b) preventing any involvement in criminal offences or other breaches of the law that could damage the confidence in the bank or in the financial markets;
(c) preventing that the confidence in the bank or in the financial markets may be affected on account of the bank's customers;
(d) preventing any acts that are so contrary to generally accepted standards that they could seriously affect the confidence in the bank or in the financial markets.

Furthermore, a bank must organise its operations in such a way as to ensure controlled and sound business operations.[199] This will include the following aspects:

(a) controlling business processes and business risks;
(b) controlling the above-mentioned integrity aspects;
(c) controlling the bank's solidity.

These requirements apply *mutatis mutandis* to Dutch branches of banks established in a non-Member State.[200]

5.6.1.1 Sound Business Operations

A bank should have clear policies, measures and procedures to control integrity risks. An integrity risk is a threat to the reputation or an existing or future threat to the capital or the result of the bank due to insufficient compliance with a statutory provision.[201] Self-evidently, this is understood to include for example, institutions

---

198. Art. 3:10 WFT.
199. Art. 3:17 WFT.
200. Art. 3:23 WFT.
201. Art. 1 Prudential Supervision Decree (definition of "integrity risk").

ensuring that they do not become involved in, and are not used for, money launder-ing, financing terrorism, insider trading, (tax) fraud, etc.

To do so a bank should provide for a management cycle aimed at integrity risk control, consisting of the following elements:

1. systematic integrity risk analysis (risk-based approach);
2. the translation of the policies into internal measures and procedures
3. information sharing and education within the institution;
4. systematic testing and adjustment of the policies, measures and procedure;
5. independent internal supervision and procedures that ensure that identified shortcomings or defects are reported to the compliance officer;[202]
6. procedures that ensure that identified shortcomings lead to a fitting adjust-ment.[203]

Furthermore, a bank must have established procedures and measures with regard to the prevention of conflicts of interest of, *inter alia*, the bank's executive and su-pervisory directors and group directors,[204] including rules regarding the provision of financial services to these persons and their family members. Such provision of services only takes place within the normal business operations and with the prior approval of the supervisory board. If the services are provided outside of the exist-ing system of employment conditions, it may only take place in the course of the normal business operations and against the usual commercial terms and conditions and collateral.[205]

A bank needs to have established procedures and measures concerning the handling and recording of incidents. An incident is a conduct or event that forms a serious threat for the sound pursuit of the business operations of the bank.[206] Incidents must be notified to DNB without delay. Following an incident the bank takes remedial actions to control the risks involved and prevent repetition.[207]

A bank must make a substantiated assessment of the integrity of persons whom they wish to appoint to an integrity sensitive position.[208] This includes the management positions just under the top management (second echelon) and other positions to which an authority is linked that entails a substantial risk for the sound

---

202. As referred to in Art. 21 Prudential Supervision Decree.
203. Art. 10 Prudential Supervision Decree.
204. A group director is defined as every person who determines the policy within a group (Art. 1 Prudential Supervision Decree).
205. Art. 11 Prudential Supervision Decree.
206. Art. 1 Prudential Supervision Decree (definition of "incident").
207. Art. 12 Prudential Supervision Decree.
208. Art. 13 Prudential Supervision Decree.

business operations.[209] The assessment must at least satisfy the following requirements: (i) the identity of the person concerned must be verified; (ii) the information
and references supplied by the person concerned must be verified to ensure that
they are correct and complete.

Banks should know their customers and refrain from doing business with
parties that could affect the confidence in the bank or in the financial markets.
Therefore, banks should have customer due diligence (**CDD**) procedures and
measures in place. CDD is closely related to the prevention of money laundering
and the financing of terrorism;[210] however, it is also relevant in relation to the
sound business operations of a bank in order to prevent that confidence in the bank
or in the financial markets could be damaged due to its customers. The bank must
implement procedures and measures regarding the following elements of CDD:

1. client acceptance;
2. client identification and verification;
3. risk classifications pertaining to clients, products or services;
4. client, account and transaction monitoring and review and risk management;
5. record keeping.[211]

In addition, DNB has provided technical rules relating to protected accounts (*afgeschermde rekeningen*).[212]

Banks must also have procedures in place concerning the provision of back-
to-back loans. A back-to-back loan is a credit instrument whereby cash or financial
instruments are made available to the borrower, for which collateral is provided
to the lender, directly or indirectly, from the own liquid assets of the borrower.[213]

Such an instrument is particularly vulnerable to abuse. If the bank intends to
provide a back-to-back loan, it must investigate whether the loan will be used for
legitimate purposes. When a back-to-back loan is provided, the credit documentation concerned must specify the collateral arrangements.[214]

Finally, banks must, at the request of DNB, investigate their records for certain
persons or institutions, who in the opinion of the Minister of Finance, in connection with suspected terrorist activities, could harm the integrity of the financial

---

209. Art. 1 Prudential Supervision Decree (definition of "integrity sensitive position").
210. See paragraph 10.5.
211. Art. 14 Prudential Supervision Decree.
212. Regulation on Protected Accounts pursuant to the WFT (*Regeling afgeschermde rekeningen
     Wft*) in conjunction with Art. 14(6) Prudential Supervision Decree.
213. Art. 1 Prudential Supervision Decree (definition of "back-to-back loan").
214. Art. 15 Prudential Supervision Decree.

sector. The outcome of the investigation must be provided to DNB within a term specified by DNB.[215]

5.6.1.2 Controlled Business Operations

The business operations of a bank must comprise:

    (a) a clear and adequate organisational structure;
    (b) a clear and adequate division of tasks, authorities and responsibilities;
    (c) an adequate recording of rights and obligations;
    (d) clear reporting lines; and
    (e) an adequate system of information provision and communication.[216]

The business operations are aligned with the nature, the size, the risks and the complexity of the bank's activities and must be recorded in a transparent manner. The effectiveness of the structure of the organisation and of the procedures and measures have to be audited at least annually in an independent manner by the bank's internal audit function. Identified deficiencies must be remediated.[217]

The internal control function of a bank that may provide investment services or investment activities, has the task of:

    (a) establishing and implementing an audit plan to examine and assess the soundness and effectiveness of the systems, internal control procedures and rules of the bank;
    (b) making recommendations based on the results of these activities;
    (c) verifying whether these recommendations are followed up; and
    (d) reporting at least annually to the executive board and the supervisory board with regard to matters concerning the internal audit and the measures taken in the event of identified deficiencies.[218]

In addition, the business operations of a bank must consist of the following elements:

    – an adequate segregation of duties and responsibilities;[219]

---

215. Art. 16 Prudential Supervision Decree.
216. Art. 17(1) Prudential Supervision Decree.
217. Art. 17(2-4) Prudential Supervision Decree.
218. Art. 17a Prudential Supervision Decree.
219. Art. 18 Prudential Supervision Decree.

- a correct, timely and complete documentation of all rights and obligations of the bank;[220]
- an information system that enables effective control of the business processes and the risks and that provides for internal and external information requirements;[221]
- an independent and adequate compliance function. The compliance function has the task of monitoring compliance with statutory rules as well as internal rules. If it concerns a bank that may provide investment services or investment activities, the compliance function has the required authority, resources, expertise and access to all necessary information to be able to perform its tasks independently and effectively. In this case the compliance function also has the task of:
  - (a) advising persons who are responsible for providing investment services or for performing investment activities with regard to the compliance with the statutory rules and internal rules;
  - (b) supervising the soundness and effectiveness of the internal rules and procedures;
  - (c) assessing the effectiveness of the procedures and measures regarding the remedy of identified deficiencies; and
  - (d) reporting at least annually to the executive board and the supervisory board with regard to matters concerning the compliance with statutory rules and internal rules.[222]

5.6.1.3 Risk Management

A bank pursues a policy aimed at managing relevant risks. Such risks include, in particular, the concentration risk, credit and counterparty risk, liquidity risk, market risk, operational risk, interest-rate risk resulting from non-trading activities, residual risk, securitisation risk and insurance risk. A bank also takes into account the risks that follow from the macroeconomic environment in which the firm operates and that are related to the stage in the economic cycle. The policy is laid down in procedures and measures to manage the relevant risks and is integrated in the business processes. These procedures and measures also consist of authorisation procedures, imposing limits, monitoring limits and procedures and measures for emergency situations and are aligned with the nature, the size, the risk profile and the complexity of the activities. The procedures and measures are recorded and

---

220. Art. 19 Prudential Supervision Decree.
221. Art. 20 Prudential Supervision Decree.
222. Art. 21 Prudential Supervision Decree.

communicated to all relevant business units of the bank. The bank must have an independent risk management function that carries out independent risk management in a systematic manner that is aimed at identifying, measuring and evaluating the risk to which banks are or can be exposed.[223] A bank verifies in a systematic manner that these procedures and measures are complied with and ensures that identified shortcomings or deficiencies are remediated.[224]

The risk management of a bank that may provide investment services or carry out investment activities also has the task of:

(a) exercising control with regard to the soundness and effectiveness of the risk management procedures and measures;
(b) exercising control with regard to the extent in which the bank and its employees comply with these procedures and measures;
(c) exercising control with regard to the soundness and effectiveness of the measures that have been taken to remediate identified shortcomings or deficiencies; and
(d) reporting at least annually to the executive board and the supervisory board, in particular whether measures have been taken in the event of identified shortcomings.[225]

A bank has established solid, effective and comprehensive strategies and procedures on the basis of which it continuously verifies whether and ensures that, the level, composition and division of its own funds are in accordance with the size and the nature of its current and potential future risks. The bank verifies in a systematic manner that these strategies and procedures are complied with and ensures that the identified shortcomings or deficiencies are remediated.[226]

If a bank makes use of internally developed models, it assesses the validity of these models and the underlying assumptions and variables in a systematic manner by, among others, comparing the projections of the model with the actual outcomes.[227]

---

223. Art. 23 and following Prudential Supervision Decree. Arts. 23a-23e elaborate on the procedures and measures as referred to in Art. 23(3) Prudential Supervision Decree concerning credit and counterparty risk, liquidity risk, operational risk, interest-rate risk and securitisation risk.
224. Art. 24 Prudential Supervision Decree.
225. Art. 24b Prudential Supervision Decree.
226. Art. 24a Prudential Supervision Decree.
227. Art. 25 Prudential Supervision Decree.

5.6.2 *Outsourcing*[228]

If a bank outsources activities to third parties, this may not hamper the supervision of the bank or have a negative effect on the quality of the bank's internal audit function.[229] The tasks and duties of the day-to-day policymakers (i.e. the members of the executive board) are not to be outsourced.[230]

The bank must have an adequate policy and procedures and measures with regard to the outsourcing of activities on a structural basis.[231] Furthermore, it must have adequate procedures, measures, expertise and information to be able to assess the execution of the activities that have been outsourced on a structural basis.[232] The outsourcing must be recorded in a written agreement, regulating in any case the following:

(a) the mutual exchange of information, including agreements about providing information requested by DNB and the AFM;

(b) the possibility for the bank to at all times make changes in the manner in which the outsourced activities are carried out;

(c) the obligation of the third party to enable the bank to continue to comply with the WFT;

(d) the possibility for DNB and the AFM to carry out on site inspection at the third party's premises;[233] and

(e) the manner in which the agreement is terminated, and the manner in which it is ensured that the bank is able, after the termination of the agreement, to carry out the activities again itself or have another third party carry out these activities.[234]

These requirements do not apply to activities that are outsourced to a group company domiciled in a Member State.[235]

The above requirements apply *mutatis mutandis* to Dutch branches of banks established in a non-Member State.[236]

---

228. Chapter 5 of the Prudential Supervision Decree in conjunction with Art. 3:18 WFT.
229. Arts. 27(1) and 28 Prudential Supervision Decree.
230. Art. 27(2) Prudential Supervision Decree.
231. Art. 29 Prudential Supervision Decree.
232. Art. 30 Prudential Supervision Decree.
233. The supervisors will only make use of this possibility when it is not possible to determine in another manner that the rules regarding the outsourced activities are complied with (Art. 31(3) Prudential Supervision Decree).
234. Art. 31 Prudential Supervision Decree.
235. Art. 32 Prudential Supervision Decree.
236. Art. 3:23 WFT.

5.6.3   *Corporate Governance*

In addition to the provisions of the WFT addressing corporate governance issues, the Dutch Corporate Governance Code (*Nederlandse corporate governance code*) applies to Dutch-based banks that are listed.[237] However, this code does not apply to all licensed banks; non-listed banks often comply on a voluntary basis.

On 9 September 2009, the Dutch Banking Association (*Nederlandse Vereniging van Banken*) drew up the Banking Code (*Code Banken*).[238] The Banking Code is a response to the report "Restoring Trust" ("*Naar herstel van vertrouwen*") which was published by the Advisory Committee on the Future of Banks (*Adviescommissie Toekomst Banken*) on 7 April 2009. This code applies to banks possessing a licence under the WFT. It is expressly recommended that Dutch branches of banks established in another Member State also apply the Banking Code. The Banking Code contains principles regarding:

- the composition, the expertise, the tasks and working methods of the supervisory board and executive board;
- the responsibilities of the supervisory board and executive board as regards risk management;
- the internal audit function; and
- the remuneration policy.

The Banking Code came into effect on 1 January 2010. All banks shall report every year in their annual report regarding the manner in which they have applied the principles of the Banking Code. Compliance with the Banking Code shall be monitored by an independent monitoring committee. The Minister of Finance has announced plans to provide a statutory basis for the Banking Code. In addition, the Government is preparing several statutory measures to improve the governance of banks.[239]

---

237. www.corpgov.nl. The Dutch Corporate Governance Code is a code of conduct as referred to in Art. 2:391(4) Civil Code.
238. www.nvb.nl.
239. Such as a draft legislative proposal to, *inter alia*, introduce requirements regarding the expertise of supervisory board members.

5.6.4   *Role of the Bank's External Auditor*

5.6.4.1   Auditor's Task

Dutch-based banks must provide DNB within six months of the end of the financial year with the annual accounts, the annual report and other information[240].[241] Foreign banks operating from a branch in the Netherlands must provide DNB within six months of the end of the financial year with the annual accounts, the consolidated accounts and the annual report. The annual accounts shall be accompanied by an auditor's statement regarding fair presentation. Furthermore, Dutch-based banks, branches of banks established in another Member State and banks established in a non-Member State operating from a branch in the Netherlands must submit statements to DNB. These statements must be certified periodically by an external auditor.[242]

The instruction to audit the bank's financial statements given to the external auditors must include high-level testing and assessment with regard to the adequacy of the structure of the organisation and risk management.[243]

If DNB considers that an auditor is no longer equipped to issue opinions and statements in relation to the bank, DNB may decide that an auditor is no longer authorised to do so.[244] This may occur, for example, on account of the increasing scale and complexity of the bank.

5.6.4.2   Auditor's Reporting Obligation

An auditor auditing the annual accounts of Dutch-based banks, branches of banks established in another Member State and banks established in a non-Member State operating from a branch in the Netherlands must notify DNB as soon as possible of any circumstance noted during the audit activities which:

1. is contrary to the regulatory requirements applicable to the bank;
2. threatens the bank's continuity;
3. causes the auditor to withhold a statement regarding the fair presentation or to have reservations.[245]

---

240. Referred to in Arts. 2:361(1), 2:391(1), and 2:392(1)(a) to (h) Civil Code.
241. Art. 3:71 WFT.
242. Arts. 3:72(7), 3:77 and 3:81 WFT.
243. Art. 22 Prudential Supervision Decree.
244. Art. 1:78 WFT.
245. Arts. 3:88, 3:90 and 3:91 WFT.

If it concerns a breach of regulatory requirements supervised by the AFM, the AFM must be notified.[246] Furthermore, the auditor must provide DNB and the AFM as soon as possible with the following information:

(a) the auditor's report issued to the executive board and the supervisory board;
(b) the management letters;
(c) correspondence between the auditor and the bank directly relating to the auditor's statement concerning the fair presentation of the annual financial accounts; and
(d) on DNB's request, a further explanation of this information.[247]

If the bank wishes to provide the information itself, instead of the auditor, it may do so. The auditor must, however, ascertain whether the information is actually provided to the regulators.[248]

6. CONDUCT OF BUSINESS SUPERVISION

Banks are subject to the conduct of business supervision exercised by the AFM. This supervision is focused on orderly and transparent financial market processes, integrity of relations between market players and due care in the provision of services to clients. Part 4 of the WFT contains rules which a financial corporation (*financiële onderneming*), including a bank, has to observe when providing financial services. These include rules for informing customers (transparency) and the duty of care. These rules apply to banks when offering, advising on, or acting as an intermediary regarding financial products, including savings accounts, loans, mortgages, insurance products, investments, etc.

For the purposes of the conduct of business supervision on banks, a distinction can be made between banks that do and banks that do not provide investment services or perform investment activities.[249] Regarding the conduct of business rules in relation to providing investment services or performing investment activities, including offering units in a collective investment scheme, reference is made to the paragraphs dealing with the conduct of business rules that apply to investment firms, see paragraph 4.1.5.5 of Chapter 2.

---

246. Art. 4:27(1) WFT.
247. Art. 136 Prudential Supervision Decree in conjunction with Art. 3:88(4) WFT and Art. 107 Conduct of Business Decree (*Besluit Gedragstoezicht financiële ondernemingen Wft*) in conjunction with Art. 4:27(4) WFT.
248. Art. 137 Prudential Supervision Decree and Art. 108 Conduct of Business Decree.
249. For the meanings of these terms see paragraph 4.1.1 of Chapter 2.

6.1 Complaints Procedure

A bank that provides investment services must have an internal complaints procedure and it must be associated with the Netherlands Financial Services Complaints Tribunal (*Klachteninstituut Financiële Dienstverlening* or **Kifid**), the designated disputes body handling disputes in respect of the provision of financial services.[250]

6.2 Information Obligation

Banks must supply their customers with accurate, clear, understandable and not misleading information about the products that they sell and the services they provide insofar as this is reasonably relevant for an adequate assessment of that service or product. This information must be provided prior to sale and the bank must during the term of a contract inform the customer with regard to material changes in the information provided.[251] The information obligation implies the following:

1. Prior to the conclusion of the agreement, the customer must be provided with at least the following information:[252]
   (a) the statutory name and – if other than the statutory name – trade name or trade names;
   (b) the nature of the financial services;
   (c) the internal complaints procedure and the disputes body to which the bank is associated;
   (d) the fact that the bank is registered in the register held by DNB and the AFM.
2. If it concerns an agreement at a distance,[253] the following information must

---

250. Art. 4:17 WFT and Arts. 39-42 Conduct of Business Decree with regard to the complains procedure and Arts. 43-48 Conduct of Business Decree with regard to the disputes body.
251. Arts. 4:19 and 4:20 WFT. On application, the AFM may grant dispensation, if the applicant demonstrates that it cannot reasonably comply with these requirements and that the objectives which these requirements seek to achieve are achieved in other ways (Art. 4:20(7) WFT). If the financial service is provided through an intermediary, the information shall be supplied by this intermediary, unless the bank and the intermediary have agreed that the bank will comply (Art. 4:21 WFT).
252. Art. 57 Conduct of Business Decree.
253. An agreement at a distance is defined as:
   (a) a contract regarding a financial service or financial product concluded between a financial enterprise and a consumer in the context of a system organised by the financial enterprise for distance sales or services, which contract is established exclusively by using one or more distance communication technologies;
   (b) a contract intended to accrue a fund to pay for the provision of the funeral of a natural person, concluded between a funeral expenses and benefits in kind insurer and a

also be provided:[254]

(a) the name of the Chamber of Commerce where the bank is registered, and the number of the registration;

(b) the principal characteristics of the financial product;

(c) the risks related to the financial product;

(d) the total costs or, if the exact costs cannot be specified, the method for calculation of the costs, so as to enable the customer to verify the costs;

(e) whether or not other amounts than set out under d. can be payable by the customer;

(f) the additional costs related to the use of distance communication technology;

(g) the manner of payment by the customer and the manner in which the distance agreement will be carried out;

(h) restrictions to the period of validity of the provided information (for example if a special offer is made which only lasts for a certain period);

(i) the minimum term of the distance agreement;

(j) whether the customer has the contractual right of early termination of the distance agreement and whether a penalty would be payable in such case;

(k) (i) whether the customer has the right to dissolve the agreement at a distance without incurring a penalty and without giving a reason during 14 calendar days starting the day of the agreement, or, if this is later, during 14 calendar days from the day where the consumer has received all required information;[255] and (ii) the duration of and the conditions for exercising that right, including information about the amount that the consumer may have to pay, the consequences of not exercising that right and the manner in which that right can be exercised;

---

consumer in the context of a system organised by the funeral expenses and benefits in kind insurer for distance sales or services, which contract does not entail an investment risk for the latter and is established exclusively by using one or more distance communication technologies (Art. 1:1 WFT).

254. Art. 77 Conduct of Business Decree. Where the telephone is used for making unsolicited calls to promote the conclusion of a distance agreement, pursuant to Art. 79 Conduct of Business Decree additional rules apply with regard to the provision of information.

255. As referred to in Art. 4:28 WFT. Arts. 4:28-4:20 WFT contain provisions with regard to agreements at a distance.

   (l) the existence of guarantee funds or other compensation schemes applicable to the distance agreement not falling under the Deposit Guarantee Scheme Directive[256] and the Investor-Compensation Schemes Directive;[257]

  (m) the language or languages in which the terms and conditions of the distance agreement, and the required information, will be provided, and the language or languages in which the financial service provider will communicate during the term of the agreement;

   (n) the law applicable prior to the conclusion of the agreement, the law that will govern that agreement and the competent court; and

   (o) the remaining conditions of the distance agreement.

3. During the term of a credit agreement involving a variable lending fee, the bank shall inform the customer of any change in the lending fee, whereby it shall also inform the customer about changes in the effective annual interest rate. Furthermore, the bank must, at the customer's request, provide an itemised summary of the outstanding balance. Up to one year after the completion of a credit agreement, customers are entitled to an itemised statement, at their request.[258]

4. During the term of an agreement at a distance, customers are entitled, upon their request, to receive a copy of the terms and conditions of the agreement.[259]

5. If the bank is acting as a broker (e.g. for insurance products), it must inform the customer of, *inter alia*, the manner in which it is remunerated and its relationship (i.e. the contractual obligations) with the party offering the financial product. The bank must disclose any shares that are held in the party offering the financial product and vice versa.[260] Furthermore, the bank's advertisements also have to comply with the relevant requirements.[261]

---

256. Directive 94/19/EC of the European Parliament and the Council of 30 May 1994 on deposit-guarantee schemes.

257. Directive 1997/9/EG of the European Parliament and the Council of the European Union of 3 March 1997 concerning the investor-compensation schemes.

258. Art. 68 Conduct of Business Decree.

259. Art. 80 Conduct of Business Decree.

260. Art. 4:72 WFT.

261. Detailed advertising rules are provided by Arts. 52-53 Conduct of Business Decree and Arts. 2:1-2:3 Further Conduct of Business Regulation (*Nadere regeling gedragstoezicht financiële ondernemingen Wft*) in conjunction with Art. 54 Conduct of Business Decree.

6.3   **Financial Information Leaflet**

If the bank offers a complex product,[262] it is obliged to make a Financial Information Leaflet (*Financiële Bijsluiter*) available on its website and supply this at the request of a customer.[263] A Financial Information Leaflet must include the following information:[264]

  (a) the purpose of the Financial Information Leaflet;
  (b) the nature and purpose of the complex product;
  (c) the financial risks of the complex product, which are demonstrated by means of a risk indicator;
  (d) the customer's obligations;
  (e) whether or not a contractual right exists to cancel the agreement regarding the complex product prematurely, and the costs and other consequences attached to such a cancellation;
  (f) the consequences if the customer dies; and
  (g) example investment returns and the costs of the complex product.

A Financial Information Leaflet may not contain any information on subjects other than the above.[265] Additional detailed rules are provided for a Financial Information Leaflet for different categories of complex products.[266]

6.4   **Credit Prospectus**

If a bank offers credit it must have a credit prospectus available and supply this prospectus free of charge to any consumer who so requests.[267] The credit prospectus must contain the following data:

  (a) a description of the procedure to be followed for a credit application;

---

262. Art. 1(d) Conduct of Business Decree contains a list of financial products that are designated complex products.
263. Art. 65 Conduct of Business Decree in conjunction with Art. 4:22(1) WFT.
264. Art. 66(1) Conduct of Business Decree.
265. Art. 66(3) Conduct of Business Decree.
266. Arts. 3:1-3:10 Further Conduct of Business Regulation.
267. Art. 4:33 WFT. Pursuant to Art. 111 Conduct of Business Decree certain parties are excluded from the obligation to have a credit prospectus available, such as mortgage lenders and parties that are obliged to have a Financial Information Leaflet available.

(b) a general description of the criteria underlying the assessment of the consumer's creditworthiness, including at least two representative examples of the application of those criteria;

(c) a statement of:

  1°. the fact that the credit provider participates in a credit registration system;

  2°. the name and registered office of the institution that maintains that system; and

  3°. the purpose and working method of that system, showing the specific situations in which the provider may ask for data regarding the consumer's creditworthiness; and that data regarding credit granted will be supplied by the provider to (and which is registered by) the institution that maintains the said system;

(d) such indications or descriptions of the credit offered to show whether it is revolving credit or another type of credit;

(e) a description of the general conditions under which the provider is prepared to enter into credit agreements, including, where applicable, the conditions in respect of:

  1°. security rights to be established for the benefit of the provider;

  2°. the amount owed by the consumer becoming due and payable before the term; and

  3°. the consumer's entitlement to full or partial early repayment;

(f) if the establishment of a credit agreement obliges the consumer to enter into another agreement:

  1°. a description of the clause to this effect; and

  2°. a statement that the consumer has the right to decide the other party with which the other agreement will be entered into;[268]

(g) a statement that the customer, if he fails to fulfil his payment obligation, shall owe compensation only after a notice of default;[269] and

(h) a note[270] reading as follows: "The effective annual interest rate is a price indication for the credit that incorporates all the costs of the credit".[271]

If revolving credit is involved, the following information must also be included in the prospectus:

---

268. Unless Art. 33(b)(1°) of the Consumer Credit Act (*Wet op het consumentenkrediet*) does not apply to the credit.
269. Unless Art. 34(b) of the Consumer Credit Act does not apply to the credit.
270. As referred to in Art. 53(10) Conduct of Business Decree.
271. Art. 112(1) Conduct of Business Decree.

(a) four representative credit limits;[272]
(b) the points of departure in calculating the theoretical term;
(c) where applicable: the level of compensation that will be owed if the customer still fails to fulfil his payment obligation after a notice of default; and
(d) where applicable: the level of compensation owed in the case of early repayment by the consumer.[273]

If it does not concern revolving credit, the following information must be included in the prospectus:

(a) four representative credit sums;[274]
(b) at least one example of a calculation that shows the manner in which – based on the credit sum, the monthly payment and the term – the amount can be determined regarding the total lending fee owed by the consumer for the regular fulfilment of the agreement;
(c) where applicable: the level of the compensation that will be owed if the consumer fails to fulfil his payment obligation after a notice of default; and
(d) where applicable: the level of the compensation owed in the case of early repayment by the consumer, and at least one example of a calculation showing the manner in which the amount of this compensation is determined.[275]

6.5 Duty of Care

6.5.1 *Offering Credit*

Before concluding a credit contract, a bank must, in the customer's interest, obtain information on the customer's financial position and assess, in order to prevent over-extension of credit to the consumer, whether concluding the contract would be justified. The bank is prohibited from entering into a credit contract where this would not be justified as regards over-extension of credit to the customer.[276]

---

272. Together with the other features of the credit referred to in Art. 53(1) and (2) Conduct of Business Decree.
273. Art. 112(3) Conduct of Business Decree.
274. Together with the other features of the credit referred to in Art. 53(1) and (2) Conduct of Business Decree.
275. Art. 112(4) Conduct of Business Decree.
276. Art. 4:34 WFT.

There is a prohibition against entering into a credit agreement where the credit sum or credit limit exceeds EUR 1,000, if the bank does not have sufficient information, laid down in writing or on another durable medium, about the customer's financial position in order to assess whether entering into the agreement is justified and in order to avoid over-extension of credit.[277]

Before entering into a credit agreement with a consumer where the credit sum or credit limit exceeds EUR 250, the bank must consult the credit registration system in which it participates for details of credit previously granted to the consumer.[278]

To avoid over-extension of credit, the bank must lay down the criteria on which it bases the assessment of a customer's credit application – and it must apply these criteria in assessing a credit application.[279]

6.5.2 *Advising and Performing Portfolio Management Activities*

If a bank advises[280] a customer, or if it performs portfolio management activities:

(a) it must, in the interest of the customer, obtain information about the customer's financial position, knowledge, experience, objectives and risk tolerance, insofar as this is reasonably relevant to the advice or the portfolio management;

(b) it must ensure that its advice or manner of managing the portfolio, insofar as reasonably possible, is partly based on the information referred to under (a); and

(c) it must, where the advice concerns financial products other than financial instruments, explain the considerations underlying its advice insofar as this is necessary for a proper understanding of the advice.[281]

If the bank, in providing a financial service other than an investment service, refrains from advising, it has to make this known to the customer.[282]

---

277. Art. 113 Conduct of Business Decree.
278. Art. 114 Conduct of Business Decree.
279. Art. 115 Conduct of Business Decree.
280. Art. 1:1 WFT defines "to advise" as follows: "to recommend, in the pursuit of a profession or business, one or more specific financial products to a particular consumer or, in the case of a financial instrument or insurance, client".
281. Art. 4:23(1) WFT.
282. Art. 4:23(2) WFT.

6.5.3   Unsolicited Communications

The use of automatic calling systems without human intervention, faxes or electronic messages for transmitting unsolicited information to a consumer in order to promote the conclusion of a distance agreement shall only be permitted with the consumer's prior consent. The use of other long-distance communication technologies for transmitting unsolicited information or making unsolicited announcements to a consumer in order to promote the conclusion of a distance agreement will be permitted, unless the consumer concerned has indicated that he does not wish to receive information or announcements transmitted by means of these technologies. Where electronic messages are used, the bank must disclose (i) its real identity; and (ii) a valid postal address or number to which the recipient may address a request for termination of such communication.[283]

6.6   Commission

A bank may not pay or receive commission with regard to the brokerage services or advice regarding a complex product or a mortgage that is not necessary for the provision of the relevant service. The foregoing does not apply, *inter alia*, if the brokers, before providing the service, informs the customer extensively, accurately and in a clear manner of the existence, the nature and the amount or, if the amount cannot be identified, the manner of calculating the commission.[284]

The initial commission which is paid to a broker may not exceed half the sum of that initial commission and the total ongoing commission in respect of the agreement concerned. The ongoing commission is paid to a broker proportionally during a minimum period of ten years after the conclusion of the agreement concerned. If the term is less than ten years, the commission will be paid proportionally during that term.[285] If an agreement regarding a complex product or mortgage is terminated prematurely during the first five years after its conclusion, otherwise than through the death of the insured party or through the sale of the immovable property to which the complex product relates, the initial commission shall be reduced proportionally.[286]

---

283. Art. 81 Conduct of Business Decree.
284. Art. 149a Conduct of Business Decree.
285. Art. 150 Conduct of Business Decree.
286. Art. 151 Conduct of Business Decree.

6.7   Market Conduct Aspects of the Operations

Banks that also provide investment services or perform investment activities must comply with the provisions regarding the operational structure with regard to orderly and transparent financial market processes, integrity in relations between market parties and due care in the provision of services to clients and unit holders.[287]

A bank that does not provide investment services or perform investment activities needs to comply with specific provisions concerning orderly and transparent financial market processes, integrity in relations between market parties and due care in the provision of services, meaning (i) safeguarding the provision of information to clients or consumers; and (ii) safeguarding due care in the provision of services to clients or consumers.[288] Consequently, a bank that advises a customer must, insofar as this advice results in the conclusion of an agreement, retain the obtained information, as well as the data concerning the financial product sold, for a minimum period of one year from the moment that the advice was issued.[289] Furthermore, if a bank provides credit, it must retain the information, as well as the credit agreement, for a minimum period of five years from the day on which that agreement was fulfilled.[290]

Finally, it is of note that a Dutch branch office of a bank must comply with the rules with regard to sound business conduct in respect of operating in markets in financial instruments.[291] This means that a bank must:

   (a) take adequate measures in order to control conflicts of interest with regard to transactions in financial instruments;[292]

   (b) take adequate measures:

       (i) in order to prevent price-sensitive information from becoming known outside the circle of persons who need to be aware of this information as part of their duties, profession or position;

---

287. As referred to in Art. 4:14(2)(c) under 1° to 6° WFT.
288. Art. 4:15(2) and (3) WFT. Pursuant to Art. 4:15(4) the AFM may, on application, whether or not for a fixed period, grant a full or partial dispensation from these requirements, if the applicant demonstrates that it cannot reasonably comply with those provisions and that the objectives which this section seeks to achieve are achieved in other ways.
289. Art. 32 Conduct of Business Decree.
290. Art. 33 Conduct of Business Decree.
291. Art. 5:68(1) WFT. Pursuant to Art. 5:68(3) WFT the AFM may, on application, whether or not for a fixed period, grant a full or partial dispensation from these requirements, if the applicant demonstrates that it cannot reasonably comply with those provisions and that the objectives which this section seeks to achieve are achieved in other ways.
292. Art. 20 Market Abuse Decree (*Besluit marktmisbruik Wft*).

    (ii) in order to ensure that persons associated with the bank exercise the utmost care in dealing with information that they know or should reasonably suspect must be classified as price-sensitive;[293]

(c) designate a person to be responsible for the internal supervision of compliance with these provisions (i.e. a compliance officer), and lay down rules with regard to the exercising of that supervision;[294] and

(d) keep a record of the transactions in financial instruments that it conducts on its own account, which record shall contain the following details:
    (i) the transactions conducted each day;
    (ii) the financial instruments to which each transaction relates;
    (iii) the date and time when each transaction was carried out;
    (iv) where applicable, the identity of the third party that carried out the transaction; and
    (v) the price or prices for which the transactions were carried out.[295]

A bank that does not provide investment services or perform investment activities which owns a qualifying holding[296] in an issuer or whose transactions in financial instruments[297] during the past calendar year amounted to EUR 20 million or more must have a code of conduct for private transactions by persons associated with the bank who are directly or indirectly involved in the bank's transactions in financial instruments or who otherwise regularly have or may have inside information as part of their duties, profession or position. The bank must ensure that all those

---

293. Art. 21 Market Abuse Decree.
294. Art. 22 Market Abuse Decree.
295. Art. 23 Market Abuse Decree.
296. A qualifying holding is a direct or indirect holding representing 10% or more of the bank's issued capital or the right to exercise, directly or indirectly, 10% or more of the voting rights in the bank, or the right to exercise, directly or indirectly, equivalent control over the bank, whereby in determining the number of voting rights of a party in an enterprise, the voting rights shall also include the voting rights which it has or is deemed to have under Art. 5:45 WFT (Art. 1:1 WFT (definition of "qualifying holding").
297. These transactions in financial instruments shall not include: (a) the transactions of a foreign branch office or a subsidiary of the bank; and (b) the transactions of an enterprise based outside the Netherlands of which the enterprise concerned is a branch office (Art. 24(3) Market Abuse Decree). Moreover, the following transactions shall be disregarded: (a) transactions in bonds issued by the State of the Netherlands, other governments and government bodies, international treaty organisations and supranational bodies governed by public law; (b) transactions in financial instruments, the management of which has been transferred to a third party, on such conditions that the enterprise exerts no influence on the selection of funds or on individual transactions; and (c) transactions in index-linked funds or in units in collective investment schemes that are available only to professional market parties (Art. 24(4) Market Abuse Decree).

concerned are familiar with the code of conduct and shall supervise compliance with this code.[298] The code of conduct shall contain rules that are applicable to all designated insiders, including:

(a) the persons that determine or co-determine the bank's day-to-day policy (i.e. the members of the executive board);
(b) the persons whose duties consist of conducting or effecting transactions in financial instruments, or of offering, providing, finalising or monitoring services in relation to brokerage in financial instruments or in relation to portfolio management; and
(c) other persons who regularly possess or may possess inside information by virtue of their association with the enterprise.[299]

A bank must establish procedures relating to the designation of insiders and maintain an insider list.[300] The code of conduct regulates that an insider must avoid any mixing of business and private interests, or the reasonably foreseeable appearance thereof, with regard to transactions in financial instruments, and that an insider: (a) must disclose any private transactions that he conducts, in the manner prescribed in the code of conduct, and with due observance of the regulations laid down in the code of conduct; and (b) must ensure to the best of his abilities that third parties on whose investments he exerts or can exert influence provide the bank's compliance officer at his request with all information regarding any private transactions conducted or effected by these third parties.[301] The code of conduct may stipulate that transactions in specific categories of financial instruments need not be disclosed because their disclosure would not contribute to the objective of the code of conduct.[302] This is subject to the condition that the transactions are transactions in financial instruments that cannot involve market abuse, for example transactions in government bonds.[303]

For the sake of completeness: as regards banks that do provide investment services or perform investment activities, similar requirements apply.[304]

---

298. Art. 24(1) and (2) Market Abuse Decree.
299. Art. 25(1) and (2) Market Abuse Decree. Pursuant to Art. 25(3) Market Abuse Decree, the firm may decide not to designate a person as referred to in (a) or (b) as an insider, if this person does not or may not regularly possess inside information.
300. Art. 25(4) Market Abuse Decree.
301. Art. 26 and 27(1) Market Abuse Decree.
302. Art. 27(2) Market Abuse Decree.
303. Explanatory Memorandum to the Market Abuse Decree, Bulletin of Acts and Decrees 2006, 510, p.55.
304. On the basis of Art. 4:14(2)(c) WFT in conjunction with Arts. 35c-35f Conduct of Business Decree

7.   REGULATORY APPROVALS AND NOTIFICATIONS

The WFT prescribes certain situations in which an approval by DNB is required. The most relevant approval requirements are set out below.

7.1   Declaration of no Objection

The WFT contains provisions enabling DNB to supervise the structure of cooperative links between banks and other companies, either being banks or other enterprises. The objective of this form of supervision is to monitor and safeguard the prudent management of banks. The mechanism enabling DNB to exercise this supervision is that of a so-called "declaration of no objection" (*verklaring van geen bezwaar*, or **DNO**). This means that DNB or, in specific cases, the Minister of Finance will have to approve certain transactions concerning banks, by issuing a DNO, before they may be implemented. There are two types of DNO requirements: (a) a DNO requirement in relation to qualifying holdings in a bank; and (b) a DNO requirement for certain actions of banks. If the licence application concerns a bank established in the Netherlands in which a qualifying holding is owned, a licence will only be granted if the holder of the qualifying holding has applied for a DNO and DNB is of the opinion that the relevant provisions are complied with.[305] In that case, the DNO application is linked to the licence application.

7.1.1   *Qualifying Holdings in Banks*

A qualifying holding is a direct or indirect holding representing 10% or more of the bank's issued capital or the right to exercise, directly or indirectly, 10% or more of the voting rights in the bank, or the right to exercise, directly or indirectly, equivalent control over the bank, whereby in determining the number of voting rights of a party in an enterprise, the voting rights shall also include the voting rights which it has or is deemed to have under Article 5:45 WFT.[306] Article 5:45 WFT makes reference to the term of having shares or voting rights at its disposal. The term "share" does also include a depositary receipt for a share and an option or any other negotiable instrument to acquire a share or a depositary receipt for a share.[307] This means that all forms of disposal are included, irrespective of whether it concerns actual or potential, direct or indirect, ownership of shares or

---

305. Art. 2:12(2) WFT.
306. Art. 1:1 WFT (definition of "qualifying holding").
307. Art. 5:33(1)(b) WFT.

voting rights. There is a prohibition, except after obtaining a DNO, to hold, acquire or increase a qualifying holding or exercise any control attached to a qualifying holding in a Dutch-based bank.[308] In determining the percentage of the holding, DNB will assess the total of all direct and indirect holdings held by the person (e.g. if a person holds two indirect holdings each of 5.5% in a bank, via different intermediary companies, the qualifying holding is considered to amount to 11% and, therefore, a DNO is required).

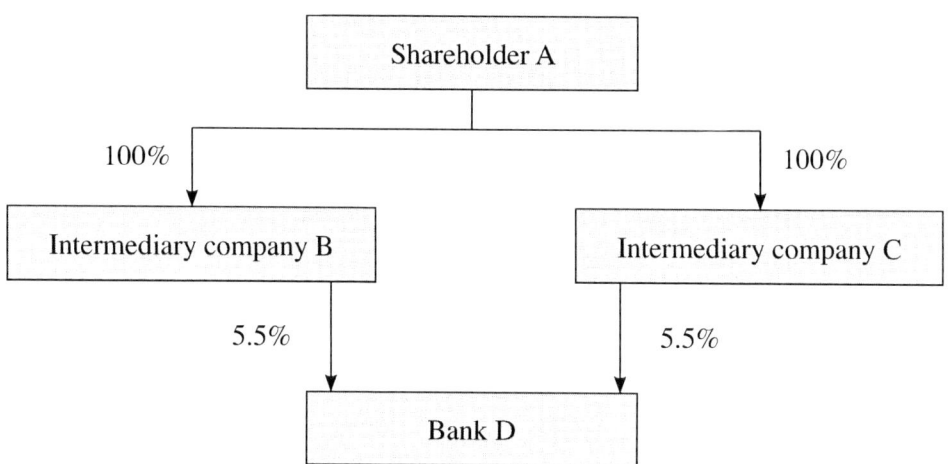

Apart from a DNO for a qualifying holding of a fixed percentage, it is also possible to apply for a DNO with a bandwidth, whereby the upper limit may be 20%, 33%, 50% or 100%. Within this bandwidth, the participation percentage is allowed to fluctuate without a new or modified DNO being required.[309] Moreover, another option is a group-DNO, which covers all of the applicant's group companies[310] collectively.[311] Hence, it is unnecessary for each individual group company to apply for a separate DNO.

---

308. Art. 3:95(1)(a) WFT. A similar requirement applies with regard to holdings in other financial institutions (Art. 3:95(1)(b)-(e) WFT, *inter alia*, a management company of an undertaking for collective investment in transferable securities (UCITS), an investment firm and an insurer.
309. Art. 3:102(1) WFT.
310. A group is an economic unit of legal persons and companies in which the group companies are organisationally linked. A group is controlled centrally.
311. Art. 3:102(2) WFT.

7.1.2   *Actions of Banks*

Unless it has obtained a DNO, a bank established in the Netherlands[312] may not, *inter alia*:

(a) decrease its own funds through a repayment of capital or a distribution of reserves;

(b) acquire or increase a qualifying holding in a financial corporation,[313] if the balance sheet total of that financial corporation exceeds 1% of the consolidated balance sheet total of the bank;[314]

(c) acquire or increase a qualifying holding in a non-financial corporation, if the (total) investment exceeds 1% of the consolidated available own funds of the bank;[315]

(d) fully or partially acquire the assets and/or liabilities of another company, if the total amount of the assets and/or the liabilities that are to be acquired exceed 1% of the consolidated balance sheet total of the bank;

(e) merge with another company, if the balance sheet total of the merger partner exceeds 1% of the consolidated balance sheet total of the bank;

(f) carry out a financial or corporate reorganisation; and/or

---

312. The DNO requirements following from Art. 3:96 WFT also apply to Dutch-licensed branches of banks established in a non-Member State (Art. 3:109 WFT).

313. A bank, an investment firm, a financial institution or an insurer.

314. A DNO is not required if it concerns a qualifying holding in a company the assets of which consist of liquid assets for more than 90%. Art. 139 Prudential Supervision Decree prescribes that the liquid assets of the company only include: (a) cash; (b) deposits payable on demand; (c) short-term receivables; and (d) assets that can be converted in a very short term and without substantial losses into cash or deposits payable on demand.

315. See preceding footnote. According to Art. 140(1) Prudential Supervision Decree in conjunction with Art. 3:96(4) WFT a DNO is issued, in the event that:
   (a) the value of the qualifying holding does not exceed 15% of the bank's regulatory capital (*toetsingvermogen*); and
   (b) the total value of the qualifying holdings of the bank in non-financial undertakings does not exceed, due to the new or increased qualifying holding, 60% of the bank's regulatory.
   According to Art. 140(2) and (3) Prudential Supervision Decree in conjunction with Art. 3:96(4) WFT a DNO is issued, only for a fixed period, notwithstanding the aforementioned, in the event that:
   (a) the qualifying holding is acquired and held in connection with a debt rescheduling or recovery programme for the non-financial corporation involved;
   (b) the qualifying holding is acquired or held in connection with an underwritten share issue; or
   (c) the qualifying holding is acquired and temporarily held in connection with a deposit transaction (*stallingsaffaire*) in the bank's own name but for the account of third parties.

(g) have a managing partner (*beherend vennoot*) join the bank.[316]

Banks may apply for a so-called umbrella DNO for all indirect qualifying holdings acquired or to be acquired through a subsidiary.[317]

7.1.3   *Application Procedure*

The procedural rules regarding a licence application apply *mutatis mutandis* to a DNO application.[318] This means, *inter alia*, that the standard DNO application forms must be used and that the decision period in principle will be to a maximum of 13 weeks upon receipt of the application.[319] The application must be submitted to DNB, which shall forward the application, together with its recommendation, to the Minister of Finance (except, of course, where DNB decides on the application).[320] The Minister of Finance decides on a DNO application if (in brief) one of the five largest Dutch banks are involved.[321] The DNO application must contain the following information:[322]

(a) an overview of the size of a qualifying holding;
(b) Integrity Test Forms with regard to the applicant or the holder of the DNO, who, based on its qualifying holding, might determine or co-determine or would determine or co-determine the policy of the bank, including relevant documentation;[323]

---

316. Art. 3:96(1) WFT.
317. Art. 3:102(3) WFT.
318. Art. 1:105(1)(c) WFT.
319. However, with regard to a DNO application pursuant to Art. 3:95(1) WFT, DNB is already applying a decision period, as prescribed in EU Directive 2007/44/EC, of a maximum 62 workdays.
320. Art. 3:95(3) and 3:96(2) WFT.
321. Art. 3:97(1) WFT. The decision-making authority of the Minister of Finance will lapse after the implementation of EU Directive 2007/44/EC in the Netherlands.
322. Art. 138 Prudential Supervision Decree in conjunction with Arts. 3:95(2) and 3:96(2) WFT. With regard to a DNO application pursuant to Art. 3:95(1) WFT, DNB is already making use of the list of information required for the assessment, as published by CEBS, Committee of European Insurance and Occupational Pensions Supervisors (**CEIOPS**) and Committee of European Securities Regulators (**CESR**).
323. Pursuant to Art. 3:99 WFT the fit and proper qualities of the applicant and the holder of a declaration of no objection that, based on its qualifying holding, might determine or co-determine the policies of the Dutch bank must be beyond doubt.

(c) documents from which the financial position[324] and the legal group structure[325] of the applicant or holder of the DNO are apparent.

A DNO concerning a qualifying holding in a bank[326] will be issued, unless:

(a) this would lead to an influence on the bank that would jeopardise its sound and prudent operations;
(b) this might or would have the effect of the bank becoming affiliated to persons in a formal or actual control structure that is so lacking in transparency that it would constitute an impediment to the adequate exercise of supervision of the bank; or
(c) this might or would lead to an undesirable development in the financial sector.[327]

If the applicant is a bank licensed in another Member State, or its parent company or a person otherwise controlling it is so licensed, and the Dutch-based bank it wishes to acquire a qualifying holding in would then become its subsidiary, DNB will liaise with the regulator of the Member State involved before issuing a DNO.[328]

A DNO concerning an action of a bank[329] will be issued, unless:

(a) this might or would be contrary to the solvency requirements[330] applicable to the bank
(b) this might or would be contrary in other ways to sound and prudent operations; or
(c) this might or would lead to an undesirable development in the financial sector.[331]

---

324. Under normal circumstances, being certified annual figures and financial statements for the last two financial years (if available), a certified opening balance sheet, declarations by foreign supervisory authorities; auditor's reports; and/or, only in the case of natural persons, a certified statement of assets and liabilities or the most recent tax return.
325. Under normal circumstances, being a structure chart showing the current and future shareholding structure or control structure with all direct and indirect shareholders with their respective interests.
326. As referred to in Art. 3:95(1)(a) WFT.
327. Art. 3:100 and 3:97(2) WFT.
328. Art. 162(1) WFT.
329. As referred to in Art. 3:96(1) WFT.
330. As referred to in Art. 3:57(1) and (2) WFT. See paragraph 5.2.
331. Arts. 3:101 and 3:97(2) WFT.

A DNO may be subject to conditions and limitations in view of the above-mentioned considerations[332].[333] The bank will be informed by DNB of the issuance of a DNO in relation to any qualifying holding in it. Furthermore, the issuance, as well as the modification or the withdrawal, of a DNO will be published in the Government Gazette, unless publication would or might lead to a disproportionate advantage or disadvantage for interested parties.[334]

If a qualifying holding is acquired without having obtained a DNO, this will in principle not affect the validity of the acquisition. However, a resolution that was adopted (partly) by exercising control attached to the qualifying holding may be declared void by the competent District Court on the demand of DNB. In such case, the decision will be declared void by the District Court only if the decision would have been different or would not have been adopted if the control concerned would not have been exercised.[335] Self-evidently, in the event of non-compliance with the DNO requirements, DNB may take formal measures vested in it pursuant to the WFT.[336] Moreover, DNB may, by issuing an instruction, order any party that does not comply with the DNO requirements to adhere to a particular line of conduct within a term specified by DNB.[337]

On 21 March 2009, the EU Directive regarding the prudential assessment of acquisitions and increase of holdings in the financial sector[338] should have been implemented in the Netherlands. This directive amends, *inter alia*, the Recast Banking Directive regulating situations regarding the acquisition or increase of a qualifying holding in a bank. Currently a legislative proposal for the implementation of this directive into the WFT is being discussed.[339] DNB has announced that, until the implementation has been effectuated, the current provisions of the WFT will be applied in conformity with the directive as far as possible. The legislative proposal shows that some significant changes to the current system will be implemented, *inter alia*:

(a) a DNO application will be handled by DNB in all cases and an obligation to provide the Minister of Finance with information will be introduced;

---

332. As referred to in Arts. 3:100 and 3:101 WFT.
333. Art. 3:104(1) WFT.
334. Art. 3:105(1), (2) and (5) WFT.
335. Art. 3:104(1) WFT.
336. See paragraph 9.3.
337. Art. 3:104(3) WFT.
338. Directive 2007/44/EC of the European Parliament and of the Council of 5 September 2007 amending Council Directive 92/49/EEC and Directives 2002/83/EC, 2004/39/EC, 2005/68/EC and 2006/48/EC as regards procedural rules and evaluation criteria for the prudential assessment of acquisitions and increase of holdings in the financial sector.
339. Parliamentary Papers II 2009–2010, 32 292, no. 2.

(b) DNB will have a maximum of 62 working days as from the date of the receipt of the application to decide on the application. If DNB requests additional information, the decision period shall be interrupted by a maximum of 20, and in specific cases 30, working days;

(c) if DNB has not rejected the application within the decision period, it shall be deemed to be approved;

(d) DNB may reject the application only if: (a) the fit and proper qualities of the applicant or of the and persons who would or might determine the day-to-day policy of the bank are not beyond doubt; (b) the persons who would or might determine the day-to-day policy are not experts; (c) the financial soundness of the proposed acquirer, considering the business of the bank, is not safeguarded; (d) the bank will not be able to continue to comply with the prudential requirements of the WFT; (e) there are reasonable grounds to suspect that, in connection with the proposed acquisition, money laundering or terrorist financing is being or has been committed or attempted, or that the proposed acquisition could increase the risk thereof; or (f) the information provided by the applicant is incomplete or incorrect; and

(e) a list specifying the information that must be provided to DNB in relation to the application shall be made publicly available (the information required shall be proportionate and adapted to the nature of the proposed acquirer and the proposed acquisition).[340]

7.1.4   *Notifying Obligation*

In addition to the DNO requirements, anyone who has a qualifying holding in a bank must notify DNB beforehand of any change in his qualifying holding:[341]

(a) as a result of which the size of this holding increases beyond 20%, 33%, 50% or 95% or becomes 100%, or as a result of which the financial enterprise concerned becomes a subsidiary; or

(b) as a result of which the size of this holding falls below 10%, 20%, 33%, 50%, 95% or 100%, or as a result of which the financial enterprise concerned ceases to be a subsidiary.

---

340. CEBS, CEIOPS and CESR have published guidelines for the prudential assessment of acquisitions and increases in holdings in the financial sector, including a comprehensive list of information required for the assessment (Appendix II). Practice has shown that DNB is already making use of this list (http://www.c-ebs.org/getdoc/09acbe4b-c2ee-4e65-b461-331a7176ac50/2008-18-12_M-A-Guidelines.aspx).

341. Art. 3:102(1) WFT.

The same obligation applies to the bank itself as soon as it becomes aware of such changes. Furthermore, the bank must inform DNB in July of each year of the identity of its qualifying holders insofar as it is aware of their identity.[342]

7.2   Liquidation or Winding-up

A Dutch-based bank that has decided to dissolve or wind up its business, either fully or in part, must consult DNB on the manner in which the dissolution or winding-up will be effected. The bank must, therefore, notify DNB at least 13 weeks before the decision is implemented.[343] The foregoing applies *mutatis mutandis* to a bank established in a non-Member State that has decided to dissolve or wind up its Dutch branch, either fully or in part.[344]

The liquidation of a Dutch private limited company or public limited company in general comprises two stages: (a) the dissolution of the company; and (b) the winding-up of its assets and liabilities. The dissolution "reduces" the legal existence of the company; it continues to exist only to the extent required for the purpose of the liquidation of its assets and liabilities and it cannot transact any business other than is necessary for the winding-up. The winding-up consists of the settlement of the accounts and the realisation of the non-financial assets for the purpose of making a final distribution to the shareholders (and perhaps other possible parties so entitled by virtue of the articles of association). As of the moment of the dissolution, the period of winding-up commences. The liquidators are in charge of the winding-up, which comprises the settlement of all debts of the company and the realisation of its non-financial assets. The liquidators must deposit the final accounting with the Commercial Register, as well as at the Company's office (if such office still exists). Furthermore, they must publish a notice in a nationally distributed daily newspaper, stating where the final accounting and the plan of distribution have been deposited for public inspection. Upon publication of such notice in the newspaper, a two-month period commences during which any creditor or beneficiary may institute opposition to the final accounting and/or the plan of distribution. Upon termination of the two-month period, the liquidators will become obliged to pay the distribution to the beneficiaries (unless objections were raised).[345]

---

342. Art. 3:103(2) WFT.
343. Art. 3:30 WFT.
344. Art. 3:44 WFT.
345. Art. 19 et seq Civil Code.

7.3 Notifications

The prospective appointment of a (co-)policymaker of a bank, i.e. an executive board member or a supervisory board member, must be pre-announced to DNB. The bank may not carry out the intended change before DNB has consented to the change. DNB will take a decision concerning consent: (a) within six weeks of having received the notification; or (b) if DNB requested further information, within two weeks of having received the notification, within four weeks of having received that information, but in any event within 13 weeks of having received the notification.[346] Before DNB consents to the appointment, it will assess whether the nominee meets its standards of integrity and/or expertise.[347] The same applies to proposed changes in the persons who determine the day-to-day policy of a branch.[348]

The bank must also notify DNB in writing of a change in the information on the basis of which DNB has assessed the integrity of a person (i.e. a change in the antecedents), immediately after it has been informed of the change.[349]

Furthermore, a bank must notify DNB within two weeks of a change in:[350]

(a) its name or address;
(b) its legal form;
(c) its registered office, its name given in the articles of association and its trade names;
(d) the number of its registration in the Commercial Register;
(e) its articles of association;
(f) its control structure; and
(g) the address(es) of its EU branches.

Finally, a bank with a branch in another Member State must notify DNB and the host regulator within two weeks in writing of a change in the address of the branch and a change with regard to the applicability of a deposit guarantee system to the branch. Such bank must also notify both regulators in writing of its intention to

---

346. Art. 3:29 WFT in conjunction with 33 of the Prudential Supervision Decree. The bank notifies DNB of the prospective appointment, using the Prospective Appointment Notification Form (available on DNB's website).
347. See paragraph 4.2.1.
348. Art. 3:29 WFT in conjunction with Art. 36 of the Prudential Supervision Decree.
349. Art. 3:29 WFT in conjunction with Art. 34 of the Prudential Supervision Decree.
350. Art. 3:29 WFT in conjunction with Art. 35 of the Prudential Supervision Decree.

discontinue carrying out its business operations from the branch. The change may not be implemented during the first four weeks after the notification.[351]

8. CREDIT INSTITUTIONS ESTABLISHED OUTSIDE THE NETHERLANDS

8.1 Credit Institutions Established in other Member States

Like Dutch banks wishing to carry on activities in other Member States, banks established in other Member States can also benefit from the European passport as well when they want to start performing banking activities in the Netherlands, whether through the establishment of a branch or as a cross-border service provider.

8.1.1 *Branch*

A bank established in another Member State (its home state) may pursue the business of a credit institution through a branch in the Netherlands (the host state). The following provisions apply.

DNB (as host state regulator) will receive a notification from the home state regulator of the intention of the foreign bank to carry on its business from a branch located in the Netherlands.[352] This notification needs to include the following information:[353]

(a) the Member State where the bank plans to set up the branch, i.e. the Netherlands;

---

351. Art. 3:29 WFT in conjunction with Art. 37 of the Prudential Supervision Decree.
352. Vice versa Arts. 2:108 and 2:109 WFT. See paragraph 4.5.1.
353. According to Art. 25 of the Recast Banking Directive a bank that wishes to establish a branch within another Member State shall notify its home regulator and provide the following information when effecting the notification:
     (a) the Member State within the territory of which it plans to establish a branch;
     (b) a programme of operations setting out, inter alia, the types of business envisaged and the structural organisation of the branch;
     (c) the address in the host Member State from which documents may be obtained; and
     (d) the names of those to be responsible for the management of the branch.
     The above-mentioned programme of operations should usually include at least the following information regarding the operations of the branch: business plan, organisational structure, systems and controls, financial information and investment activities (if applicable). For a more detailed explanation reference is made to CEBS, Guidelines for passport notifications, 27 August 2009, also including a standard notification form for branch establishment (Annex 2).

(b) the address of the branch;

(c) a statement of the activities that the bank intends to carry out from the branch;

(d) the name and private address of the persons who shall determine the day-to-day policy of the branch, i.e. the branch managers;

(e) a description of the proposed policy with regard to the conduct of business in a controlled and sound manner; and

(f) a description of the operational structure for the controlled and sound conduct of business.

After receiving this notification, DNB must, without delay, inform the bank of its receipt. Within two months of receiving the notification from the home state regulator, DNB may inform the other regulator which conditions the bank should observe for reasons of public interest in the pursuit of its business from its Dutch branch. DNB must send the bank a copy of this.[354] The Dutch branch may start its operation after the two-month period or immediately on receiving the conditions letter.[355] The bank is allowed to perform the activities listed in Annex I to the Recast Banking Directive, except for those activities that are either ruled out under its home licence or (while allowed under its home licence) which are not included in the received notification.[356] The investment services and activities and ancillary services provided for in Sections A and B of Annex I to the Markets in Financial Instruments Directive[357] (**MiFID**) are also subject to mutual recognition according to the Recast Banking Directive.

The foreign credit institution will be entered in the public register kept by DNB. The register states which banking activities the bank is allowed to carry out through its branch.[358]

8.1.2   *Cross-border Services*

A licensed bank established in another Member State that intends to conduct its business as a cross-border service provider (i.e. not through a branch) to the Netherlands may start doing so after it has notified its home state regulator of this intention.[359] The bank is allowed to perform the activities listed in Annex I

---

354. Art. 2:14 WFT.
355. Art. 2:15 (1) WFT.
356. Art. 2:15 (2) and Art. 3:39 (1) WFT.
357. Directive 2004/39/EC of the European Parliament and of the Council of 21 April 2004 on markets in financial instruments.
358. Art. 1:107 WFT.
359. Art. 2:18 (1) WFT.

to the Recast Banking Directive, except for those activities that are either ruled out under its home licence or (while allowed under its home licence) the received notification expressly provides otherwise or does not specify the performance of those activities.[360]

8.1.3   Supervision and Enforcement

A Dutch branch of a licensed bank established in another Member State will – primarily – be subject to the prudential supervision of its home state regulator. DNB will, however, supervise the liquidity of the branch. Banks established in another Member State which carry on their business from branches situated in the Netherlands must be sufficiently liquid. If a branch expects or may reasonably expect that its liquidity does not or will not comply with the applicable rules, it must, without delay, inform DNB of this. It is significant that DNB, on application, may grant a dispensation, fully or in part, whether or not for a fixed term, of these requirements, if the applicant shows proof that it cannot reasonably comply with these provisions and that the objects which these provisions seek to attain shall be attained otherwise.[361] Furthermore, DNB supervises compliance with the Act on the prevention of money laundering and financing of terrorism[362] (*Wet ter voorkoming van witwassen en financieren van terrorisme*, **WWFT**) and the Sanctions Act 1997 (*Sanctiewet 1997*) and regulations,[363] as well as the administrative organisation and internal control system to ensure compliance. In other respects the bank and the branch remain under the prudential supervision of the home state regulator.

Non-compliance with the above-mentioned WFT requirements constitutes a violation of the WFT. In such a case, DNB may impose several measures to enforce compliance, such as giving an instruction[364] (*aanwijzing*), appointing a trustee[365] (*curator*), or imposing a cease and desist order[366] (*last onder dwangsom*) or an administrative fine[367] (*bestuurlijke boete*).[368] DNB may also give an instruction to follow a certain line of business if it "becomes aware of signs of a development" which may jeopardise its own funds, its solvency or its liquidity, also in circumstances where there is not a breach or a threat of a breach of the WFT.[369] Since the

---

360. Arts. 2:18 (2) and 3:39 (2) WFT.
361. Art. 3:63 in conjunction with Art. 3:64 WFT.
362. See paragraph 10.5.
363. See paragraph 10.6.
364. Art. 1:75 WFT.
365. Art. 1:76 WFT.
366. Art. 1:79 WFT.
367. Art. 1:80 WFT.
368. See paragraph 9.3.
369. Art. 1:75 (2) WFT.

WFT requirements regarding own funds and solvency do not apply to branches, DNB's right to give such an instruction would have to be based on concerns on the liquidity situation; more precisely: DNB would have to take the position that it has become aware of signs of a development that may jeopardise the liquidity of the bank. In this context, the bank's liquidity principally means the liquidity of the Dutch branch. Furthermore DNB may, under such circumstances, decide to appoint a trustee with regard to all or part of the activities and without first giving an instruction where urgent intervention is required.[370]

If a bank with a Dutch branch or which provides services to the Netherlands fails to comply with an instruction, DNB would notify the home state regulator. If the bank, despite the measures taken by the home state regulator (or if that regulator has taken insufficient measures or no measures at all), still does not act in compliance with the WFT, DNB may decide that the bank must discontinue the conclusion of contracts in the Netherlands. DNB shall publish a notification of such decision in the Government Gazette as soon as the appeal period has expired or, where an appeal has been lodged, as soon as a final and conclusive decision has been rendered on the appeal.[371]

Legal measures taken by DNB are subject to objection by DNB and administrative appeal.[372]

In the case of a bank licensed in another Member State, having a branch in the Netherlands or providing services to the Netherlands, and the home state regulator has informed DNB of the withdrawal of the licence of that bank, DNB shall publicly disclose this notification.[373]

8.2 Credit Institutions Established outside the EEA

8.2.1 *Branch*

The European passport is not available to banks established outside the EEA. A bank established in a country that is not a Member State may pursue the business of a credit institution through a branch in the Netherlands only to the extent DNB has granted that bank a licence to do so.[374]

---

370. Art. 1:76 (3) WFT.
371. Art. 1:58 WFT.
372. See paragraph 9.4.
373. Art. 1:61(2) WFT.
374. Arts. 2:20 and 2:21 WFT.

8.2.1.1   Licence Application

The licensing procedure, including the decision term, and the licence requirements are to a large extent the same as those for Dutch-based banks.

The licence application must contain the following information:[375]

(a) a statement of the name, address, telephone and fax number of the bank;
(b) a statement of its legal form;
(c) if the bank is a legal person, a statement of the registered office, the name according to the articles of association and the trade name or names;
(d) if the bank is listed in the Trade Register, a statement of the registration number;
(e) the address of the branch;
(f) if available, a certified copy of the articles of association;
(g) a business plan, in which it must be specified which activities the bank wants to carry out from the branch;
(h) details enabling DNB to assess the expertise of the persons determining the day-to-day policy of the branch;[376]
(i) details enabling DNB to assess the trustworthiness of the persons who determine or co-determine policy of the branch;[377]
(j) a description of the proposed policy with regard to the conduct of business in a controlled and sound manner from the branch;
(k) a description of the operational structure with regard to the controlled and sound conduct of business from the branch;
(l) if applicable, a description of the consolidated supervision; and
(m) documents from which the bank's minimum amount of own funds, the bank's expected solvency and the bank's liquidity are apparent.

---

375. Art. 10 Financial Enterprises Market Access Decree in conjunction with Art. 2:21(2) WFT.
376. Pursuant to Art. 10(2) Financial Enterprises Market Access Decree these details include: (a) a statement of the name, date of birth, place of birth, nationality, private address, telephone and fax number and position of the person in question; (b) a curriculum vitae; (c) a list of the relevant diplomas; (d) a copy of a valid identity document; and (e) a list of referees.
377. Pursuant to Art. 10(3) Financial Enterprises Market Access Decree these details include: (a) a statement of the name, date of birth, place of birth, nationality, private address, telephone and fax number and position of the person in question; (b) a copy of a valid identity document; (c) details with regard to the designated antecedents; and (d) a list of referees. DNB, in cooperation with the AFM, has drawn up Integrity Test Forms for this purpose. This requirement shall not apply if the integrity of the person concerned has already been tested by DNB or the AFM (Art. 10 (4) of the Financial Enterprises Market Access Decree).

If a bank also intends to provide investment services or perform investment activities in the Netherlands bank, the licence application must also contain a description of:[378]

(a) the operational structure with regard to orderly and transparent financial market processes, integrity in relations between market parties and due care in the provision of services to clients and unit holders;[379]

(b) the measures taken to protect clients' rights;[380] and

(c) the proposed policy with regard to preventing and managing conflicts of interest between itself and its clients, and among its clients.[381]

8.2.1.2   Licence Requirements

Again, the licence requirements are largely similar to those for Dutch-based banks.[382]

a. Management[383]

The day-to-day policy of a branch must be determined by at least two natural persons and these persons shall perform their activities in this respect from the Netherlands. Persons determining the day-to-day policy of the branch are supposed to have sufficient expertise in relation to the business and operations of the financial undertaking. In addition, the fit and proper qualities of these persons, as well as of the persons determining or co-determining the policy of the branch, are supposed to be beyond doubt.[384]

b. Sound Business Operations[385]

The branch shall pursue adequate policies securing sound operations.[386]

---

378. Art. 11 Financial Enterprises Market Access Decree in conjunction with Art. 2:22(2) WFT.
379. As referred to in Art. 4:14 WFT.
380. Art. 4:87 WFT.
381. Art. 4:88 WFT.
382. See paragraph 4.3.
383. Art. 2:21(1)(a), (b) and (e) WFT.
384. Art. 3:8, 3:9 and 3:21 WFT.
385. Art. 2:21(1)(c) WFT.
386. As referred to in Art. 3:10(1) WFT and as further described in Arts. 10-16 Prudential Supervision Decree.

c. Controlled Business Operations[387]

The branch shall organise its operations in such a way as to safeguard controlled and sound business operations.[388]

d. Consolidated Supervision[389]

A bank which has been established in a non-Member State with a branch in the Netherlands that is a subsidiary of the bank established in a non-Member State, shall be deemed to be under sufficient consolidated supervision in the state where the parent bank is established.[390]

e. Own Funds[391]

The minimum amount of own funds shall be at least EUR 5 million.[392]

f. Solvency[393]

The solvency requirement aims to ensure that the branch holds sufficient own funds in relation to the size of its liabilities and the nature and extent of its business risks.[394]

g. Liquidity[395]

The liquidity requirements mean that the branch must be able to fulfil its short-term payment obligations.[396]

h. Separate Accounts[397]

---

387. Art. 2:21(1)(d) WFT.
388. Art. 3:17(1) and (2) WFT and Arts. 17-26 Prudential Supervision Decree.
389. Art. 2:21(1)(f) WFT.
390. Art. 3:46 WFT.
391. Art. 2:21(1)(g) WFT.
392. Art. 48 Prudential Supervision Decree in conjunction with Art. 3:53(1) and (3) WFT.
393. Art. 2:21(1)(h) WFT.
394. Art. 3:57(1) and (2) WFT.
395. Art. 2:21(1)(i) WFT.
396. Arts. 3:63(1) and (2) WFT.
397. Art. 2:21(1)(j) WFT.

A bank having its registered office in another Member State with a branch in the Netherlands shall keep at least one set of separate accounts relating to the branch, in such a way as to enable DNB to supervise compliance with the liquidity requirements[398].[399]

On application, DNB may grant a full or partial dispensation from the above requirements under (b), (d), (g), (h) and/or (i), if the applicant demonstrates that it cannot reasonably comply with those requirements and that the objectives which such requirements seek to achieve are achieved in other ways.[400]

If the bank intends to also provide investment services or perform investment activities, DNB, will only grant a banking licence if the applicant demonstrates that it will also comply with the provisions regarding:[401]

(a) the operational structure with regard to orderly and transparent financial market processes, integrity in relations between market parties and due care in the provision of services to clients and unit holders;[402]
(b) the measures taken to protect clients' rights;[403] and
(c) the rules applicable to the trading process and the settlement of transactions in a multilateral trading facility, if the applicant intends to operate a multilateral trading facility.[404]

After a licence is granted, the bank will be registered in the public register maintained by DNB. The register states which banking activities the bank is allowed to carry out.[405]

Having obtained a licence, the foreign bank is allowed to perform at least the activities listed in Annex I to the Recast Banking Directive, unless the licence expressly states otherwise.[406]

8.2.2 *Cross-border Activities*

If a bank established in a country that is not a Member State intends to operate in the Netherlands as a cross-border service provider (i.e. other than through a

---

398. Arising from Art. 3:63 in conjunction with Art. 3:64 WFT.
399. Art. 3:75 WFT.
400. Art. 2:21(3) WFT.
401. Art. 2:22(2) WFT.
402. As referred to in Art. 4:14(2)(c) under 1° to 6° WFT.
403. Art. 4:87 WFT.
404. Art. 4:91a WFT.
405. Art. 1:107 WFT.
406. Art. 3:43 in conjunction with Art. 3:32 WFT.

branch) it is not subject to a licence requirement. It will, however, need to observe Article 3:5 of the WFT containing a prohibition to attract, obtain or have the disposal of repayable funds beyond a restricted circle in the Netherlands in the pursuit of a business from others than professional market parties.[407]

9. SUPERVISORY POWERS AND ENFORCEMENT

9.1 Supervision

DNB, as supervisory authority, is empowered to demand information from any party for the purpose of the supervision of compliance with the rules laid down by or pursuant to the WFT.[408] In addition, the designated supervisory officials employed by DNB have the following powers listed in General Administrative Law Act (*Algemene wet bestuursrecht*, or **AWB**),[409] *inter alia*:

- general authority to demand information.[410] This authority is not limited as to the parties from whom information may be requested. Therefore, in principle information may be requested from anyone;
- conducting on-site investigations;[411]
- demanding inspection of business data and documents and making copies of these data and documents (or, if this is not possible, taking these data and documents for a short period of time for the purpose of making copies).[412]

The AWB provides for an obligation to cooperate with DNB and its supervisory officials within a reasonable set term.[413] DNB is given the discretion to exercise its supervisory powers, but it may only use its statutory powers to the extent reasonably necessary for the fulfilment of its task.[414]

Banks must periodically submit so-called statements (*staten*), whether or not on a consolidated basis, to DNB for the purpose of its prudential supervision.[415]

---

407. See paragraph 10.2
408. Art. 1:74(1) WFT.
409. See Arts. 1:72 and 1:73 WFT.
410. Art. 5:16 AWB.
411. Art. 5:15 AWB.
412. Art. 5:17 AWB.
413. Art. 5:20 AWB.
414. Art. 5:13 AWB.
415. Art. 3:72(1) WFT.

If an event occurs or has occurred which seriously affects or may seriously affect the financial position of the bank, DNB may prescribe that one or more statements must temporarily be submitted with a higher frequency or within a shorter period.[416] Again periodically, these statements must be accompanied by an auditor's report.[417] This reporting requirement also applies with regard to Dutch branches of banks having their registered offices in another Member State.[418]

9.2   Duty of Confidentiality and Exchange of Information

The WFT provides for rules on secrecy that oblige DNB to ensure the confidentiality of confidential data or information from and about banks. The basic rule is that DNB is prohibited to use confidential data or information in any further or other way than is required for the performance of its duties or required pursuant to the WFT.[419] DNB, however, may supply the AFM or a supervisory authority of another Member State with confidential data or information, provided certain safeguards are in place.[420] Furthermore, DNB may exchange confidential information with other authorities, such as the criminal authorities, receivers (in bankruptcy proceedings), administrators (if emergency regulations are declared by the court), and the central banks (again, provided certain safeguards are in place).[421]

9.3   Enforcement

The WFT empowers DNB to take formal measures in cases of non-compliance with the WFT and its implementing regulations. The principles and factors set out in the Enforcement Policy (*Handhavingsbeleid*) adopted by the AFM and DNB serve as directives for the assessment of concrete cases on the basis of which DNB determines what reaction to a breach of the WFT would be appropriate.[422]

---

416. Art. 3:72(6) WFT.
417. Art. 3:72(7) WFT.
418. Art. 3:77 WFT.
419. Art. 1:89(1) WFT.
420. Art. 1:90 WFT.
421. Arts. 1:91-1:93 WFT.
422. Government Gazette, 11 July 2008, 132, p.30.

9.3.1 Instruction[423]

If a bank or its qualifying shareholder(s) fails to comply with the provisions laid down by or pursuant to the WFT, DNB may issue an instruction (*aanwijzing*) to adhere to a particular line of conduct within a reasonable term specified by DNB.[424] DNB may also give an instruction to a bank if it becomes aware of signs of a development that may jeopardise the bank's own funds, solvency or liquidity.[425] The language of this provision gives DNB considerable leeway in this respect.

9.3.2 Appointment of a Trustee[426]

In the event of non-compliance, DNB may decide to appoint one or more persons as a trustee (*curator*) with regard to all or certain bodies or representatives of a bank. This means that the relevant bodies or representatives may only exercise their powers after obtaining the trustee's approval and with due observance of the trustee's instructions. Such decision may only be taken:

(a) after the bank has failed to comply, either fully or in part, with an instruction[427] issued by DNB within the specified term; or
(b) if the breach seriously jeopardises the adequate functioning of the bank; or
(c) if the breach seriously jeopardises the interests of consumers.

In the latter two cases the bank must have had the opportunity to submit its view on the proposed decision.

In addition, DNB may appoint a trustee, if it becomes aware of signs of a development that may jeopardise the bank's own funds, solvency or liquidity. Such decision may only be taken:

(a) after the bank has failed to comply, either fully or in part, with an instruction[428] issued by DNB within the specified term; or
(b) if urgent intervention is required and the bank has had the opportunity to submit its view on the proposed decision.

---

423. Art. 1:75 WFT.
424. Art. 1:75(1) WFT. With regard to qualifying shareholders, reference is also made to the authority to issue an instruction pursuant to Art. 3:104(3) WFT in the event of non-compliance with Art. 3:95(1) WFT.
425. Art. 1:75(2) WFT.
426. Art. 1:76 WFT.
427. As referred to in Art. 1:75(1) WFT.
428. As referred to in Art. 1:75(2) WFT.

The appointment of a trustee is communicated to the bank. From the date of this announcement the bank's bodies or representatives that are placed in trusteeship may exercise their powers only with the prior approval of the trustee. Orders issued by the trustee must also be complied with. If any person who is part of the body concerned nonetheless performs acts without having obtained the required approval of the trustee, he will in principle be jointly and severally liable for any loss or damage resulting from such acts.[429] The trusteeship is, in principle, a measure that does not affect legal acts with third parties. However, legal acts are capable of annulment if the counterparty knew or should have known that the required approval had not been granted.[430]

9.3.3   *Cease and Desist Order*[431]

In the event of a breach of certain provisions listed in the WFT, DNB can impose a cease and desist order (*last onder dwangsom*) on the infringer. This means that the infringer is ordered to take or desist from a certain action. The cease and desist order is a remedial measure and is intended to end the breach and/or prevent the continuation or repetition of the breach. If the infringer fails to comply with the order within a certain term, a penalty payment is forfeited. In addition, in such case, the cease and desist order will be made public by DNB, unless publication of the decision is or might be considered counterproductive to achieving the object of DNB's supervision.[432] If the infringer wishes to prevent the publication, it may, pending a decision on the objection,[433] apply for a preliminary relief[434] and request the preliminary relief judge to suspend the publication. In such case, the publication will be suspended until the preliminary relief judge has rendered judgment. The case will be heard behind closed doors.

As mentioned above, a cease and desist order can only be imposed on the infringer. This will most definitely be the bank itself, because most of the relevant provisions of the WFT address the institution. However, the AWB provides that not only the perpetrator (*pleger*), but also, *inter alia*, the co-perpetrator (*medepleger*), individuals who ordered the offence (*opdrachtgevers*) and the individuals *de facto* in charge (*feitelijk leidinggevers*), are considered infringers.[435] This means

---

429. Art. 1:176(5)(d) WFT.
430. Art. 1:176(5)(e) WFT.
431. Art. 1:79 WFT and Arts. 5:31d-5:39 AWB.
432. Art. 1:99 WFT.
433. See further paragraph 9.4.
434. As referred to in Art. 8:81 AWB.
435. Art. 5:1(2) AWB, respectively Art. 5:1(3) AWB in conjunction with Art. 51 Criminal Code (*Wetboek van Strafrecht*).

that breaches by a legal entity may be attributed to the individuals who ordered the violation or who were *de facto* in charge at the time when the violation occurred. Depending on the circumstances of the case, such individuals include the bank's supervisory board members, managing directors and heads of department. More specifically this means that DNB has the authority also to impose a cease and desist order on those parties. It appears from established criminal case law that an individual will be *de facto* in charge if, although so authorised and reasonably so required, he fails to take measures to prevent this prohibited conduct and consciously accepts the considerable risk that this conduct will arise. The moment the individual *de facto* in charge becomes aware of the unlawful conduct is relevant in this respect. If he then fails to intervene, he could be liable. Knowledge of similar facts committed previously by the legal entity could also lead to liability.

9.3.4   *Administrative Fine*[436]

In the event of a breach of certain provisions listed in the WFT, DNB can impose an administrative fine (*bestuurlijke boete*) on the infringer. This is a punitive sanction, implying an unconditional obligation to pay a sum of money. A punitive sanction means that the fine is imposed with the intention to punish the infringer. For the imposition of an administrative fine a limitation period of five years applies after the breach was committed.[437]

The WFT provides for a rather flexible statutory penalty system, which is based on three penalty categories:

1. Category 1 (reporting requirements etc.): a penalty system applies, which means that fixed penalty amounts are provided by law. The maximum penalty amounts to EUR 10,000.
2. Category 2 (provisions governing operations etc.): a flexible system applies – a basis penalty amount of EUR 500,000 and maximum penalty amount of EUR 1 million are prescribed by law; and
3. Category 3: a flexible system applies – a basis penalty amount of EUR 2 million and a maximum penalty amount of EUR 4 million are prescribed by law.[438]

With regard to the latter two categories DNB must explicitly consider whether circumstances like the gravity, duration, and degree of blame should have an in-

---

436. Art. 1:80 WFT and Art. 5:40-5:54 AWB.
437. Art. 5:45 AWB.
438. Art. 1:81(2) WFT.

creasing or decreasing effect on the penalty amount. DNB must take into account the financial capacity of the infringer. In addition, the penalty amounts will be doubled if the offence is repeated within five years, and, if the proceeds of the offence exceed EUR 2 million, the penalty amounts may be determined at not more that than twice the proceeds realised.[439]

The imposition of an administrative fine will be made public by DNB, unless publication of the decision is or might be considered counterproductive to achieving the object of DNB's supervision.[440] If the infringer wishes to prevent the publication, it may, pending a decision on the objection,[441] apply for a preliminary relief[442] and request the preliminary relief judge to suspend the publication. In such a case, the publication will be suspended until the preliminary relief judge has passed judgment. The case will be heard behind closed doors. Furthermore, DNB will publicise a decision to impose an administrative fine if this has become irreversible by law, unless publication of the decision is or might be considered counterproductive to achieving the object of DNB's supervision.[443]

The aforementioned with regard to the imposition of a cease and desist order on perpetrators, co-perpetrators, individuals who ordered the offence and individuals *de facto* in charge also applies to the imposition of an administrative fine. For both natural persons and legal persons the same penalty amounts apply.

9.3.5 Public Warning[444]

DNB can issue a public warning (*openbare waarschuwing*) upon violation of certain prohibitory provisions of the WFT and, insofar as relevant, *inter alia*, if: (i) a bank licensed in another Member State having a branch in the Netherlands or providing services to the Netherlands fails to comply with a decision of DNB that it must discontinue the conclusion of contracts;[445] (ii) a Dutch licensed bank which conducts its business from a branch in another Member State fails to comply with DNB's decision that it must discontinue the conclusion of contracts in the host Member State;[446] and (iii) a Dutch bank which conducts its business in another Member State, either by the establishment of a branch or by way of the provision

---

439. Decree on Administrative Fines Financial Sector (*Besluit bestuurlijke boetes financiële sector*).
440. Art. 1:97 WFT.
441. See further paragraph 9.4.
442. As referred to in Section 8:81 AWB.
443. Art. 1:80 WFT.
444. Arts. 1:94-1:96 WFT.
445. As referred to in Art. 1:58(2) WFT.
446. As referred to in Art. 1:59(2) WFT.

of services, fails to comply with DNB's decision that it may no longer conduct its business from the branch or as a cross-border service provider in the host Member State[447].[448]

A public warning shall not be issued before five working days have elapsed after the date on which the bank involved was informed of this. During this five-day period the bank may, if it wishes to prevent the publication, pending a decision on the objection,[449] apply for a preliminary relief[450] and request the preliminary relief judge to suspend the publication. In urgent cases, if the protection of the interests which the WFT seeks to protect does not allow delay, DNB may issue a public warning immediately.[451]

9.3.6 Special Prudential Measures

The WFT provides for special measures to require a bank that does not meet the requirements with regard to business operations and the regulatory capital to take the necessary actions to address the situation.[452] These measures include the following:

If a bank does not satisfy the requirements laid down by or pursuant to the WFT with regard to the business operations and the regulatory capital then the WFT requires the bank:

(a) to maintain a higher regulatory capital;[453]
(b) in connection with the solvency requirements, to pursue a specific policy with regard to provisions or to treat its assets in a specific manner; or
(c) to limit the risks to which it is exposed.[454]

DNB may only take such measures when the bank is in breach of the WFT.

If, based on the SREP,[455] DNB is of the opinion that the strategies, procedures and measures or the qualifying capital of the bank do not guarantee a controlled and lasting cover of its risks, DNB may require the bank to maintain a higher regulatory capital if other measures cannot reasonably ensure that these requirements will be satisfied within a reasonable period.[456] It is noted, however, that the ICAAP

---

447. As referred to in Art. 1:77(1) WFT.
448. Art. 1:94 WFT.
449. See further paragraph 9.4.
450. As referred to in Section 8:81 AWB.
451. Art. 1:96 WFT.
452. Implementing Art. 136 of the Recast Banking Directive.
453. I.e. higher than prescribed by Art. 3:57 WFT.
454. Art. 3:111a(1) WFT.
455. Referred to in Art. 3:18a WFT (see paragraph 5.2.2.2).
456. Art. 3:111a(2) WFT.

belongs to the institution and supervisors should not dictate how it is applied. The task of DNB is to review and evaluate the ICAAP and the soundness of the internal governance processes. The dialogue between an institution and its supervisor is a key part of the SREP. DNB will report to the bank in writing on the outcome of the SREP. If DNB is of the opinion that a bank's strategies, procedures and measures or its regulatory capital do not guarantee a controlled and lasting cover of its risks, DNB should specify which additional measures it deems necessary and, if appropriate additional measures are not available or will not be effective, what amount of additional regulatory capital is needed.[457]

9.3.7 *Modification, Withdrawal or Limitation of the Licence, DNO or Dispensation*

If the licence holder no longer complies with the rules laid down by or pursuant to the WFT, or no longer complies with the conditions or limitations attached to the licence, DNB may modify, withdraw or limit a licence, either fully or in part, or attach further conditions to the licence.[458]

The same rules apply with regard to a DNO and some kinds of dispensations granted by DNB.[459] Furthermore, DNB may withdraw a DNO, if the holder of a declaration of no objection fails to adhere to the instruction issued by DNB.[460] DNB may attach further limitations or conditions to a DNO or withdraw a DNO if circumstances occur or facts become known in respect of the act regarding which the DNO was issued which might or would:

(a) lead to an influence on the bank that would jeopardise its sound and prudent operations;
(b) have the effect that the bank becomes affiliated to persons in a formal or actual control structure that is so lacking in transparency that it would constitute an impediment to the adequate exercise of supervision;[461] or
(c) lead to an undesirable development in the financial sector.[462]

---

457. This follows from the DNB Policy Rule Principles Application Pillar 2 Capital Accord Basel 2 (*Beleidsregel uitgangspunten toepassing tweede pijler Kapitaalakkoord Bazel 2*), July 2008. Reference is also made to Committee of European Banking Supervisors, Guidelines on the Application of the Supervisory Review Process under Pillar 2 CP03 revised), 25 January 2006.
458. Art. 1:104(1) WFT.
459. Art. 1:104(1) WFT in conjunction with Art. 1:105(1)(c) and (d) WFT.
460. An instruction as referred to in Art. 1:75 WFT.
461. Only in case of a DNO granted to a qualifying holder in a bank (Art. 3:95(1)(a) WFT).
462. Only in case of a DNO granted to a qualifying holder in a bank (Art. 3:95(1)(a) WFT) or to a bank pursuant to Art. 3:96(1) WFT.

In the decision to withdraw a licence, DNB may also stipulate that the bank must wind up its business, either fully or in part, within a period to be specified by DNB. During the winding-up, whether or not stipulated by DNB, the bank or its bankruptcy liquidator (*curator*) shall be classified as a licensed enterprise.[463]

9.3.8   *Emergency Regulation*

Should the above measures not lead to a recovery, and should no improvement in the development of the solvency and the liquidity of a Dutch licensed bank[464] in reason be expected, DNB may request the court to declare the "emergency regulation" (*noodregeling*) applicable to a bank.[465] If the emergency regulations are declared applicable, the court will appoint a delegated judge (*rechter-commissaris*)[466] and one or more administrators (*bewindvoerders*); for the latter DNB may make nominations.[467] The court may empower the administrators to transfer all or part of the obligations of the bank and/or to wind up, in full or in part, the bank's business.[468] This means the emergency regulations may involve a restructuring and/or winding-up procedure. Under the emergency regulation, the administrators, solely and exclusively, exercise all powers of the bodies of the bank concerned, and these bodies must provide the receivers all the assistance they require.[469] Upon the imposition of an emergency regulation, the bank can no longer be forced to fulfil its obligations under any debts.[470]

The emergency regulation will apply for a period determined by the court, which may be one and a half years at most, subject to the right of the administrators to apply for an extension, once or more, in each case for another one and a half

---

463. Art. 1:104(3) WFT.
464. DNB may request that the emergency regulations be applied to Dutch licensed banks. These provisions do not apply to a branch of a licensed bank established in another Member State. According to Art. 3:202 WFT it is, however, possible to request the application of emergency regulations to a branch of an unlicensed bank established in another Member State. This led to the application of the emergency regulation to the Dutch branch of Landsbanki Islands hf., although this concerned an Icelandic licensed bank. On 13 October 2008, the District Court of Amsterdam considered that, even though this was not proven, it must be assumed that the banking licence of Landsbanki Islands hf. was withdrawn, and therefore, that the Dutch branch was now a branch of an unlicensed bank established in another Member State, falling within the scope of Art. 3:202 WFT (District Court of Amsterdam, 13 October 2008, LJN: BF8586).
465. Art. 3:160 WFT.
466. Pursuant to Art. 3:173 WFT the delegated judge will supervise the restructuring or winding-up procedure and the administration of the bank's assets.
467. Art. 3:160(4) WFT.
468. Art. 3:163 WFT.
469. Art. 3:175 WFT.
470. Art. 3:76 WFT.

years at most.[471] The court's decision is published.[472] The decision of the court may be appealed at a higher court and at the Supreme Court.[473]

A normal requirement under the Dutch Bankruptcy Act (*Faillissementswet*) to declare a company bankrupt is that the company has ceased paying its due debts. However, after the emergency regulation has been applied to a bank, the district court may, on the application of the administrators, on the proposal of the delegating judge or on its own initiative, having heard DNB, declare the bank with its seat in the Netherlands bankrupt if it appears that such institution has a negative own equity and that the objects of the emergency regulation were realised or can no longer be realised, and therefore regardless of whether the bank has actually ceased paying its due debts. The emergency regulation shall cease to have legal effect if the bank is declared bankrupt.[474] In any event, no decision shall be given on an application for the declaration of bankruptcy of a bank without DNB having been given an opportunity to state its views in respect thereof. DNB shall withdraw the licence when a bank is declared bankrupt.[475]

9.4   Procedure and Legal Remedies

DNB is an administrative authority.[476] According to the AWB administrative authorities are in their decision-making processes bound by general principles of proper administration (*algemene beginselen van behoorlijk bestuur*). Administrative decisions, including the imposition of a administrative measure and the granting of a licence, a dispensation or a DNO, taken by administrative authorities must be properly prepared, whereby the administrative authority is obliged to collect evidence concerning the relevant facts and interests that need to be balanced.[477] Apart from the emergency regulations, being a civil measure, the above-mentioned measures are considered administrative measures.

During the preparation phase, an administrative authority should, before issuing a decision to which the party concerned according to expectations will raise objections, provide an opportunity to the party concerned to express its views if (i) the decision is based on information regarding the party concerned and (ii) that

---

471. Art. 3:168 WFT.
472. Art. 3:163(5) WFT.
473. Art. 3:191 WFT.
474. Art. 212m Bankruptcy Act.
475. Art. 212k Bankruptcy Act.
476. See paragraph 1.3.
477. Arts. 2:4 (impartiality), 3:2 (proper preparation), 3:3 (prohibition of misuse of power), 3:4 (balancing of interests and principle of proportionality) and 3:46 (sound reasoning) AWB.

information is not provided by the party concerned.[478] A party concerned need not be heard if: (i) the need for expedition precludes this; (ii) the party concerned has already been given an opportunity to explain its point of view and since then no new facts or circumstances have been raised; or (iii) the intended objective of the decision can merely be achieved if the party concerned has not already been notified.[479] In addition or in derogation of these general applicable rules, the WFT provides certain specific procedural requirements.[480]

A party who disagrees with the imposition of a formal measure (or another formal decision of DNB) may lodge an objection with DNB within six weeks after the day on which that decision was announced.[481] In this case DNB will fully review its initial decision. This means that DNB will review the lawfulness as well as the suitability of the decision. As part of the objection procedure there will be a closed hearing to provide for an opportunity for the party concerned to explain the grounds of its objection.[482] DNB will in principle have to come to a decision on this objection within six weeks, but may extend this term by another four weeks.[483]

Filing an objection will have no suspensory effect,[484] except regarding the payment of a fine.[485] In the event of an urgent interest – for instance, if the imposed formal measure has immediate effect and may lead to irreversible damage, those concerned may, after the objection has been lodged, apply to the preliminary relief judge of the administrative court (*bestuursrechter*) in Rotterdam[486] for a preliminary relief.[487] This means that the judge will be requested to take a provisional decision – for instance, to suspend the effect of the imposed measure until it has been tried by a court.

---

478. Arts. 4:8 AWB.
479. Art. 4:11 AWB.
480. Art. 1:76(2)(b) and (c) WFT prescribing that a trustee may only be appointed, without issuing an instruction first, if the breach seriously jeopardises the adequate functioning of the bank or the interests of consumers and the bank has had the opportunity to submit its view on the proposed decision. Pursuant to Art. 1:76(4)(b) the same applies when DNB intends to appoint a trustee after becoming aware of signs of a development that may jeopardise the bank's own funds, solvency or liquidity, without issuing an instruction first. According to Arts. 1:95, 1:96 and 1:97 DNB must inform the interested party involved beforehand of its intention to issue a public warning or publish an imposed cease and desist order or administrative fine.
481. Art. 7:1 AWB and Art. 6:7 AWB. Pursuant to Art. 7:1a AWB the party lodging an objection may request DNB to agree to a direct appeal to the administrative court in Rotterdam. This would mean that the objection procedure is skipped.
482. Art. 7:2 AWB.
483. Art. 7:10 AWB.
484. Art. 6:17 AWB.
485. Art. 1:85 WFT.
486. Art. 8:81(1) AWB in conjunction with Art. 110(1) WFT.
487. As referred to in Art. 8:81 AWB.

If the objection is rejected by DNB, those concerned may apply within six weeks to the administrative court in Rotterdam[488] for judicial review of the case, and may subsequently appeal against the court's decision to the Trade and Industry Appeals Tribunal (*College van Beroep voor het bedrijfsleven*, or **CBb**). The administrative court and the CBb both review the lawfulness (and not the suitability) of DNB's decision. This means that these courts will marginally review DNB's discretionary power, in accordance with the relevant provisions of Dutch law,[489] and, within the boundaries of the general principles of proper administration, to impose formal measures. The administrative court in Rotterdam and the CBb are both independent courts.

The objection procedure described above is in principle private and the proceedings and their outcome will not be in the public domain. An appeal to the administrative court and the CBb is in principle dealt with in a public procedure.[490] In very limited circumstances[491] the court can rule that there will be a closed hearing.[492] The decisions of the courts are also public and in principle these decisions are published on the internet, in anonymised form.

9.5 Criminal Liability

Breaches of the most important provisions of the WFT, particularly breaches the provisions for which penalty category 3 applies, also constitute an economic offence under the Act on Economic Offences (*Wet op de economische delicten*, or **WED**).[493] Possible sanctions are a fine of up to, in principle, EUR 76,000 for legal entities and EUR 19,000 for individuals and/or imprisonment of up to six months, or (in case of intentional violations) two years.[494]

---

488. Art. 110(1) WFT.
489. The relevant EU Directives have in principle no direct effect within the Netherlands. However, to interpret the provisions of Dutch law, the court might also fall back on the EU Directives on which the provisions are based.
490. Art. 6:62(1) AWB.
491. Based on the European Convention for the Protection of Human Rights and Fundamental Freedoms.
492. Art. 6:62(2) AWB.
493. Art. 1(2°) WED.
494. Art. 6(1)(1°) and (3°) WED in conjunction with Art. 23(4) Criminal Code.

9.6   Civil Liability

In addition, violations of provisions of the WFT may lead to civil liability on the basis of contract or tort (*onrechtmatige daad*) under general rules of civil law. However, the validity of a legal act under civil law performed contrary to the rules laid down by or pursuant to the WFT cannot be affected on that account, except where specifically otherwise provided by the WFT.[495] This means that in principle a violation of the WFT will not lead to transactions being void (*nietig*) or voidable (*vernietigbaar*).

10.   MISCELLANEOUS

10.1   Deposit Guarantee Scheme[496]

As is apparent from the foregoing, the worst scenario is that a bank may eventually go bankrupt. Pursuant to the WFT there is a deposit guarantee scheme which seeks to compensate deposit holders in the event that a bank is unable to fulfil its obligations ensuing from deposit-related claims.[497] The scheme is not a fund to which participating institutions have to contribute an annual premium. Rather, DNB pays the compensation to the deposit holders that are eligible for compensation, and then is reimbursed for this by the participating institutions. Payment will be effected by DNB no later than three months after the due submission of claims. DNB will be subrogated in, and by way of assignment succeeds to, the rights of the claimant against the bank concerned, insofar as it has paid the claim of that deposit holder.[498] The total sum paid by DNB will be apportioned among the other (i.e. non-insolvent) participating institutions in accordance with an apportionment percentage set by DNB for each such institution, which is based on the size of its balance sheet.[499] Revenues which DNB subsequently realises from the insolvent

---

495. Art. 1:23 WFT.
496. In addition to the deposit guarantee scheme, an investor compensation scheme is also implemented (Art. 3:259(1) WFT). The investor compensation scheme deals with investors (having deposited moneys or securities in connection with portfolio management transactions, which latter concept encompasses not just portfolio management in the narrow sense but also brokerage and custody/administration activities). Hereafter only creditors will be mentioned, but the situation for investors is largely the same.
497. Art. 3:259(2) WFT.
498. Art. 3:261 WFT.
499. Art. 3:262 WFT and Arts. 21-23 Decree on Special Prudential Measures, Investor Compensation and Deposit Guarantees WFT (*Besluit bijzondere prudentiële maatregelen, beleggerscompensatie en depositogarantie Wft*).

bank pursuant to the subrogation and assignment referred to above, shall be paid on to the participating institutions that have reimbursed DNB.[500]

Certain deposits made by certain types of deposit holders are excluded from compensation. Broadly speaking, professional investors and professional market parties, directors and managers of the bank and holders of at least 5% of the bank's capital as well as their close relatives and third parties acting on their behalf and larger companies are excluded.[501] Deposits that fall under the protection include repayable credit balances in accounts as well as debt certificates registered in the holder's name but not, for example, bearer bonds. The covered deposits may also include subordinated claims. To the extent that the deposits carry interest, accrued interest is covered as well. When determining the value of the established claims, DNB shall set the claims off against the possible claims of the bank vis-à-vis the applicant.[502] Compensation is limited to a maximum of EUR 100,000 per deposit holder for the total amount of his claims, irrespective of, for example, the number of his deposits.[503] The scheme provides for situations of joint accounts. Absent contractual arrangements providing otherwise, each holder is entitled to a proportional part of the balance. For each deposit holder the maximum of EUR 100,000 applies.

Banks must, upon request, make information available about the applicable deposit guarantee scheme. The information must be such as to enable deposit holders to check whether a claim is covered by the deposit guarantee scheme or by a similar foreign scheme. The information must be made available in the Dutch language or, where it concerns a similar scheme applicable to a branch office, in the official language of the host Member State.[504] The bank, however, may not use information on the deposit guarantee scheme for advertising purposes, but may state in advertisements that the deposit guarantee scheme applies to it.[505] The aim of this prohibition is to prevent both competition distortions and the undermining of the stability of the banking system or of creditors' confidence. A bank established in a non-Member State operating a branch in the Netherlands must likewise make information available, in the Dutch language, about the applicable guarantee scheme.[506]

---

500. Art. 3:265(2) WFT.
501. Art. 20(1) Decree on Special Prudential Measures, Investor Compensation and Deposit Guarantees WFT, referring to Annex B.
502. Art. 25(1) Decree on Special Prudential Measures, Investor Compensation and Deposit Guarantees WFT.
503. Art. 26(4) Decree on Special Prudential Measures, Investor Compensation and Deposit Guarantees WFT.
504. Art. 3:263 WFT.
505. Art. 3:264 WFT.
506. Art. 3:267 (3) and (4) WFT.

The scheme being based on an EU directive,[507] protection of depositors has been harmonised throughout the Member States. The principle is home country control. Thus, as Dutch licensed banks fall within the scope of the deposit guarantee scheme,[508] the cover provided by the Dutch scheme not only relates to deposits at the bank's head office (which is in the Netherlands), but also to any of its branches in other Member States. If the host Member State deposit guarantee scheme exceeds the level and/or scope of cover provided by the Dutch deposit guarantee scheme, the bank may opt for supplementary cover of the scheme of the host Member State.

The other side of this coin is that licensed banks established in another Member State, operating a branch in the Netherlands, fall within the scope of the deposit guarantee scheme of their country of origin. However, if the cover of the deposit guarantee scheme of the country of origin is more limited than the cover of the Dutch deposit guarantee scheme, the bank may opt for membership of the Dutch deposit guarantee scheme in addition to the cover of the scheme in its country of origin.[509] On 4 July 2009, the Decree on Special Prudential Measures, Investor Compensation and Deposit Guarantees WFT was amended to provide for further rules as regards membership of the deposit guarantee scheme of banks established in another Member State that has a branch in the Netherlands.[510] To become a member of the Dutch scheme specific requirements must have been complied with,[511] including:

(a) there being no operational and legal risks that stand in the way of a good execution of the Dutch deposit guarantee scheme;
(b) the bank concerned and the manager of the deposit guarantee scheme of the country of origin having proven that there are sufficient safeguards that they will comply with their obligations arising from the membership of the Dutch deposit guarantee scheme;

---

507. Directive 94/19/EC of the European Parliament and of the Council 30 May 1994 on deposit guarantee schemes, amended by Directive 2009/14/EC of the European Parliament and of the Council of 11 March 2009.
508. Art. 3:258(1) WFT.
509. Art. 3:266(1)(b) and (3) WFT.
510. Arts. 29a-29j Decree on Special Prudential Measures, Investor Compensation and Deposit Guarantees WFT. These provisions include, *inter alia*, procedural rules, requirements applicable to the bank concerned, measures to be taken in the event of non-compliance. These amendments undoubtedly result from the collapse of the Icelandic Landsbanki Islands hf. in 2008. Landsbanki Islands hf. operated a Dutch branch and did opt for supplementary cover from the Dutch deposit guarantee scheme.
511. Art. 29b(3) Decree on Special Prudential Measures, Investor Compensation and Deposit Guarantees WFT.

(c) the bank concerned and the manager of the deposit guarantee scheme of the country of origin having sufficiently demonstrated to DNB that the supplementary membership will not affect the Dutch scheme in a way that the possible appeal of the deposit holders of the bank will constitute a danger to the stability of the Dutch financial sector or the protection by the Dutch scheme of deposit holders.

Furthermore, a collaboration agreement and an accession agreement will be concluded between DNB and the manager of the deposit guarantee scheme of the country of origin and the bank concerned, respectively. DNB may attach conditions or limitations to a supplementary membership of the Dutch deposit guarantee scheme with a view to the stability of the Dutch financial sector or the protection by the Dutch scheme of deposit holders.[512] In cases of non-compliance DNB will notify the home state regulator. If the bank, despite the measures taken by the home state regulator, would then still not act in compliance with the WFT, or if that regulator has taken insufficient measures or no measures at all, DNB may decide that the bank must discontinue the conclusion of contracts in the Netherlands or, with prior consent from the home state regulator, terminate the accession agreement subject to 12 months' notice.[513] The collaboration agreement and the accession agreement will lay down that DNB may modify or terminate the agreements with immediate effect, or terminate the supplementary membership with immediate effect if special circumstances as provided by law, including unforeseen circumstances, arise.[514]

DNB may decide, whether or not on application, that the Dutch deposit guarantee scheme will apply also to banks established in a non-Member State operating a branch in the Netherlands.[515]

10.2   Prohibition to Receive Repayable Funds

In addition to the prohibition to be active as a bank without a licence, Article 3:5(1) WFT contains a general prohibition for any party to attract, obtain or have

---

512. Art. 29b(5) Decree on Special Prudential Measures, Investor Compensation and Deposit Guarantees WFT. Art. 29d and 29f Decree on Special Prudential Measures, Investor Compensation and Deposit Guarantees WFT provide for specific requirements regarding these agreements.
513. Art. 29c Decree on Special Prudential Measures, Investor Compensation and Deposit Guarantees WFT.
514. Art. 29d Decree on Special Prudential Measures, Investor Compensation and Deposit Guarantees WFT.
515. Art. 3:267(1) WFT.

the disposal of repayable funds beyond a restricted circle in the Netherlands in the pursuit of a business from others than professional market parties.[516] This prohibition is not applicable to: (i) licensed banks; (ii) Member States and their regional or local government authorities; or (iii) parties attracting, obtaining or having the disposal of repayable funds as a result of offering securities in accordance with the relevant provisions of the WFT and regulations pursuant thereto.[517] With regard to the latter, this also means that this prohibition does not apply to parties attracting repayable funds as a result of offering bonds to which the obligation to have a prospectus generally available does not apply[518] (i.e., *inter alia*, parties offering securities to fewer than 100 persons other than qualified investors or when the denomination per security is at least EUR 50,000[519]). Some parties are exempted from this prohibition, *inter alia*, bailiffs (*gerechtsdeurwaarders*), notaries (*notarissen*), licensed money transaction offices (*geldtransactiekantoren*) and licensed trust offices (*trustkantoren*).[520] On application, DNB may, whether or not for a fixed period, grant a dispensation from the prohibition if the applicant demonstrates that the interests which prudential rules seek to protect are sufficiently protected in other ways.[521] It is noted that such dispensation may be granted if the holder of a dispensation will be able at all times to fulfil its obligations with regard to the funds it attracts from creditors. This kind of security may be provided if all the applicant's obligations are guaranteed by, *inter alia*: the applicant's parent company which has positive consolidated own funds; a bank having its registered office in a state designated by the Minister of Finance where banking supervision offers sufficient guarantees;[522] or a company designated by DNB, or if the applicant is granted an authorisation by DNB or the AFM pursuant to the WFT.[523] In addition, the integrity of the members of the applicant's executive board and supervisory board has to be tested by DNB.[524]

---

516. For an explanation of the concepts of " repayable funds", "beyond a restricted circle", "business", " professional market party" see paragraph 3.1.
517. Art. 3:5(2) WFT.
518. Art. 5:2 WFT.
519. Art. 5:3 WFT.
520. Arts. 19-24a Exemption Regulations WFT (*Vrijstellingsregeling Wft*).
521. Art. 3:5(4) WFT.
522. All EU Member States, Australia, Canada, Japan, the United States and Switzerland (Art. 4 of the Decree on Designated States of the Act on Financial Supervision (*Besluit aangewezen staten Wft*)).
523. Art. 27 of the Decree on the Scope of the Provisions of the Act on Financial Supervision (*Besluit reikwijdtebepalingen Wft*).
524. Art. 27 of the Decree on the Scope of the Provisions of the Act on Financial Supervision.

10.3   Protection of the Term "Bank"

Any party not being a licensed credit institution is prohibited from the use of the term "bank" or translations or forms thereof in its name or in the conduct of its business, unless this is done in a context which clearly shows that it does not operate in the financial markets.[525] The objective of this prohibition is to avoid confusion about the nature of a corporation that uses the term "bank". Some parties are exempted from this prohibition, *inter alia*, collective investment schemes incorporated by a bank, subsidiaries of a bank if the obligations of the subsidiary are guaranteed by that bank and any financial enterprise, persons or companies acting as intermediaries for banks.[526] On application, DNB may, whether or not for a fixed period, grant a dispensation from the prohibition if the applicant demonstrates that the interests which this part seeks to protect are sufficiently protected in other ways.[527]

10.4   Bank Secrecy

There is no statutory law in the Netherlands on the duty of confidentiality owed by banks to their customers. There are, however, certain statutory rules which deal with aspects of bank secrecy. Article 10 of the Dutch Constitution (*Grondwet*) of the Netherlands lays down the principle of protection against disclosure of personal data. The Act on the Protection of Personal Data (*Wet bescherming persoonsgegevens*) provides for detailed regulations applicable in all cases where personal data relating to individuals are compiled and used. These specific statutory provisions also apply to banks. However, a general statutory rule on bank confidentiality does not exist; the duty of confidentiality which under Dutch law a bank generally owes its customer is based on the contractual relationship between the bank and its customers. This relationship more often than not is governed by the General Banking Conditions[528] (*Algemene Bankvoorwaarden*) which have been developed by the Dutch Banking Association (*Nederlandse Vereniging van Banken*). Pursuant to Article 2 of the General Banking Conditions banks must exercise due care in providing services and will thereby to the best of their ability take into consideration the interests of the customer. The duty of care and the duty to take into consideration the interests of customers are considered, *inter alia*, to contain the duty to

---

525. Art. 3:7 WFT.
526. Arts. 26-31 Exemption Regulations WFT.
527. Art. 3:5(4) WFT.
528. www.nvb.nl.

maintain customer data confidentiality. These duties would, however, also apply to the relationship between a bank and its customer even if the General Banking Conditions did not apply. These duties are generally considered applicable on the basis of the principle of reasonableness and fairness which is a cornerstone of the Dutch law of contract.[529]

10.5 Act on the Prevention of Money Laundering and Financing of Terrorism

10.5.1 Introduction

On 1 August 2008, the Act for the Prevention of Money Laundering and Financing of Terrorism (*Wet ter voorkoming van witwassen en financieren van terrorisme*, **WWFT**) entered into effect.[530] The WWFT implements the Third EU Money Laundering Directive[531] in the Netherlands. The WWFT applies to, *inter alia*, financial institutions, including banks. The aim of the WWFT is to combat the laundering of the proceeds of crime and the financing of terrorism. The WWFT introduces a risk-oriented and principle-based approach and creates flexibility for the institutions. At the same time it implies greater responsibility. The institutions have to assess the risk exposure entailed by certain customers and products and have to align their efforts accordingly. Mandatory rules are no longer imposed on institutions on how to comply, but rather what has to be complied with. An institution, however, must ensure that its employees are familiar with the provisions of the WWFT and that they receive training in order to enable them to recognise unusual transactions.[532] The WWFT imposes requirements regarding, *inter alia*, CDD and the reporting of unusual transactions.

---

529. See Arts. 6:2 and 6:248 Civil Code.
530. The WWFT replaced the (former) Identification (Provision of Services) Act (*Wet identificatie bij dienstverlening*) and the (former) Disclosure of Unusual Transactions Act (*Wet melding ongebruikelijke transacties*), and incorporated most of their provisions.
531. Directive 2005/60/EC of the European Parliament and of the Council of 26 October 2005 on the prevention of the use of the financial system for the purpose of money laundering and terrorist financing. Among other things, the Third EU Money Laundering Directive implements the 40 Recommendations to combat money laundering, developed by the Financial Action Task Force on Money Laundering (FATF). The FATF is an inter-governmental body whose purpose is the development and promotion of national and international policies to combat money laundering and terrorist financing. The FATF has published 40 Recommendations to combat money laundering and nine Special Recommendations on Terrorist Financing. The Kingdom of the Netherlands is a Member State of the FATF.
532. Art. 35 WWFT.

10.5.2   CDD Requirements

CDD requirements also apply to banks under the WFT.[533] The background to these requirements is, however, much more general, namely to counter that the confidence in the bank or in the financial markets could be damaged due to its customers and not solely the prevention of money laundering and the financing of terrorism.
Pursuant to the WWFT, CDD measures must be applied when;[534]

- establishing a business relationship;
- carrying out occasional transactions amounting to EUR 15,000 or more, whether the transaction is carried out in a single operation or in several operations which appear to be linked;
- there is a suspicion of money laundering or terrorist financing;
- there are doubts about the veracity or adequacy of previously obtained customer identification data;
- the risk of involvement with money laundering or terrorist financing of an existing customer makes it necessary.

The CDD measures shall comprise:[535]

- identifying the customer, and also where applicable the ultimate beneficial owner, and verifying the customer's identity;
- ascertaining the purpose and the intended nature of the business relationship; and
- conducting ongoing monitoring of the business relationship.

To verify the identity of the customer, only documents, data and information from reliable and independent sources must be used.[536]

---

533. Art. 14 Prudential Supervision Decree in conjunction with 3:10 and 3:17 WFT. See paragraph 5.6.1.1.
534. Art. 3(1) and (3) WWFT.
535. Art. 3(2) WWFT.
536. Art. 11 WWFT. Art. 4 Regulation implementing the WWFT (*Uitvoeringsregeling Wet ter voorkoming van witwassen en financieren van terrorisme*) contains a non-exhaustive list of documentation that can be used for this purpose (i.e. in the case of a natural person, a valid passport or Dutch identity card, and in the case of a legal person, an extract from the Trade Register).

10.5.3 Reporting Requirements

Banks must report executed or intended unusual transactions to the Financial Intelligence Unit (**FIU**).[537] For determining whether a transaction qualifies as an unusual transaction, the following subjective and objective indicators are laid down:[538]

- based on the subjective indicator, a bank must report any transaction when there is an indication of money laundering or terrorist financing;
- based on the objective indicator, a bank must report: (i) a money exchange transactions amounting to EUR 15,000 or more in cash when money is changed into a different currency or into larger denominations; (ii) money transfer transactions amounting to EUR 2,000 or more in cash; and (iii) transactions with countries designated by the Minister of Finance and the Minister of Justice.

10.5.4 EC Regulation 1781/2006

On 1 January 2007, the EC Regulation on information on the payer accompanying transfers of funds[539] came into force. This is intended to counter the use of wire transfers for terrorist financing and money laundering. The Regulation has a direct effect in the Netherlands and sanctions on non-compliance have been provided for in the WWFT.[540]

10.5.5 Supervision and Enforcement

DNB is the designated authority for the supervision of banks for compliance with the provisions of the WWFT.[541] Supervision primarily targets the adequacy of the administrative organisation and internal control. These must enable: (i) an institution to conduct CDD; and (ii) employees to recognise and report an unusual transaction to the FIU. DNB can take administrative measures for non-compliance,

---

537. Art. 16 WWFT.
538. Art. 4 Order in Council implementing the WWFT (*Uitvoeringsbesluit en Wet ter voorkoming van witwassen en financieren van terrorisme*) in conjunction with Art. 15 WWFT. Reference is made to Annex I to the Order in Council implementing the WWFT.
539. Regulation (EC) No 1781/2006 of the European Parliament and of the Council of 15 November 2006 on information on the payer accompanying transfers of funds, transposing the Financial Action Task Force Recommendation VII on wire transfers into EU legislation.
540. Arts. 24, 26 and 27 WWFT.
541. Art. 1(a) Decree designation supervisory authorities WWFT (*Besluit aanwijzing toezichthouders Wet ter voorkoming van witwassen en financieren van terrorisme*).

including issuing an instruction or imposing a cease and desist order or an administrative fine.[542]

10.5.6   Criminal Liability

Breaches of the most important provisions of the WWFT constitute also an economic offence under the WED.[543] Possible sanctions are a fine of up to, in principle, EUR 76,000 for legal entities and EUR 19,000 for individuals and/or imprisonment of up to six months, or (in the event of intentional violations) two years.[544] A bank may also be held liable under the Criminal Code[545] for negligent money laundering (*schuldwitwassen*). This would include any person receiving or holding moneys who must reasonably suspect that they are proceeds of crime.

10.6   Sanctions Regulation

Sanctions are political instruments in the foreign and security policy of the United Nations and the EU. They are mandatory instruments, used in response to breaches of international laws and human rights, or to effect change when legal or democratic principles are not being adhered to. Sanctions also play a role in the fight against terrorism. Sanctions can be derived from regulations, common positions or directions from international organisations. Sanctions imposed by the United Nations are incorporated as soon as possible by the EU into European legislation.

EU sanctions regulations have direct effect in the Dutch legal system. The content of the regulations concerned indicate the kind of sanctions involved, their purport, and the states, territories, persons or entities they are aimed at. EU sanctions regulations may, in principle, impose either of two types of financial sanctions.

10.6.1   Freezing of Funds or Economic Resources

An order to freeze assets is aimed at particular persons and entities, including (alleged) terrorists and terrorist groups. On the electronic Combined Targeted

---

542. See paragraph 9.3.
543. Art. 1(2°) WED.
544. Art. 6(1)(2°) and (4°) WED in conjunction with Art. 2(3) Criminal Code.
545. Art. 420quater Criminal Code. Possible sanctions are a fine of up to EUR 760,000 for legal entities and EUR 76,000 for individuals and/or imprisonment of up to one year. The Supreme Court on 7 October 2008, in a criminal procedure, ruled that tax fraud is considered a predicate offence to money laundering. This means that if a person receives or holds moneys that are proceeds from tax fraud, he may be liable under the Criminal Code.

Financial Sanctions List (**EU freeze list**), the targeted persons and entities can be verified.[546]

10.6.2   *Measures against the Provision of Financial Services*

It is prohibited to provide financial services to, or for the benefit of, a person or entity included in the EU freeze list. Furthermore, a prohibition or restrictive measure against the provision of financial services may also be aimed at specific countries and regions. These are not included in the EU freeze list.[547]

In addition, under the Sanctions Act 1977 the Netherlands may autonomously take national measures against Dutch persons or organisations, or persons or organisations based in the Netherlands.[548]

10.6.3   *Supervision and Enforcement*

In the Netherlands a breach of the EU sanctions regulations constitutes a breach of the Sanctions Act 1977 (*Sanctiewet 1977*).[549] DNB is the designated authority for the supervision of banks for compliance with the provisions of the Sanctions Act 1977.[550] Banks need to ensure adequate administrative organisation and internal control measures in this respect.[551] DNB can take administrative measures for non-compliance, including imposing a cease and desist order or an administrative fine.[552]

10.6.4   *Criminal Liability*

Breaches of the Sanctions Act also constitute an economic offence under the WED.[553] Possible sanctions are a fine of up to EUR 760,000 for legal entities and

---

546. For a consolidated list of persons and entities under financial sanctioning measures, see: http://ec.europa.eu/external_relations/cfsp/sanctions/list/consol-list.htm.
547. For an up-to-date overview, see: http://ec.europa.eu/external_relations/cfsp/sanctions/measures.htm.
548. An example is the Sanctions Regulation on Terrorism 2007 (*Sanctieregeling terrorisme 2007*).
549. Art. 2 Sanctions Act 1977.
550. Art. 1 Ministerial Designation Supervisory Authorities Sanctions Act 1977 (*Aanwijzing rechtspersonen Sanctiewet 1977*) in conjunction with Art. 10(2)(a) Sanctions Act 1977.
551. Art. 2 of the Regulation Supervision Sanction Act 1977 (*Regeling toezicht Sanctiewet 1977*), issued by DNB, jointly with the AFM, on the basis of the Sanctions Act 1977 in conjunction with the Transfer Decree Sanctions Act 1977 (*Overdrachtsbesluit Sanctiewet 1977*).
552. See paragraph 9.3.
553. Art. 1(2°) WED.

EUR 76,000 for individuals and/or imprisonment of up to one year, or (in the event of intentional violations) six years.[554]

---

554. Art. 6(1)(1°) and (3°) WED in conjunction with Art. 23(4) Criminal Code.

Chapter 2

Securities Regulation

1.   GENERAL INTRODUCTION

1.1   General

Securities law is traditionally not a separate area of law within the Dutch legal system. More generally defined areas of the law such as civil law, corporate law and administrative law have shaped it over time.

Securities regulations in the Netherlands have increased considerably since the beginning of the 1980s. Areas which until relatively recently were not, or were scarcely, regulated are now subject to occasionally quite strict regulations in the form of a variety of laws, implementing regulations and policy statements. Although several other factors can be identified, the two main reasons for this development seem to be the desire to strengthen investor protection in the securities markets and the issuing of a number of EEC Directives covering almost all aspects of the issue and trading of securities (see paragraph 1.5).

A number of government and semi-government authorities are involved in drafting and implementing these regulations. This has resulted in the regulations having different objectives, different definitions and partially overlapping subject matters, all of which serves only to enhance the complexity of the regulatory framework.

1.2   The Securities Markets

When discussing securities markets in general, several distinctions can be made. First, the distinction between the "exchange" markets and the "over-the-counter" (OTC) markets. In the Netherlands, the exchange markets are concentrated on the recognised securities exchanges operated by Euronext Amsterdam (part of NYSE Euronext) for common stocks and bonds, options and futures (see paragraph 4.3). As in many other countries, the OTC markets are largely unstructured and are operated mainly through a computer and telephone communication network. Multilateral Trading Facilities or MTFs are unregulated trading facilities operated by an investment firm where buy and sell orders for financial instruments of third parties are brought together.

The second distinction is the type of security which might involve the bond market, the stock market or the markets for other securities (options, futures). Almost all major Dutch corporations have their stock listed on Euronext Amsterdam and a number of them on one or more foreign stock exchanges as well. The bond market can be divided into the government bond market which, although initially conducted through Euronext Amsterdam, is subject to its own rules (see paragraph 4.3.5) and the market for bonds issued by corporations. Other securities, such as options and futures, are traded on specialised options and futures exchanges and also on the OTC markets.

A third distinction can be made between domestic and international markets. Traditionally, the rules and procedures applied in the Dutch domestic market have differed substantially from those of the international markets. However, these differences have been eroded by the general internationalisation of securities trading and the rise of the Euro-markets. The Dutch securities markets have become inseparably linked to the international markets. A substantial part of Dutch stocks and Dutch government bonds are now traded abroad, mainly on the London markets. Dutch corporations and Dutch finance subsidiaries of foreign multinationals issue securities on the Euro-markets. A number of foreign enterprises, including US enterprises, are listed on Euronext Amsterdam so trade their stocks in the Netherlands.

Other relevant distinctions are those between the primary and secondary markets and between the retail and institutional wholesale markets.

Services in the securities industry are provided by commercial and investment banks, investment firms, market makers and fund managers. The Netherlands imposes few restrictions on combining these services. As a result, the main commercial banks are engaged not only in typical banking and lending activities but also in brokerage, underwriting, investment advice, fund management and a range of other activities.

1.3 The Authority for the Financial Markets

The Authority for the Financial Markets (*Stichting Autoriteit Financiële Markten* or AFM)) is the authority with principal responsibility for the enforcement and administration of most securities laws, in particular in the area of conduct of business supervision, in the Netherlands. Under the main Dutch securities statute, the Financial Supervision Act (*Wet op het financieel toezicht* or WFT), the AFM has been designated the "watchdog" of the Dutch securities markets and, in that role, supervises the various securities exchanges and the off-exchange market and grants licences to and supervises investment firms (broker-dealers, portfolio managers).[1] The AFM was founded in 1988 and commenced supervising the Dutch securities exchanges in early 1989.

The AFM is governed by a three to five member Executive Board and a Supervisory Council consisting of three to five members as well. The day-to-day administration of the statutes for which the AFM is responsible is delegated to a progressively increasing staff in the AFM's Amsterdam office.

The other main authority, other than the Dutch Minister of Finance, who bears ultimate responsibility for most securities regulations, involved in the enforcement of securities laws, is the Dutch Central Bank (*De Nederlandsche Bank N.V.* or DNB). DNB is responsible for, *inter alia*, prudential supervision of investment undertakings, investment firms and credit institutions. For a more detailed description of the roles and responsibilities of DNB and the AFM, see paragraphs 1.3 and 1.4 of Chapter 1.

1.4 Sources of Securities Law: Financial Supervision Act (WFT)

The primary sources of securities law are:

(a) Statutes;
(b) Royal Decrees (*Koninklijke Besluiten*);
(c) Ministerial regulations;
(d) Regulations issued under statutes by government or semi government authorities such as the AFM and DNB; and
(e) Policy statements and other statements of general applicability.

In addition to these formal sources, there are statements which have been given in response to individual questions dealing with, for instance, matters of interpretation

---

1. Art. 1:25 WFT.

of the regulations. In principle, these statements are not generally binding but a certain policy can sometimes be construed from the repeated issue of several of these individual statements. Case law in this field is scarce and, with a few exceptions, does not play an important role.

The main statute and other regulations of general application (excluding the regulations of the various securities exchanges) are found in the Financial Supervision Act (WFT)[2] and its implementing regulations. The WFT entered into force on 1 January 2007, to replace and combine seven then existing financial supervision acts, including the Securities Transactions Supervision Act of 1995.[3] The latter statute had replaced the 1985 Securities Trading Act[4] and the 1914 Exchange Act[5] in 1992. The WFT's implementing regulations were issued partly as Royal Decrees, partly as regulations of the Ministry of Finance, and partly as regulations of the AFM and DNB. The main regulations include:

(a) The Financial Enterprises Market Access Decree;[6]
(b) The Prudential Supervision Decree;[7]
(c) The WFT Exemption Regulation[8] issued by the Ministry of Finance;
(d) The Conduct of Business Decree;[9] and
(e) The Further Conduct of Business Regulation[10] issued by the AFM.

The WFT and its implementing regulations deal with, *inter alia*, the primary offer of securities (see paragraph 2), public take-over bids, the supervision of investment firms (broker-dealers, portfolio managers, see paragraph 4.1), banks (see Chapter 1), insurance companies, investment undertakings (see paragraph 5.), the supervision of securities exchanges (see paragraph 4.3) and market abuse (see paragraph 6.1).

---

2.   *Wet op het financieel toezicht* (WFT), 2006 *Staatsblad* [Stb.] 475.
3.   *Wet toezicht effectenverkeer* 1995, 1995 Stb. 574.
4.   *Wet effectenhandel*, 1985 Stb. 570.
5.   *Beurswet*, 1914 Stb. 445, *as amended*.
6.   *Besluit markttoegang financiële ondernemingen Wft*, 2006 Stb. 506.
7.   *Besluit prudentiële regels Wft*, 2007 Stb. 407.
8.   *Vrijstellingsregeling Wft*, 2006 Staatscourant [Stcr.] (Government Gazette) 229.
9.   *Besluit gedragstoezicht financiële ondernemingen Wft*, 2006, Stb. 520.
10. *Nadere Regeling gedragstoezicht financiële ondernemingen Wft*, 2006 Stcr. 233.

1.5 Harmonisation of European Securities Law

An increasing number of elements in Dutch securities regulations are the result of implementation of EEC directives. These directives are aimed at two different objectives. First, the EEC wished to liberalise capital movements in relation to securities operations in the European Community.[11] Second, in the late seventies the EC Commission shifted its attention to harmonisation (referred to officially as "co-ordination") of national securities regulations. The concept behind these directives is that harmonisation of the investor protection rules in each of the EC Member States will ultimately encourage the creation of a genuine European capital market and a level playing field.

Important elements of some of these directives are to be found in the European Code of Conduct Recommendation (1977)[12] which outlined a set of basic rules of conduct for participants in the securities markets. Many of the principles laid down in this non-binding recommendation can be identified in the directives which followed. The directives referred to below have been declared applicable in all states which are part of the European Economic Area (EEA). The EEA currently consists of all European Union Member States as well as Norway, Liechtenstein and Iceland. References to Member States below include these other EEA states.

1.5.1 Stock Exchange Admission Directive[13]

The Stock Exchange Admission Directive lays down minimum requirements for the admission of securities to official listing on a stock exchange situated or operating within a Member State.

The main purpose of this directive is to facilitate crossborder listings within the EEA. This includes both the admission to official stock exchange listing in a Member State of securities from another Member State and the simultaneous listing of securities on a number of European stock exchanges. The directive contains, *inter alia*, minimum capitalization requirements and obligations with respect to the supply of information to holders of the listed securities.

---

11. Capital Movements Directives: First Directive for the implementation of Article 67 of the Treaty, Official Journal of the European Communities [O.J. Eur.Comm.] (No. 43) 919 (1960) and Second Council Directive adding to and amending the First Directive for the implementation of Article 67 of the Treaty No. 63/21, O.J. Eur. Comm. (1963) 62.

12. Commission Recommendation concerning an European code of conduct relating to transactions in transferable securities No. 77/534, O.J. Eur. Comm. (No. L 212) 37 (1977), as *amended by* O.J. Eur. Comm. (No. L 294) 28 (1977).

13. Directive on the admission of securities to official stock exchange listing and on information to be published on those securities No. 2001/34, O.J. Eur. Comm. (No. L 184) 1 (2001).

1.5.2   *Prospectus Directive*[14]

This directive harmonises the requirements for the prospectus to be published when securities are offered to the public or admitted to stock exchange listing.

The directive applies the principle of "mutual recognition" of a prospectus approved by the competent authority in any Member State. Once approved in a Member State as an adequate prospectus for a public offer or listing, the prospectus must, as a general rule, be recognized by other Member States in which the securities are offered or admission to official listing is sought.

1.5.3   *Transparency Directive*[15]

The Transparency Directive harmonises the information which must be published on a yearly, half-yearly and quarterly basis by companies whose shares are listed on a stock exchange situated or operating in a Member State. It also contains a number of other provisions which deal with the position of holders of listed securities. This directive also provides for an obligation to disclose the acquisition or disposal of a major holding in a listed company (see paragraph 3.3). This aims to enhance the transparency of the securities markets.

1.5.4   *Investment Undertakings or UCITS Directive*[16]

The Investment Undertakings Directive harmonises the rules on the authorisation, structure and investment policy of, and information to be provided by, undertakings for collective investment in transferable securities (so-called UCITS), such as mutual funds. The directive applies the home-state control principle and mutual recognition of supervisory standards and licences, so that an investment undertaking with a single licence obtained in a Member State can operate throughout the European Economic Area (see paragraph 5).

---

14. Directive on the prospectus to be published when securities are offered to the public or admitted to trading No. 2003/71, O.J. Eur. Comm. (No. L 354) (2003).
15. Directive on the harmonisation of transparency requirements in relation to information about issuers whose securities are admitted to trading on a regulated market No. 2004/10, O.J. Eur. Comm. (No. L 390) 38 (2004).
16. Directive on the coordination of laws, regulations and administrative provisions relating to undertakings for collective investments in transferable securities (UCITS) No. 2009/65, O.J. Eur. Comm. (No. L 302) 332 (2009).

1.5.5   *Market Abuse Directive* [17]

The Market Abuse Directive sets minimum rules on the prohibition and punishment of insider trading and market manipulation. It also contains the obligation for issuers of listed securities to disclose price sensitive information.

1.5.6   *Recast Banking Directive* [18]

Although the Recast Banking Directive focuses primarily on banking activities (see Chapter 1), it also contains provisions as to the supply of services by banks for the issue and trading of securities. Essentially, this directive provides for the mutual recognition of banking licences issued by Member States. Mutual recognition in this case means, *inter alia*, that, subject to certain limitations, licensed banks in a Member State must be allowed to establish a branch office or to provide services in another Member State. The activities in which, subject to the limitations of its home-state licence, such a bank may be engaged include the provision of services in the field of securities. [19]

1.5.7   *Markets in Financial Instruments Directive* [20] *(MiFID)*

The MiFID provides for the freedom of establishment and freedom to provide services for investment firms active in the securities business.

    Just as the Banking directives enabled banks to operate on an EEA-wide scale on the basis of a single licence (the "European passport"), this directive enables investment firms in any Member State to set up a branch office or to provide investment services in other Member States on the basis of the licence granted by their home Member State.

---

17. Directive on insider dealing and market manipulation No. 2003/6, O.J. Eur. Comm. (No. L 96) 16 (2003).
18. Directive relating to the taking up and pursuit of the business of credit institutions (recast) No. 2006/48, O.J. Eur. Comm. (No. L 177) 1 (2006).
19. These services include: trading in financial instruments for one's own account or for the account of customers, participation in securities issues, portfolio management, safekeeping and the administration of securities.
20. Directive on markets in financial instruments No. 2004/39, O.J. Eur. Comm. (No. L 45) 1 (2004).

1.6 Definition of Securities and Financial Instruments

Dutch law originally did not provide for an entirely uniform and consistent definition of exactly what is covered by the term "securities". The applicable definition depended in each case on the objective of the regulation at issue. The WFT[21] has now introduced the following general definition of the term securities:

> (a) a tradable share or equivalent tradable instrument or right (excluding apartment rights);
> (b) a tradable bond or other tradable debt instrument; and
> (c) each other tradable instrument issued by a legal entity, company or institution which upon exercise or conversion entitles the holder thereof to receive an instrument as referred to under (a) or (b) or to cash settlement.

This definition would essentially seem to cover all conceivable tradable equity and debt instruments and most tradable bond or share options. The term "financial instrument", as introduced by the MiFID, also comprises securities but has a much broader meaning:[22]

> (a) securities;
> (b) money market instruments;
> (c) units in an investment undertaking, other than being securities;
> (d) options, futures, swaps, forward rate agreements and any other derivative contracts relating to securities, currencies, interest rates or yields, or other derivative instruments, indices or financial measures which may be settled physically or in cash;
> (e) options, futures, swaps, forward rate agreements and any other derivative contracts relating to commodities that must be settled in cash or may be settled in cash at the option of one of the parties, otherwise than by reason of a default or other termination event;
> (f) options, futures, swaps and any other derivative contracts relating to commodities that can only be physically settled, provided they are traded on a regulated market or through a multilateral trading facility;
> (g) options, futures, swaps or forward rate agreements other than those referred to under (f) and any other derivative contracts relating to commodities which can be physically settled and are not intended for commercial purposes, and which have the characteristics of other derivative financial instruments;

---

21. Art. 1:1 WFT.
22. Art. 1:1 WFT.

(h) derivative instruments for the transfer of credit risk;

(i) financial contracts to settle differences; or

(j) options, futures, swaps, forward rate agreements and any other derivative contracts relating to climate variables, freight rates, emission rights, inflation rates or other official economic statistics that must be settled in cash or may be settled in cash at the option of one of the parties, otherwise than by reason of default or any other termination event, as well as any other derivative contracts relating to assets, rights, obligations, indices or measures (other than those referred to above) which have the characteristics of other derivative financial instruments.

2.   REGULATION OF SECURITIES OFFERINGS

2.1   Introduction

Until the Securities Trading Act[23] was introduced in 1986, there was no securities legislation in the Netherlands which specifically regulated the public offering of newly issued securities. In the case of securities listed on Euronext Amsterdam, the stock exchange regulations ensured that an adequate prospectus was made available in respect of these securities by the issuer. These rules did not, however, apply to unlisted securities or securities listed elsewhere.

As a result of undesired developments in the off-exchange markets, consisting mainly of the increasing occurrence of fraudulent broking and investment schemes, emergency legislation in the form of the Securities Trading Act was quickly put into place in order to counter these developments. This Act was only meant to be temporary as new overall securities legislation was being considered. This new legislation, the Securities Transactions Supervision Act 1991 (WTE 1991), replaced both the Securities Trading Act and the Exchange Act[24] and entered into force on 15 June 1992. The WTE 1991 was replaced by the WTE of 1995, and most recently by the WFT, as currently in force.

Primary market supervision in the Netherlands changed significantly on 1 July 2005. As of such date, the Prospectus Directive (see paragraph 1.5.2) was implemented in Dutch legislation (in Chapter 5 of the WFT). The prospectus rules for both listed and unlisted securities were harmonised and the AFM was appointed as the sole competent authority for prospectus supervision. In addition, the contents

---

23. *Wet effectenhandel*, see paragraph 1.4.
24. *Beurswet*, see paragraph 1.4.

requirements for both types of prospectuses were laid down in an EC regulation with direct effect in all EEA Member States.[25]

The aim of this advanced harmonisation – with even fully uniform contents requirements for prospectuses – was to facilitate pan-European securities offerings on the basis of one single offer document. This shall create a truly European capital market, which was never accomplished under the previous EC prospectus directives of 1980 and 1989. Those directives also tried to create a form of mutual prospectus recognition within the EEA but never achieved their goal due to local barriers and uncooperative supervisors.

The Prospectus Directive's system simply means that any prospectus which has been approved by the competent authority in any EEA Member State must be recognised in all other Member States. This is referred to as the "passporting" of prospectuses, comparable with the passporting of licences of banks, insurance companies, investment firms etc.

2.2 Primary Market Restrictions

2.2.1 Prohibition

The WFT prohibits (i) any offer of securities to the public in the Netherlands and (ii) the admission of securities to trading on a regulated market in the Netherlands unless a prospectus has been made generally available with respect to such offer or admission to trading.[26] Such prospectus must be approved by the AFM or the competent authority of another EEA Member State.

An "offer of securities" has been defined as the making of a sufficiently determined offer to more than one person to enter into an agreement to acquire securities or the invitation to make such an offer to acquire securities.

2.2.2 PD Securities

The Prospectus Directive only applies to so-called "PD Securities" which are securities set out in the Prospective Directive. Those PD Securities are (i) tradable shares, similar equity instruments or rights, (ii) tradable instruments which entitle the holder thereof, through exercise or conversion, to a different equity security which has been issued by the same issuer or a group company thereof, (iii) tradable instruments which entitle the holder thereof, through exercise or conversion, to

---

25. Commission Regulation (EC) No. 809 /2004, O.J. Eur.Comm. (No. L 149) 1 (2004).
26. Art. 5:2WFT.

a different security which has not been issued by the issuer or a group company thereof, (iv) tradable instruments which entitle the holder thereof, through exercise of the right attached thereto, to cash settlement, or (v) tradable bonds and other debt instruments. The securities referred to in (i) and (ii) are defined as equity securities while the instruments referred to in (iii)-(v) are defined as debt securities. This distinction is relevant, inter alia, for determining which supervisor is competent to approve the prospectus (see paragraph 2.2.3.1).

Money market instruments with a term of less than 12 months (e.g. Commercial Paper, or Certificates of Deposit), are excluded from the definition of PD Securities.

Participation rights in open-end investment undertakings are excluded from the definition as well as they are subject to a distinct supervisory regime and prospectus rules (see paragraph 5).

The offer of other financial instruments which do not qualify as PD Securities is not subject to the WFT's primary market restrictions.

2.2.3 *Issue of a Prospectus*

2.2.3.1 General

If none of the applicable exceptions or exemptions is available (see paragraph 2.2.5), the public offer or admission to trading of PD Securities will require a prospectus to be prepared, approved and made generally available. For equity securities and debt securities with a nominal value below EUR 1,000, the prospectus will have to be approved by the competent authority in the Member State in which the issuer is established. For any other type of securities, the issuer or offeror has the option to elect its home authority or another EEA authority as the competent authority (e.g. in the Member State where the offer is made or the admission to trading is sought). Issuers in third countries (i.e. non-Member States) can elect the competent authority in any EEA Member State where the offer is made or admission to trading is sought.

In the Netherlands, the AFM has been exclusively designated as the competent authority for approval of any PD prospectuses.

On the basis of the Prospectus Directive's requirements, the AFM must respond to an approval request within 10 business days of the receipt of such request (20 business days in the case of an initial public equity offering (IPO) or another securities offering by an issuer whose securities have not yet been offered to the public or admitted to trading). In practice, the AFM will not approve any prospectus in such a short timeframe but will provide its first comments only (in the form of so-called "comment sheets"). Once these comments have been incorporated, the draft prospectus is refiled and this process is repeated until the AFM indicates it has no more comments and approval can be granted.

2.2.3.2   Contents of Prospectus

In the approval process, the AFM checks if the prospectus complies with the general WFT requirements and the detailed requirements of the Prospectus Regulation which are specific to the type of security. The general WFT requirements are that the prospectus must be complete, correct and not misleading. Pursuant to the Prospectus Regulation, a prospectus must consist of a registration document which describes the issuer, a securities note which describes the relevant securities and a summary (in about 2,500 words or less) of the registration document and securities note. These three prospectus components can be combined in one single document or produced as three separate documents.[27]

The contents requirements for registration documents and securities notes differ according to the type of security being offered, e.g. equity instruments, debt instruments (with different requirements for debt securities with a nominal value of less than EUR 50,000, those with a nominal value of at least EUR 50,000 and derivative securities which may repay less than their principal amount at maturity), asset backed securities etc.

In the case of continuous debt issuance programmes such as Medium Term Note programmes, a prospectus may be produced in the form of a so-called base prospectus.[28] This type of prospectus must also consist of a registration document, securities note and summary but the specific details of any drawdown under the programme, such as issue price, term, and interest rate, may be completed at the time of the offer or admission to trading by means of final terms. Such final terms must be filed with the competent authority which has approved the base prospectus.

A PD prospectus published in the Netherlands must be prepared in Dutch or in English. The Prospectus Directive entitles the EEA host Member State to require that the prospectus summary be translated into the local language. In practice the AFM does not make use of this authority and also accepts English as the language of the summary.

2.2.3.3   Publication of Prospectus

Once the prospectus has been approved, it must be made generally available.[29] The Prospectus Directive permits various publication methods such as (i) publication in a national newspaper, (ii) making a hard copy of the prospectus available, at no

---

27. Art. 5:15 WFT.
28. Art. 5:16 WFT.
29. Art. 5:21 WFT.

charge, at the relevant securities exchange, the issuer or the investment firms involved in the offer, (iii) publication on the issuer's website and (iv) publication on the website of the relevant securities exchange. The AFM keeps a public register on its website (www.afm.nl) in which all prospectuses approved by it are listed. In the case of an initial public offering (IPO), the issuer or offeror must make the prospectus available at least six business days before the offer or admission to trading to allow investors sufficient reading time.

A base prospectus remains valid for a maximum period of 12 months after its publication. This period also applies to a registration document that has been prepared and published as a separate document.

2.2.3.4   Prospectus Supplement

Once the AFM has approved a prospectus, its contents become final and can no longer be amended. If there are any material new developments after approval of the prospectus but before the offer of the relevant securities is closed or the securities are admitted to trading, the issuer or offeror must prepare a prospectus supplement. This important new development can relate to the information contained in the prospectus or can be a material error or inaccuracy which can influence the assessment of the securities. If necessary, the prospectus summary may need to be supplemented as well.

The prospectus supplement will have to be approved by the AFM before it can be published.[30] A written request to this effect will have to be submitted to the AFM, after which the AFM has seven business days to review the draft supplement. During that period, the AFM can also provide comments on the draft first. Depending on the length of the supplement, the approval can already be given within a couple of business days and sometimes even on the same day the approval request was submitted. After it has been approved, the supplement forms part of the prospectus. It has to be made public in the same manner as a prospectus.

An investor may want to reconsider his investment decision on the basis of the new information contained in the supplement. For that reason, the Prospectus Directive has introduced a withdrawal right which applies to both a public offer and an admission to trading.[31] This withdrawal right entitles an investor who has subscribed for the relevant securities to rescind the agreement or revoke his offer.

---

30.   Art. 5:23(3) WFT.
31.   Art. 5:23(6) WFT.

2.2.3.5 Advertising Rules

The WFT also imposes certain restrictions on advertising a public offer of securities or admission to trading.[32] Such advertising materials, which may also be published before any offer is made ("pre-marketing"), must mention that a prospectus is or will be made generally available and where a copy of the prospectus may be obtained. The advertising materials may not be incorrect or misleading and must be consistent with the information which is or will be included in the prospectus. Oral or written statements by the issuer or offeror must also be consistent with the information contained in the prospectus.[33] Important information which is only provided to certain (professional) investors or during investor presentations, road shows or analyst presentations must also be included in the prospectus or in a prospectus supplement.[34]

2.2.4 *The European Passport*

2.2.4.1 Introduction

One of the main purposes of the Prospectus Directive is to create a pan-European capital market where on the basis of one single offer document securities can be offered or listed throughout the EEA. I.e., a type of European "passport" which is recognised by all EEA Member States.

As soon as a prospectus has been approved by the competent authority in one EEA Member State the relevant authority can, upon request, confirm such approval in writing to one or more competent authorities in other Member States. If subsequently a prospectus supplement is prepared, such supplement will need to be "passported" to the relevant Member States in a similar fashion. If the passport request is made before the prospectus has been approved, the relevant home authority needs to issue the confirmation to other Member States within one business day. If the request is made after the prospectus has been approved, the confirmation has to be issued within three business days after receipt of the request.[35]

---

32. Art. 5:20(1) WFT.
33. Art. 5:20(2) WFT.
34. Art. 5:20(3) WFT.
35. Art. 5:10 WFT.

2.2.4.2   Passporting from the Netherlands

Upon request the AFM will issue a confirmation of approval to other EEA Member States in accordance with the procedure in the previous paragraph. This confirmation is accompanied by the approved prospectus (and any documents incorporated by reference therein) and, if applicable, a translation of the summary. Whether the summary needs to be translated in to the local language(s) depends on the implementing legislation in the relevant Member State (e.g., in Germany, France and Belgium the summary must be made available in the local language(s)). In practice, the AFM will only send its confirmation after it has received a copy of the relevant translation(s) of the summary.

After the AFM has despatched its confirmation to the relevant competent authorities, it will not in all cases be possible to offer or list the securities in the relevant host states. In some Member States there may be local formalities which need to be considered, e.g. with respect to local advertising rules or filing requirements with the local Trade Register.

When a base prospectus has been approved (see paragraph 2.2.3.2), the confirmation of approval will only be issued in relation to the base prospectus. The final terms need only be filed with the home supervisor although CESR recommends that the final terms are also filed with the relevant host states[36]

2.2.4.3   Passporting to the Netherlands

The Prospectus Directive is based on the principle of mutual recognition which means that a prospectus approved in another Member State must also be recognised in the Netherlands. The prospectus approved in another Member State can therefore be used for a public offer or listing of securities in the Netherlands once the AFM has received the confirmation of approval. Such prospectus must be prepared in Dutch or in an internationally recognised language.

The AFM has the right to require that the summary be made available in Dutch but in practice does not require this. In the Netherlands there are no other local formalities which go beyond what is required by the Prospectus Directive so once the "passport" confirmation has been sent to the AFM the public offer or listing of the securities can take place.

---

36.   Commission of European Securities Regulators (CESR)'s Frequently asked questions regarding prospectuses: Common positions agreed by CESR Members (the latest version is available at www.cesr.eu).

2.2.5 *Exceptions/Exemptions*

2.2.5.1 General

The WFT and the WFT Exemption Regulation[37] provide a number of general exceptions to and exemptions from the prospectus requirement. All of such exceptions and exemptions are based on the Prospectus Directive in order to achieve full harmonisation. Some exceptions and exemptions are available in the case of both a public offer of securities and an admission to listing, while others are available for one of those two only.

2.2.5.2 Exceptions/Exemptions for Public Offer and Admission to Trading

The main exceptions and exemptions in the case of a public offer and an admission to trading of securities are the following:

(a) shares or depositary receipts for shares which are issued to replace already issued securities, provided that the issued share capital is not increased;

(b) securities which are offered in relation to a public exchange bid, provided that a document containing equivalent information is made generally available ;

(c) securities that are offered or allotted in the case of a merger or demerger, provided that a document containing equivalent information is made generally available;

(d) stock dividends and other shares or depositary receipts which are issued to shareholders free of charge, provided that the new securities are of the same kind as the existing ones and a document containing information on the number of shares, the characteristics thereof, the rationale for the offer and any specifics thereof is made available;

(e) securities which an employer (or one of its group companies) offers or allots to its board members or employees, provided that a document containing information on the number of securities, the characteristics thereof, the rationale for the offer and any specifics thereof is made available;

(f) debt securities which are issued or guaranteed by an EEA Member State, a local authority in a Member State or an international public organisation of which one or more Member States is a member;

(g) certain types of debt instruments which are offered by banks on a continuous basis (e.g. bank and saving certificates); and

---

37. WFT Exemption Regulation §5.1.

(h) securities which have a total issue size, calculated over a period of 12 months, of less than EUR 2,500,000.[38]

2.2.5.3   Exceptions/Exemptions in case of Public Offer Only

In the following events, no prospectus will have to be prepared for a public offer of the relevant securities:

(a) securities which are offered only to qualifying investors (see below);
(b) securities which are offered to fewer than 100 persons (who are not qualifying investors);
(c) securities with a nominal value of at least EUR 50,000 per security or which can only be purchased for a total consideration of at least EUR 50,000;
(d) securities which have a total issue size, calculated a period of 12 months, of less than EUR 100,000; and
(e) securities which have already been issued and are offered in the secondary market (unless they were only offered to qualifying investors when first issued).

A "qualified investor" is defined as:[39]

(a) a legal person or company that holds a licence or is otherwise authorised to be active on the financial markets;
(b) a legal person or company that does not hold a licence or is not otherwise authorised to be active on the financial markets and whose only corporate object is to invest in securities;
(c) a national or regional government body, central bank, international or supranational financial organisation or other similar international institution;
(d) a legal person or company having its registered office in the Netherlands that: (i) is classified as a small enterprise under rules to be laid down by decree;[40] and (ii) is registered by the AFM as a qualified investor at its own request;

---

38. This exemption is non-cumulative and may therefore not be used in combination with any other exemption.
39. Art. 1:1 WFT.
40. Pursuant to Art. 4(1) *Besluit definitiebepalingen Wft* (Decree on Definitions) small enterprises are legal persons or companies, which, according to the most recent annual accounts or consolidated accounts, fulfil at least two of the following three criteria:
    (a) the average number of employees during the financial year is fewer than 250;

(e) a legal person or company, not being a legal person or company as referred to in d above;

(f) a natural person residing in the Netherlands who satisfies the criteria to be laid down by decree[41] and who is registered by the AFM as a qualified investor at his own request; or

(g) a natural person or enterprise classified as a qualified investor in another Member State pursuant to the Prospectus Directive.[42]

2.2.5.4   Exceptions/Exemptions in case of Admission to Trading

In the following events, no prospectus will have to be prepared for an admission to trading of the relevant securities:

(a) shares (and depositary receipts for shares) which, calculated over a period of 12 months, represent less than 10% of the issued shares of the same class or type which have already been admitted to trading;

(b) shares (and depositary receipts for shares) which are issued upon a conversion or exercise of other securities and which are of the same class or type as securities which are already admitted to trading on the same stock exchange;

(c) securities which have already been admitted to trading on another securities exchange for a period of at least 18 months.

2.2.6   *Sanctions*

Violation of the prohibition on primary offers of securities or of the disclosure obligations used to constitute an economic offence under the Act on Economic

---

(b) the balance sheet total is no more than EUR 43,000,000; and

(c) the annual net turnover is no more than EUR 50,000,000.

41. Pursuant to Art. 4(2) Decree on Definitions, such natural persons are natural persons who fulfil at least two of the following three criteria:

    (a) the natural person has carried out at least 10 transactions of a significant size on the securities markets, per quarter, over the previous four quarters;

    (b) the size of the natural persons securities portfolio exceeds EUR 500,000; and

    (c) the natural person works or has worked for at least one year in the financial sector in a professional position which requires knowledge of securities investments.

42. Directive 2003/71/EC of the European Parliament and of the Council of 4 November 2003 on the prospectus to be published when securities are offered to the public or admitted to trading. This provision means that certain natural persons and small and medium-sized enterprises (SMEs) that are considered qualified investors in another Member State are also considered qualified investors in the Netherlands.

Offences.[43] However, when the WFT entered into force, the relevant articles of the WFT were – possibly erroneously – no longer included in the list of punishable violations. This means that such violations are only subject to a number of administrative sanctions, including administrative fines (see paragraph 9.3.4. of Chapter 1).

The WFT does not provide any specific civil law sanctions for violation of its provisions and thus the common civil law rules of contractual and tortuous liability apply. Transactions in violation of the WFT's provisions, such as a public offer of securities which contravenes the WFT's restrictions on primary offers are not void or voidable.[44]

2.3 Civil Liability for a Prospectus

2.3.1 *Liability of the Issuer*

Extensive and detailed requirements with respect to the contents of a prospectus do not necessarily mean that all the information contained in the prospectus is correct and complete. A prospectus issued for the purpose of a listing on Euronext Amsterdam is reviewed by the AFM to verify that it meets the requirements of the WFT and the EU Prospectus Regulation. However, the AFM does not conduct any investigation into the correctness and completeness of the prospectus. Furthermore, there is a possibility that the securities are being issued under an exception or exemption but that an (informal) offering circular or information memorandum was used regardless. Such an offering document is not subject to any official examination other than that of the lead manager.

Accordingly, it can never be excluded that some of the information in the prospectus or other offering document is incorrect, incomplete or misleading. The question then arises as to whether an investor, who has relied on such information and has suffered damage as a result, has a right of action. The damage could consist of a price devaluation of the securities upon publication of the information which is lacking or is incorrectly stated in the prospectus (e.g., the financial position turns out to be considerably worse than that stated in the prospectus).

It will first have to be determined whether the investor has any contractual right of action. This will be the case if the investor purchased the securities directly from the issuer. The investor could then invoke rescission (*vernietiging or ontbinding*)

---

43. Act on Economic Offences (*Wet op de Economische Delicten* – WED) .
44. Art. 1:23 WFT.

and/or claim damages on the basis of an error of facts (*dwaling*[45]), fraud (*bedrog*[46]) or default (*wanprestatie*[47]). If the securities were purchased from the issuer through a broker, the broker can take action on behalf of the investor.[48]

If there is no contractual relationship between the issuer and the investor, a claim could be based on the rules of tort and, more specifically, on the misleading advertising provisions thereof.[49] Case law has confirmed that these provisions equally apply to a prospectus.[50] Under these provisions, a person who makes public, or causes to be made public, information regarding goods or services which he, or the person for whom he acts, offers in the conduct of a profession or business, commits a tort if this information is misleading. If a claim based on this provision is filed, the burden of proof will be reversed in two respects. First, a person who, wholly or partly, determined or caused to be determined the content and presentation of the published information, must, as a general rule, prove the accuracy or completeness of the allegedly misleading statements. Second, if it is established that this person has committed a tort, he is liable for any loss resulting therefrom unless he is neither at fault nor responsible for any other reason.

The content and presentation of the prospectus is generally determined to a large degree by the issuer. Accordingly, the rules of tort seem to offer the investor a relatively strong position in the case of an allegedly misleading prospectus, because it is the issuer who will have to prove that the prospectus was not misleading.

2.3.2   *Liability of the Lead Manager*

In the case of an issue through a syndicate of banks or investment firms, the lead manager will generally also has an active role in preparing and verifying the information to be included in the prospectus. It can be safely assumed that the lead manager normally qualifies as "a person who, wholly or partly, determined or caused to be determined the content and presentation" of the prospectus. The Dutch Supreme Court has also confirmed that a claim can be successfully filed against a lead manager on the basis of the misleading advertising provisions.[51]

There is a tendency, derived from Anglo-American practice in the 1990s, to emphasize the syndicate's and the lead manager's responsibility for the content of

---

45.   Art. 6:228 BW.
46.   Art. 3:44 BW.
47.   Arts. 6:74-78 BW.
48.   Art. 7:411 BW.
49.   Arts. 6:194-196 BW.
50.   Judgment of 20 December 1985, Supreme Court (*Hoge Raad* [HR]), 1986 NJ No. 231.
51.   Judgement of December 2, 1994, HR, 1996 NJ No. 246 and judgement of 27 November, 2009, HR, JOR 2010 No. 43 (Word Online case).

the prospectus. An adequate due diligence investigation and verification process can reduce the syndicate's and the lead manager's potential liability in this respect. As a result, in 1993 Euronext Amsterdam issued a directive to its member firms requiring them to conduct a due diligence investigation if the firm were acting as a syndicate member in respect of an issue of securities which were to be listed on Euronext Amsterdam. The directive also contained detailed requirements as to the areas which the investigation should cover. The directive was abolished when the Prospectus Directive was implemented in 2005. However, for the reasons set out above, the lead manager will in practice generally still conduct a due diligence investigation in order to reduce or eliminate its liability risk.

3.   REGULATION OF PUBLICLY HELD COMPANIES

3.1   Introduction

Dutch publicly held companies are subject to the general corporate law provisions of Book 2 of the Civil Code as well as to the WFT's transparency requirements with respect to, *inter alia*, the provision of information to the public and periodic financial disclosure. Until 2009 – when the Transparency Directive was implemented in the WFT – most of the latter requirements were set out in the Euronext Amsterdam listing rules and did not have a statutory basis.

Companies whose securities are not listed on Euronext Amsterdam may still be subject to the prospectus and periodic disclosure requirements under the WFT if their shares or other securities are listed on another regulated securities market within the EEA.

3.2   Listing on Euronext Amsterdam

3.2.1   *General*

A stock exchange listing is a step which has far-reaching repercussions throughout the company. The company's responsibility to its shareholders becomes subject to a new, formalized structure. Many changes are made to the company's internal and external information policy.

In the period between the decision to apply for listing and admission to the exchange, a great deal has to be arranged. The company has to liaise with a firm admitted to Euronext Amsterdam, i.e., a bank or investment firm, given that only these firms are authorised to file an application for listing on behalf of the company[52] as listing agent. One or more institutions (usually the company's bankers) guide the company through the listing process.

An important issue which must, if relevant, be addressed during the preparatory period is the legal structure of the company. A corporation whose shares are to be listed must be an "N.V." and in some cases this will require modification of the company's legal form.[53] In many cases, the change to the corporate structure will lead to the company adopting a more formal management structure and also a supervisory board. Such corporate structure will also have to comply with the Dutch corporate governance code.[54] The question of whether the Company will put any anti-takeover devices into place will need to be considered at this stage as well.[55]

Both registered and bearer securities may be listed and traded. Depository receipts for bearer or registered shares can also be admitted.

Bearer securities are traditionally listed in the form of "K" or "CF" certificates. CF certificates are administered by Centrum voor Fondsenadministratie B.V. (the Centre for Securities Administration B.V.), a subsidiary of Euronext Amsterdam N.V. which administers and effects the distribution of dividend, and interest on securities. Unlike K-certificates, which are issued with interest or dividend coupons attached, CF certificates are issued with a simplified interest or coupon sheet. Euronext Amsterdam and the Dutch central securities depository, Necigef/Euroclear Netherlands (see paragraph 4.3.3.5) also accept bearer securities in permanent global or in registered form. Many of the companies admitted to listing on Euronext Amsterdam in recent years have in fact issued only one global share certificate which represents the entire issued share capital of the company or shares in registered form.

3.2.2 Admission Procedure

The Euronext Amsterdam Rulebooks distinguish between two methods of introducing securities to listing on Euronext Amsterdam: introduction through a public issue and introduction by trading.[56] In the first case, new shares are issued and offered to the general public for subscription, whereas in the second, existing shares are placed through the exchange. In both cases, an application must be made for listing of the securities concerned, signed by both the issuer and the listing agent (i.e., the firm supporting the application). The documents which need

---

52. Rulebook II of Euronext Amsterdam.
53. The only other legal forms accepted for listing of domestic entities are an unincorporated investment fund and a cooperative.
54. Dutch corporate governance code (Code Tabaksblatt), www.corpgov.nl.
55. Euronext Amsterdam abolished its restrictions on anti-takeover devices in December 2007.
56. Rulebook II art. A 2702.

to be filed with Euronext Amsterdam together with the application include a copy of the prospectus which is required to be issued and evidence of approval thereof by the competent authority.[57] Under the WFT, Euronext Amsterdam is authorised to decide on any listing application. The Euronext Rulebooks and implementing notices contain a set of general rules for the admission procedure.

These Rulebooks contain certain minimum requirements for the minimum nominal amount of securities which must be available for trading in order to be admitted to listing.[58] An issuer wishing to have its securities listed on Euronext Amsterdam must enter into a standard form listing agreement with Euronext Amsterdam. By signing this agreement, the issuer becomes bound by the provisions of the Rulebooks.

Euronext Amsterdam charges certain fees to an issuer of securities listed or to be listed on Euronext Amsterdam including an admission fee and an annual listing fee.[59]

3.2.3 *Prospectus*

Until the Prospectus Directive was implemented in 2005, Euronext Amsterdam was in charge of the review and approval process with respect to the listing prospectus. However, this task was delegated to the AFM upon such implementation (see paragraph 2.2.3).

If the securities whose listing is sought have been publicly offered or admitted for listing on a securities exchange located or operating in another EEA Member State and the prospectus used for that listing has been approved by the competent authority in the relevant Member State, then Euronext Amsterdam must also accept that prospectus (see paragraph 2.2.4).

3.3 Continuing Obligations

3.3.1 *General*

Once an issuer has listed its securities on Euronext Amsterdam, it becomes subject to the continuing disclosure obligations set out in the WFT. The obligations are

---

57. A prospectus does not always have to be issued; if, for instance, the listing is sought for shares which represent less than 10% of the issuer's issued share capital already admitted to listing, a prospectus may not be required (see paragraph 2.2.4).
58. On the Stock Market, this amount is EUR 5,000,000 for shares and EUR 200,000 for bonds. For shares there are also certain minimum free float requirements..
59. The Admission and Listing Fees Regulation (*Reglement tarieven toelating en notering*).

different for issuers of shares and debt securities and consist of ad hoc requirements to publish price sensitive information as well as periodic financial disclosure
requirements.

3.3.2   *Annual Financial Reports*

The WFT requires all issuers whose securities are admitted to trading on a regulated market to publish their annual financial report at the latest four months after
the end of each financial year and to ensure that it is publicly available for at least
five years.[60] The annual financial report must include:

-   the audited financial statements, which must include consolidated accounts
    drawn up in line with IFRS (if applicable). The IAS Regulation, which
    applies to EEA issuers, requires consolidated accounts for accounting
    periods beginning on or after 1 January 2005 to be prepared in accordance
    with IFRS;
-   the management report, which must include a fair review of the develop-
    ment of the issuer's business, an indication of any important events that
    have occurred since the end of the financial year and the likely future
    development of the issuer; and
-   a responsibility statement by the persons responsible within the issuer to
    the effect that, to the best of their knowledge, the financial statements pre-
    pared in accordance with applicable accounting standards give a true and
    fair view of the assets, liabilities, financial position and profit or loss of the
    issuer and the undertakings included in the consolidation taken as a whole.
    The statement must further provide that the management report includes
    a fair review of the development and performance of the business and the
    position of the issuer and the undertakings included in the consolidation
    taken as a whole, together with a description of the principal risks and
    uncertainties that they face.

3.3.3   *Half-yearly Financial Reports*

The WFT requires issuers of shares or debt securities to publish a half-yearly financial report covering the first six months of the financial year within two months of
the end of the relevant period and to ensure that it is publicly available for at least
five years.[61] The half-yearly report must include:

---

60.   Art. 5:25c WFT.
61.   Art. 5:25d WFT.

- the condensed set of financial statements prepared in accordance with the IAS Regulation (i.e. using IFRS), if applicable;
- an interim management report, which must include as a minimum all important events that occurred during the first six months of the financial year, and their impact on the condensed set of financial statements, together with a description of the principal risks and uncertainties for the remaining six months of the financial year. For issuers of shares, the interim management report must also include major related party transactions; and
- as with annual financial reports, a responsibility statement by persons responsible within the issuer to the effect that, to the best of their knowledge, the condensed set of financial statements (prepared in accordance with applicable accounting standards) gives a true and fair view of the assets, liabilities, financial position and profit or loss of the issuer or the undertakings included in the consolidation taken as a whole and that the interim management report includes a fair review of important events that have occurred during the first six months of the financial year, and their impact on the condensed set of financial statements, together with a description of the principal risks and uncertainties for the remaining six months of the financial year. The half-yearly report does not have to be audited (but if it is not, a statement must be included to that effect and if it is, the audit report must be reproduced in full).

3.3.4 *Interim Management Statements*

The WFT requires issuers whose shares are admitted to trading on a regulated market and who do not otherwise publish quarterly financial reports in accordance with their national legislation or rules of their regulated market or on their own initiative, to publish two interim management statements during the financial year.[62] These must be published in the period ten weeks after the beginning, and six weeks before the end, of each half-yearly period. The interim management statement must provide (i) an explanation of material events and transactions that have taken place during the relevant period and their impact on the financial position of the issuer and its controlled undertakings, and (ii) a general description of the financial position and performance of the issuer and its controlled undertakings during the relevant period.

---

62. Art. 5:25e WFT.

3.3.5   *Other Continuing Obligations*

An issuer of listed equity or debt securities must also immediately disclose any non-public price sensitive information relating to the issuer.[63] The issuer may only delay such disclosure if (a) the delay serves a legitimate interest of the issuer, (b) there is no risk that the public will be misled by the delay and (iii) the confidentiality of the information is guaranteed. A legitimate interest as referred to above may be that the outcome of non-public negotiations could be influenced by the publication or that certain internal corporate authorisations have not yet been obtained.[64] See also paragraph 6.1.6.

Furthermore, issuers of shares admitted to trading on a regulated market are required to ensure equal treatment of all shareholders who are in the same position.[65] An identical requirement applies in respect of holders of debt securities who rank *pari passu*.[66] In addition, issuers of shares must ensure that all the facilities and information necessary to enable shareholders to exercise their rights are available in the home Member State and that the integrity of the data is preserved. In particular, an issuer of shares must:

- provide information on the place, time and agenda of meetings, the total number of shares and voting rights, and the rights of holders to participate in meetings;
- make available a proxy form on paper or electronically to each person entitled to vote at a shareholders' meeting, together with a notice concerning the meeting or, on request, announcing the meeting;
- designate as its agent a financial institution through which shareholders may exercise their financial rights; and
- publish notices or distribute circulars concerning the allocation and payment of dividends and the issue of new shares, including information on any arrangements for allotment, subscription, cancellation or conversion.

Equivalent additional requirements apply in respect of issuers of debt securities.

Issuers may use electronic means for the purposes of conveying information to shareholders and holders of debt securities, provided that the decision to do so is taken in a general meeting and certain other conditions are met.

---

63.   Art. 5:25i(2) WFT,
64.   Decree on Transparency by Issuers (*Besluit uitvoeringsrichtlijn transparantie uitgevende instellingen Wft*), 2008 Stb. 579.
65.   Art. 5:25k WFT.
66.   Art. 5:25l WFT.

If a meeting relates only to holders of debt securities with a minimum denomination of EUR 50,000 (or its equivalent in another currency), then the issuer may choose any Member State as a venue for that meeting, provided that all the facilities and information necessary to enable such holders to exercise their rights are made available in that Member State.

3.3.6 *Exemptions from Periodic Reporting Requirements*

The requirement to file annual and half-yearly financial reports and interim management statements do not apply to:[67]

- States, regional or local authorities of States, public international bodies of which at least one Member State is a member, the ECB and Member States' national central banks; and
- issuers exclusively of debt securities admitted to trading on a regulated market in minimum denominations of at least EUR 50,000 (or its equivalent in another currency at the date of issue).

3.4 Major Holdings Disclosure

3.4.1 *Introduction*

The first Major Holdings Disclosure Act (WMZ)[68] entered into force in 1991 to implement the Disclosure of Major Holdings Directive.[69] According to the preamble of the directive, its objective was to increase investors' confidence in securities markets by adopting a policy of adequate information for investors, *i.e.* by increasing the transparency of the securities markets. As of 1 January 2007, the WMZ (since renamed WMZ 1996) was replaced by the WFT.

Pursuant to the WFT, an actual or potential holder of a direct or indirect interest (in terms of shares or voting rights or both) in the capital of an "N.V." is obliged to disclose its holding if the percentage of its interest reaches, exceeds or falls below, the following thresholds: 10, 15, 20, 25, 30, 40, 50, 60, 75 and 90%.[70]

The Act applies to N.Vs incorporated in the Netherlands whose shares or depository receipts are officially listed on a securities exchange located and operat-

---

67. Art. 5:25g(2) WFT.
68. *Wet melding zeggenschap in ter beurze genoteerde vennootschappen*, 1991 Stb.748.
69. No. 88/627 O.J. Eur. Comm. (No. L. 348) 62 (1988) (replaced by the Transparency Directive, see paragraph 1.5.3).
70. Art. 5:38 WFT.

ing in an EEA Member State and to non-EEA issuers whose shares or depositary receipts are listed on Euronext Amsterdam.[71]

3.4.2 *Notification and Publication*

Each time the above thresholds are reached, exceeded or passed, a notification has to be sent without delay to the AFM. The notification must be effected by means of a standard form issued by the AFM and must contain, *inter alia*, the name and address of the shareholder, the name of the corporation involved, the percentage of shares and voting rights and the composition thereof, as well as the date on which the obligation to disclose arose (which, in most cases, is the date on which the shares or voting rights were acquired or disposed of).[72] The AFM shall confirm the notification to both the issuer and the notifying party and publish the notification in a register kept on its website.[73]

The WFT also requires an issuer of listed securities to notify the AFM of any changes in an issued share capital.[74] Should such changes also cause a holder of a notifiable interest to reach, pass or fall below a threshold, such event will also have to notified to the AFM.[75]

3.4.3 *Types of Holding*

The WFT also contains provisions which deal with the various types of holdings which trigger an obligation to disclose. The AFM has published a brochure on the disclosure rules, which is available both in Dutch and in English (www.afm.nl) and contains a detailed explanation of the various types of holdings relevant under the WFT. Essentially, the relevant provisions can be summarized as follows:

(a) the WFT covers both holdings in terms of voting rights attached to shares and capital interest (i.e. shares in respect of which the shareholder does not necessarily have any voting rights). It also covers voting rights which are vested in the pledgee or usufructuary of shares when a right of pledge or usufruct is created on the shares;[76]

---

71. Art. 5:33 (1)(a) WFT.
72. Disclosure of Holding Decree (*Besluit melding zeggenschap en kapitaalbelang in uitgevende instellingen*), 2006, Stb. 509, art. 5.
73. Art. 5:49 WFT. www.afm.nl.
74. Arts. 5:34 and 35 WFT.
75. Art. 5:39 WFT.
76. Art. 5:45(2) WFT.

(b) the WFT covers direct holdings as well as holdings through a subsidiary,[77] a third party (which holds the shares or voting rights for someone else's account) or an associated party.[78] In this context, an associated party is a person with whom the shareholder has concluded an agreement providing for a lasting common policy with respect to the exercise of voting rights. The conclusion or termination of such an agreement could also trigger the disclosure requirements. In a group of companies, it is the ultimate parent company which will have to fulfil the notification requirements; other companies in the group do not need to notify as regards the same holding.[79] The acquisition or disposal of a subsidiary which holds a major holding must be disclosed;

(c) the WFT defines shares so as to include depository receipts for shares (*certificaten van aandelen*) and option rights to acquire shares or depository receipts of shares i.e. potential holdings.[80] These potential holdings include options, warrants and convertible debt obligations.

From the above, it follows that the combinations of either capital interests or voting rights that must be distinguished are: direct actual; direct potential; indirect actual; and indirect potential. The actual composition of a holding which is disclosed under the WFT must be specified in this manner (as indicated on the standard notification form issued by the AFM).

3.4.4   Exemptions

The WFT provides a number of exemptions from the requirement to notify:[81]

- Clearing and settling: shares acquired for the sole purpose of clearing and settling within a short settlement cycle.
- Custodians: shares held by custodians in their capacity as custodians, provided that they can only exercise the voting rights attached to such shares under instruction.
- Market makers: market makers are exempt from the requirement to notify the acquisition or disposal of a major holding reaching, crossing or falling below the 5% threshold when acting in the capacity of a market maker, provided that they are authorised under the WFT and do not intervene in

---

77. Art. 5:45(3) WFT.
78. Arts. 5:45(4) and (5) WFT.
79. Art. 5:45(3) WFT.
80. Art. 5:33(1)(b)(4) WFT.
81. Art. 5:46 WFT.

the management of the issuer or exert any influence on the issuer to buy such shares or back the share price.

- Trading book: voting rights attaching to shares held in the trading book of a credit institution or investment firm are not counted, provided that the voting rights held in the trading book do not exceed 5% and the credit institution or investment firm ensures that such voting rights are not exercised or otherwise used to intervene in the management of the issuer.
- Management companies and investment firms: the parent undertaking of a management company or of an authorised investment firm is not required to aggregate its holdings with those managed by the management company/investment firm, provided that the management company/investment firm exercises the voting rights independently from the parent undertaking.

3.4.5   *Sanctions for Violations*

3.4.5.1   Criminal Sanctions

Violation of the obligation to notify under the WFT constitutes an economic offence.[82] The non-intentional offender can be sentenced to imprisonment for a maximum term of six months and/or given a fine of up to EUR 19,000 (EUR 76,000 for legal entities). If the offence is committed intentionally, the offender can be sentenced to imprisonment for a maximum term of two years imprisonment and/or given a fine of up to EUR 19,000 (EUR 76,000 for legal entities).

Alternatively, the AFM can impose administrative fines (see 9.3.4 of Chapter 1 for further details).

3.4.5.2   Civil Sanctions

At the request of the corporation concerned or the holder of a 5% interest in the corporation's issued share capital, the competent District Court can impose any of the following sanctions for a violation of one of the WFT's provisions:[83]

(a) suspension of the voting rights which can be exercised on all shares which the person obliged to notify holds or is deemed to hold;

(b) rescission of a resolution of the general meeting of shareholders if it can be reasonably assumed that the resolution would not have been adopted if the offender had not exercised his voting rights; and/or

---

82.   Art. 1(2°) WED.
83.   Art. 5:52 WFT.

(c) an order to an offender to refrain from any further direct or indirect acquisition of shares issued by the relevant corporation for a maximum period of five years.

4.   REGULATION OF THE SECURITIES BUSINESS

4.1   Investment Firms

4.1.1   *Definition*

The WFT defines an investment firm as a person who provides investment services or engages in investment activities.[84] Investment services are defined as:

(a) the receipt and transmission of client orders with respect to financial instruments in the conduct of a profession or business;
(b) the execution of client orders with respect to financial instruments in the conduct of a profession or business;
(c) individual portfolio management;
(d) investment advice with respect to financial instruments in the conduct of a profession or business;
(e) the underwriting of financial instruments, or the placing of financial instruments with an underwriting commitment in the conduct of a profession or business;
(f) placing of financial instruments without an underwriting commitment in the conduct of a profession or business.

Ancillary investment services are defined as:

(a) custody and management of financial instruments for the account of clients, including safekeeping and related services such as cash or securities custody;
(b) granting credits or loans to an investor so as to enable the latter to conduct a transaction in one or more financial instruments, where the firm granting the credit or loan is a party to the transaction;
(c) advice to enterprises on capital structure, industrial strategy and related matters, and advice and services relating to mergers and the purchase of enterprises;

---

84. Art. 1:1 WFT.

(d) foreign exchange services where these are connected to the provision of investment services;

(e) investment research and financial analysis or other forms of general recommendations relating to transactions in financial instruments;

(f) services related to underwriting;

(g) investment services or activities as well as ancillary services relating to the underlying security of certain types of financial instruments with an underlying security, to the extent that these are connected to the provision of investment or ancillary services.

Investment activities are defined as:

(a) own account trading;

(b) operating a multilateral trading facility (MTF).

This rather broad definition covers the usual broking activities as well as market making and underwriting activities. It also covers the offering of investment accounts or giros (accounts through which securities transactions are effected by the investment firm).

A multilateral trading facility or MTF is a multilateral system operated by an investment firm which brings together multiple buying and selling interests in financial instruments – within the system and in accordance with its non-discretionary rules – in a way that results in a contract in accordance with the applicable rules on licensing and ongoing supervision.[85]

4.1.2   Prohibition

The WFT prohibits the rendering of investment services or engaging in investment activities in the Netherlands without a licence.[86] The rationale behind this prohibition is to protect the general public from fraudulent brokerage and other intermediary services and to provide a legal basis for supervising investment firms. The term "in the Netherlands" covers both an offer from a person outside the Netherlands to Dutch residents and from a Dutch resident to other Dutch residents.

---

85.   Art. 1:1 WFT.
86.   Art. 2:96(1) WFT.

4.1.3   Licence

Unless an exemption applies (see paragraph 4.1.6), an investment firm is required to obtain a licence from the AFM. An applicant for a licence must provide certain detailed information to the AFM[87] and must meet a number of minimum requirements regarding, *inter alia*:

4.1.3.1   Management

The day-to-day policy of an investment firm must be determined by at least two natural persons (the so-called "four eyes principle"). These persons shall perform their activities in this respect from within the Netherlands (i.e. it is not an absolute requirement that the Management Board members are Dutch residents, but the managers in charge must perform their functions in the Netherlands rather than from abroad). Persons determining the day-to-day policy should, under normal circumstances, be members of the investment firm's executive board. However, *de facto* directors are also entitled to determine the day-to-day policy. The executive board members should have sufficient expertise in relation to the business and operations of the financial undertaking. No guidelines are available as to how expertise is interpreted by the AFM. The AFM will assess a managing director's expertise by the following means: his curriculum vitae and, if necessary, a personal interview and/or an interview with his referees. In addition, the managing director's trustworthiness must be beyond any doubt. The application documents must include Integrity Test Forms, drawn up by the AFM, containing information on the managing director's criminal, private financial, business-related financial, supervisory and tax administrative and other antecedents, as well as other relevant records. The AFM will also consult various public and non-public sources. On the basis of this information the AFM will form an opinion or the person's integrity. If the person's integrity has been assessed before, by either DNB or the AFM, no new assessment will be carried out, unless a change in the relevant facts or circumstances has given reasonable cause for a reassessment. If the investment firm has a supervisory board (or a comparable body), its members must also be trustworthy and this is assessed in the same way as for managing directors.

4.1.3.2   Sound Business Operations

The investment firm shall pursue adequate policies to secure the sound of its operations. This shall concern, among other things, preventing: (a) conflicts of interests;

---

87.   Art. 2:99 WFT and Art. 42 Financial Enterprises Market Access Decree.

(b) any involvement in criminal offences and other violations of the law; (c) the confidence in the institution or in the financial markets preventing from being damaged or adversely affected on account of its clients; and (d) the performance of any acts that are so contrary to generally accepted standards that they seriously damage confidence in the institution or in the financial markets.

4.1.3.3   Control Structure

The bank shall not be affiliated to persons in a formal or actual control structure which is so lacking in transparency that it constitutes or may constitute an impediment to the adequate exercise of supervision.

4.1.3.4   Controlled Business Operations

The bank shall organise its operations in such a way as to safeguard controlled and sound business operations. This concerns, among other things, the control of business processes and business risks, transparency, integrity risks and financial risks.

4.1.3.5   Own Funds

The minimum amount of own funds must be between EUR 35,000 and 730,000, depending on the type of investment services or activities.

4.1.3.6   Solvency

The solvency requirements aim to ensure that investment firms hold sufficient own funds in relation to the size of their liabilities and the nature and extent of their business risks so as to maintain sufficient buffers to absorb any potential losses. The level of actual solvency is expressed as a percentage of the risk-weighted assets.

The AFM can also grant a licence if the applicant for a licence can demonstrate that the objectives of the WFT have been adequately achieved in a different manner.[88]

4.1.4   Prudential Supervision

An investment firm licensed under the WFT must comply with the minimum own funds and minimum solvency requirements set out in the WFT and its implement-

---

88.   Art. 2:96(2) WFT.

ing regulations.[89] Compliance with these prudential supervision rules, which are similar to the prudential rules applicable to banks, is not supervised by the AFM but by DNB which is generally in charge of prudential supervision in the Netherlands (see Chapter 1). Like banks, investment firms need to periodically report to DNB on their financial position and DNB can adopt certain measures if such financial position deteriorates. See Chapter 1 for further details.

4.1.5   *Continuing Licence Obligations*

The WFT's continuing obligations not only apply to investment firms but also to credit institution, which are active in the securities business.

4.1.5.1   Organisational Requirements

The WFT requires investment firms and credit institutions to establish policies and procedures which are adequate to ensure compliance with the provisions of the WFT and to maintain and operate effective organisational and administrative arrangements with a view to taking all reasonable steps designed to prevent conflicts of interest from adversely affecting the interests of clients.[90] It identifies the key elements necessary for the proper functioning of a firm:

(a) appropriate and proportionate systems, resources and procedures to ensure the performance of its investment services and activities;
(b) appropriate control of outsourcing so as not to impair the quality of the firm's internal controls and the ability of the regulator to monitor the firm's compliance with its obligations;
(c) sound administrative and accounting procedures;
(d) internal control mechanisms;
(e) effective procedures for risk assessment;
(f) effective control and safeguard arrangements for information processing systems;
(g) record keeping for all services and transactions sufficient to enable the regulator to monitor compliance with the WFT;
(h) adequate arrangements for safeguarding clients' financial instruments and funds;
(i) rules governing personal account transactions by managers, employees and tied agents; and

---

89. Art. 3:53 WFT and Art. 3:57 Prudential Supervision Decree.
90. Art. 4:14 WFT.

   (j) complaints handling – but this applies only to complaints from retail clients.

The implementing rules, set out in the Conduct of Business Decree, elaborate on the general organisational requirements and in particular on three key functions:

   (a) compliance – this must operate independently and have the necessary authority, resources, expertise and access to information to enable it to discharge its responsibilities properly; a compliance officer must be appointed;

   (b) risk management – risks relating to a firm's activities, processes and systems should be identified and managed and a risk management function established where this is appropriate, given the nature, scale and complexity of the firm's business; and

   (c) internal audit – an internal audit function must be established where this is appropriate.

An investment firm must also have a code of conduct for private transactions by persons associated with the bank who are directly or indirectly involved in the firm's transactions in financial instruments or who otherwise regularly have or may have inside information as part of their duties, profession or position. See paragraph 6.7 of Chapter 2 for further details.

4.1.5.2   Outsourcing

Where an investment firm, or a credit institution providing one or more investment services or performing investment activities, outsources any of its critical or important operational functions or investment services or activities, it must exercise due skill, care and diligence when entering into, managing or terminating the outsourcing arrangement, and must satisfy the relevant conditions.[91]

    There are restrictions in relation to the appointment of a party in a third country to provide portfolio management services in respect of an investment firm's retail clients.

    Outsourcing is an arrangement of any form between an investment firm and a service provider by which that service provider performs a process, a service or an activity which would otherwise be undertaken by the investment firm itself.

    There is no special obligation to notify outsourcing arrangements to the investment firm's or credit institution's regulator, although in the case of an investment firm, if the outsourcing of investment services and activities or critical and impor-

---

91.   Art. 4:16 WFT.

tant functions constitutes a material change of the conditions for the authorisation of the investment firm, notification will be required.

An operation is regarded as "critical and important" if a defect or failure in its performance would materially impair:

- the continuing compliance of the investment firm with the conditions and obligations of its authorisation or its other obligations under the WFT;
- its financial performance;
- the soundness or the continuity of its investment services or activities.

Any investment firm outsourcing a critical or important operational function, or investment service or activity, must ensure that the arrangement complies with the following conditions:[92]

- the respective rights and obligations of the investment firm and of the service provider must be clearly allocated and set out in a written agreement;
- the service provider must have the ability, capacity, and any authorisation required by law to perform the outsourced functions, services or activities reliably and professionally;
- the service provider must carry out the outsourced services effectively, and to this end the firm must establish methods for assessing the standard of performance of the service provider;
- the service provider must properly supervise the carrying out of the outsourced functions, and adequately manage the risks associated with the outsourcing;
- appropriate action must be taken if it appears that the service provider may not be carrying out the functions effectively and in compliance with applicable laws and regulatory requirements;
- the investment firm must retain the necessary expertise to supervise the outsourced functions effectively and manage the risks associated with the outsourcing, and must supervise those functions and manage those risks;
- the service provider must disclose to the investment firm any development that may have a material impact on its ability to carry out the outsourced functions, effectively and in compliance with applicable laws and regulatory requirements;
- the investment firm must be able to terminate the arrangement for outsourcing where necessary without detriment to the continuity and quality of its provision of services to clients;

---

92.   Arts. 36-38j Conduct of Business Decree.

> – the service provider must co operate with the competent authorities of the investment firm in connection with the outsourced activities;
> – the investment firm, its auditors and the relevant competent authorities must have effective access to data related to the outsourced activities, as well as to the business premises of the service provider, and the competent authorities must be able to exercise those rights of access;
> – the service provider must protect any confidential information relating to the investment firm or its clients;
> – the investment firm and the service provider must establish, implement and maintain a contingency plan for disaster recovery and periodic testing of back-up facilities where that is necessary, having regard to the function, service or activity that has been outsourced.

4.1.5.3   Transaction Reporting

Transaction reporting applies to all firms which execute transactions in instruments admitted to trading on a regulated market (whether or not the transaction is executed on the regulated market in question). This includes securities broker-dealers, commodity dealers and asset managers. The requirements also impact on exchanges, multilateral trading functions (MTFs) and other providers of transaction reporting services.[93]

The scope of the transaction reporting framework is extended to apply to all financial instruments admitted to trading on a regulated market including money market instruments, units in collective investment undertakings, and commodity, interest rate and foreign exchange derivatives, and requires daily reporting to the AFM.

4.1.5.4   Conflicts of Interest

The MiFID approach to conflicts of interest places an emphasis on addressing conflicts through organisational or administrative arrangements and only where these are not sufficient to prevent damage to clients through disclosure. The scope of the relevant conflicts of interest is defined as, broadly, conflicts between investment firms and their clients or between one client and another arising in the course of providing investment and ancillary services. Conflicts will only arise where the interests of the firm (or relevant persons or other specified persons) conflict with the duty a firm owes to a client or where there is a conflict between the interests of two or more clients to each of whom a firm owes a duty.

---

93.   Art. 4:90e (3) WFT.

An investment firm shall maintain and operate effective organisational and administrative arrangements with a view to taking all reasonable steps designed to prevent conflicts of interest from adversely affecting the interests of its clients.[94]

Ways of managing conflicts of interest include:

- effective procedures to prevent or control the exchange of information between relevant persons where this exchange might harm the interests of one or more clients;
- separate supervision of staff whose principal function involves carrying out activities on behalf of, or who provide services, to clients whose interests may conflict or who otherwise represent different interests that may conflict, e.g. separate reporting lines for proprietary trading and fund management activities;
- the removal from persons principally engaged in one activity of remuneration incentives based on revenues generated by another activity where a conflict may arise in relation to those activities, e.g. research analysts should not be remunerated basedon sales activities;
- measures to prevent or limit inappropriate influence being exercised, e.g. management should not coerce research analysts into favouring particular securities; and
- measures to prevent or control the simultaneous or sequential involvement of a relevant person in separate services or activities where such involvement might impair the proper management of conflicts of interests.

Where organisational or administrative arrangements are not sufficient to prevent damage to clients, the investment firm must clearly disclose the conflict of interest to the client before carrying on business for the client.[95]

4.1.5.5   Conduct of Business Rules

The MiFID has introduced three categories of "client" – eligible counterparties, professional clients and retail clients – each of which has a different position under the WFT's conduct of business rules.[96]

---

94.   Art. 4:88 WFT.
95.   Art. 4:88(2) WFT.
96.   Art. 4:18a WFT.

Eligible counterparties

Certain conduct of business obligations (e.g. best execution and order handling rules) do not apply to investment firms and credit institutions when they bring about or enter into transactions with eligible counterparties or in respect of any ancillary service directly related to those transactions.[97]

Eligible counterparty status is limited to dealing (and related ancillary services), so in relation to other activities/services, for example, investment advice or portfolio management, an "eligible counterparty" will be a professional client. Entities which are automatically categorised as eligible counterparties ("per se" eligible counterparties) are:[98]

- investment firms, credit institutions and insurance companies;
- investment undertakings and their management companies, and pension funds and their management companies;
- own account dealers in commodities and/or commodity derivatives, and "locals" on derivatives markets;
- national governments and their corresponding offices, including public bodies that deal with public debt, central banks and supranational organizations.

These "per se" eligible counterparties may nonetheless request, either on a general basis or on a trade-by-trade basis, to be treated as professional or retail clients in order to obtain the protections.

Opting up professional investors – criteria

Investment firms have the option to recognise as eligible counterparties entities other than per se eligible counterparties, provided that such entities meet the predetermined proportionate requirements, including the quantitative thresholds. In addition to the per se eligible counterparties, investment firms may recognise as eligible counterparties large undertakings meeting two out of the three size criteria (see "Professional investors" below).[99] Private individuals and other persons that are not "large undertakings" cannot be treated as eligible counterparties.

Opted-up professional investors can only be categorised as eligible counterparties in respect of the services or transactions for which they qualify as professional investors.

---

97.   Art. 4:18b(1) WFT.
98.   Art. 1:1 WFT.
99.   Art. 4:18b(2) WFT.

Importantly, MiFID provides that where prospective counterparties are located in different jurisdictions, the investment firm must defer to the status of the counterparty as determined by the rules of the Member State in which the counterparty is established. This means that, in categorising clients, investment firms doing cross-border business will not be able to rely on the approach of their own home Member State regulator to opting clients up to eligible counterparty status but instead will have to have regard to the approach of the host Member State regulator where the client is established.

Notification/confirmation requirements

Clients must be notified of their categorisation and, in the case of opted-up eligible counterparties, give express confirmation to be treated as such. This may be in the form of a general agreement or in respect of each individual transaction. Clients must also be informed in a durable medium of their right to request a different categorisation.[100]

Opting down to client category

An investment firm may treat an eligible counterparty as a professional or retail client (thereby affording it greater protections under the WFT). An eligible counterparty may also request such treatment.

Professional investors

As with eligible counterparties, there are those who automatically fall within the definition of professional investors[101] and those who may be treated as professionals at their request and provided that they meet the criteria laid down. Per se professional clients may request retail client treatment.

Per se professionals include all the categories of per se eligible counterparties and, in addition:

- large undertakings meeting two of the following size criteria:
  · balance sheet total: EUR 20,000,000;
  · net turnover: EUR 40,000,000;
  · own funds: EUR 2,000,000; and

---

100. Art. 4:18a(1) WFT.
101. Art. 1:1 WFT.

> – investors whose main activity is to invest in financial instruments, including entities dedicated to the securitisation of assets or other financial transactions.

Clients not falling within this definition, such as small companies and individual investors, may be treated as professional clients if they so request (in accordance with the procedures laid down) and meet two out of the three criteria relating to investment experience, size of portfolio and knowledge. (The criteria are substantially the same as those which must be met by a natural person in order to be authorised by a Member State as a "qualified investor" under the Prospectus Directive; see paragraph 2.2.5.3)

The procedure for professional client opt-up involves:[102]

> – written client request to be treated as a professional client;
> – written warning of protections and compensation rights which may be lost; and
> – the client's written acknowledgement that he is aware of the consequences of losing such protections.

The latter must be contained in a document which is separate from the contract.

The onus is placed on professional clients to keep firms informed of changes which might affect the clients' categorisation as "professional". However, if a firm becomes aware that an elective professional client no longer fulfils the conditions which made him eligible for professional treatment, it must take appropriate action.

Anyone who is not an eligible counterparty or a professional investor is considered a retail client, which therefore is a residual category.

Suitability

MiFID has introduced "know your customer" and suitability requirements which apply when an investment firm provides investment advice or discretionary portfolio management. These requirements apply to both retail and (in a more limited form) professional clients. The obligation will in practice extend to "eligible counterparties" for whom investment advice or portfolio management services are provided as eligible counterparty status is only available in relation to the execution of orders and related ancillary services.

When providing investment advice or portfolio management to a client an investment firm must obtain the necessary information regarding a client's:

---

102. Art. 4:18c WFT.

- knowledge and experience in the investment field relevant to the specific type of product or service; and
- financial situation and investment objectives,
- to enable the firm to make a suitable recommendation.[103] This test is tougher than the appropriateness test, which requires a firm to assess knowledge and experience but not its financial situation or objectives. (See below "Appropriateness")

There are criteria to be satisfied in relation to the "necessary" information for the firm to be able to meet the suitability test. The information obtained must be necessary for the firm to:

- understand the essential facts about the client; and
- have a reasonable basis for believing that the recommendation/transaction:
  - meets the client's investment objectives;
  - is such that the client is able financially to bear any related investment risks; and
  - is such that the client has the necessary experience and knowledge to understand the risks involved.

In the case of a professional client, the investment firm may assume that the client has the necessary experience and knowledge in relation to the products, transactions and services for which he is so classified. In addition, where an investment firm provides investment advice to a per se professional client, the firm can assume that the client is able to bear any related investment risks consistent with his investment objectives.

A firm is entitled to rely on the information provided by a client unless it is aware or ought to be aware that the information is manifestly out of date, inaccurate or incomplete. If a firm does not obtain the relevant information it may not make a recommendation to the client. Where a firm (A) receives an instruction on behalf of a client through the medium of another investment firm (B) A can rely on information about the client provided by B (who will be responsible for its completeness and accuracy). In addition, B will remain responsible for the appropriateness for the client of any recommendations or advice provided.

---

103. Art. 4:23 WFT.

Appropriateness

The scope for providing execution-only services has been circumscribed by the introduction of a requirement to assess "appropriateness" for the client. An investment firm is required to assess the appropriateness of a product or service if:[104]

- the transaction relates to a financial instrument;
- the service does not include the provision of investment advice or portfolio management (if the service does include either of these, the relevant obligation is to assess "suitability", rather than "appropriateness");
- the service is provided to a retail client or professional client; and
- the firm has not taken advantage of the carve-out in relation to non-complex financial instruments (see below "Carve-out for non-complex financial instruments").

Investment firms required to assess the appropriateness of a product or service are required to ask their clients to provide information regarding their knowledge and experience in the relevant investment field so as to enable the investment firm to assess whether the investment service or product envisaged is appropriate for the client. Investment firms should determine, using this information, whether the relevant client (or potential client) has the necessary experience and knowledge to understand the risks involved in relation to the specific type of product or service offered or demanded.

To meet the appropriateness test a firm must (to the extent appropriate to the nature of the client and the nature and extent of the service/product to be provided) obtain information on:

- the types of service, transactions and investments with which the client is familiar;
- the nature, volume and frequency of the client's transactions in investments and the period over which they have been carried out; and
- the level of the client's education, profession or relevant former profession.

There is no need for investment firms to verify this information, unless they are aware (or ought to be aware) that the information is manifestly out of date, inaccurate or incomplete.

---

104. Art. 4:24 WFT.

If, having carried out the appropriateness test, the investment firm determines that the product or service is not appropriate for the client, it must warn the client of this fact.

If a client refuses to provide the information required to enable an investment firm to satisfy the appropriateness test, or provides insufficient information to enable it to do so, the investment firm will be able to provide the product/service without undertaking the appropriateness test, provided it has warned the client that it is therefore unable to determine whether the product or service to be provided is appropriate for it. However, the investment firm should ensure that the provision of required information by a client is encouraged.

If its client is classified as a professional client, for the purposes of the appropriateness test, an investment firm can assume that the client has the necessary experience and knowledge to understand products or services in relation to which it is so classified.

Carve-out for non-complex financial instruments

A firm which provides services consisting solely of the execution and/or reception and transmission of client orders (with or without ancillary services) relating to "non-complex" financial instruments can provide such services without carrying out the appropriateness test if:[105]

- the service is provided at the initiative of the client;
- the client has been clearly informed that in the provision of this service the firm is not required to undertake the appropriateness test, and the corresponding protections in the relevant conduct of business rules will not apply; and
- the firm has complied with the applicable rules relating to conflicts of interest.

MiFID specifies a number of instruments which are "non-complex" for the purposes of the "appropriateness test". These are shares admitted to trading on a regulated market or equivalent third country market; money market instruments; bonds or other debt instruments (excluding convertible instruments); and investment undertakings.

---

105. Art. 4:24(4) WFT.

Client order handling/best execution

MiFID requires that investment firms have procedures and arrangements which provide for the prompt, fair and expeditious execution of client orders and specifies conditions which must be met in relation to the aggregation and allocation of orders. In addition, unexecuted client limit orders held by firms in shares admitted to trading on a regulated market must be made public to facilitate their earliest possible execution.[106]

The requirements relating to prompt, fair and expeditious execution of client orders are expressly disapplied in relation to orders from eligible counterparties.

As regards limit order exposure, in respect of transactions executed between eligible counterparties, the obligation to disclose client limit orders should only apply where the counterparty is explicitly sending a limit order to an investment firm for its execution.

The client order handling provisions are not applicable to transactions concluded on a regulated market or under the rules of an MTF as between members and participants (but they would apply with respect to their clients when firms execute their orders on a regulated market or MTF).

The procedures and arrangements for the prompt, fair and expeditious execution of client orders are subject to the following conditions:

– prompt and accurate record keeping and allocation;
– sequential and prompt execution of comparable client orders (unless the characteristics of the order or prevailing market conditions make this impracticable or the interests of the client require otherwise);
– notification to retail clients of any material difficulty in relation to the carrying out of orders.

Where a firm is responsible for overseeing or arranging the settlement of an executed order, it must take reasonable steps to ensure that any client financial instruments or client funds received in settlement of the order are promptly and correctly delivered to the account of the appropriate client.

The "best execution" obligation under MiFID applies to three investment services undertaken with respect to financial instruments: execution of client orders, reception and transmission of orders on behalf of clients, and portfolio management. The core best execution obligation is an obligation on investment firms to "take all reasonable steps to obtain [...] the best possible result for their clients

---

106. Art. 4:90a WFT.

taking into account price, costs, speed, likelihood of execution and settlement, size, nature or any other consideration relevant to the execution of the order".

Where the client is a retail client the best possible result is to be determined in terms of the total consideration, representing the price of the financial instrument and the costs related to execution, including all expenses incurred by the client directly related to the execution of the order. These include execution venue fees, clearing and settlement fees and any other fees paid to third parties involved in the execution of the order. For the purpose of the best execution regime, the term "execution venue" means a regulated market, an MTF, a systematic internaliser,[107] or a market maker or other liquidity provider or an entity that performs a similar function in a third country. The investment firm's own commissions and costs are to be taken into account when assessing best execution as between different execution venues. Investment firms will also be required not to structure their commissions in such a way as to discriminate unfairly between execution venues.

In respect of retail clients, of the factors to be taken into account in taking steps to obtain best execution, total consideration (the price of the financial instrument less costs associated with execution on the relevant execution venue) is paramount. Speed, likelihood of execution and settlement, size, nature of the transaction, market impact and implicit transaction costs should be given precedence over the immediate price and cost consideration only insofar as they are instrumental in delivering the best possible result in terms of the total consideration to the retail client. There is no such guidance in relation to execution for professional clients.

MiFID does not otherwise specify the relative importance of the factors to be taken into account for non-retail clients. Rather, it provides four sets of characteristics to be taken into account in determining the importance of the factors:

- the client;
- the order;
- the financial instruments that are the subject of the order; and
- the execution venues to which the order may be directed.

The importance of the factors will, in particular, vary depending on the nature of the financial instrument, for example, likelihood of settlement will be a more significant factor in respect of an OTC derivative carrying ongoing counterparty risk than in respect of a cash equity transaction. The obligation should be applied in a manner which takes into account the different circumstances associated with the execution of orders related to different types of instruments.

---

107. Arts. 4:91f-91k WFT.

MiFID excludes from the scope of the conduct of business obligations under MiFID the execution of client orders and the reception and transmission of orders where the service is provided to an eligible counterparty. In addition, where a client gives a specific instruction, an investment firm must follow that instruction in executing the client's order.

MiFID disapplies the best execution obligation as between participants dealing on a regulated market or MTF (although this does not affect any best execution obligations the participants may have to their clients for whom they trade on the regulated market or MTF). For firms seeking to avoid the best execution obligation, dealing over a regulated market or MTF provides the opportunity to deal without becoming subject to the best execution obligation in relation to the participants.

Investment firms subject to the best execution requirement must establish and implement effective arrangements to ensure compliance with their obligations.[108] This includes establishing and implementing a written order execution policy. The policy must be reviewed annually and whenever a material change occurs which affects the ability of the firm to comply with the best execution requirement on a consistent basis using the venues set out in the policy. In addition, the effectiveness of the policy must be monitored, including regular assessment of whether the execution venues included in the policy provide for the best possible result for the client or whether changes need to be made.

The order execution policy must include, by instrument:

– the execution venues used to execute client orders; and
– the factors affecting the choice of execution venue.

If the firm has retail clients, the policy will also need to reflect specific content requirements. Investment firms which provide best execution are required to provide appropriate information to their clients on their order execution policy, and to obtain client consent to it. The policy must:

– specifically draw attention to (and express client consent must be obtained to) the possibility of execution away from a regulated market or MTF (consent may be in the form of a general agreement);
– (for retail clients only) include an account of the relative importance the firm assigns to the factors (price, costs speed, likelihood of execution and settlement, size, nature or any other relevant consideration), or the process by which the firm does so;

---

108. Art. 4:90b WFT.

- list the execution venues on which the firm places specific reliance in meeting its best execution obligation; and
- include a warning that specific instructions from a client may prevent the firm from taking the steps that it has designed and implemented in its policy to give best execution.

Material changes to the policy must be notified to clients. Investment firms must be able to demonstrate to their clients, at their request, that they have executed orders in accordance with their policy.

Client agreement and information obligation

Investment firms must also conclude a client agreement with their non-professional clients which meets certain minimum requirements as to their contents.[109] For agreements concluded at a distance, additional requirements apply (see 6.2 of Chapter 1). The client agreement shall contain at least the following information:

(a) the services, distinguished by type, which the investment firm shall perform for the client in the context of the agreement;

(b) a specification of any restrictions with regard to the markets on which transactions in financial instruments will be settled on the client's behalf;

(c) the costs, distinguished by type, other than the costs which are charged to the client in relation to an offer of securities as referred to in Chapter 5.1 of the WFT, as well as the calculation underlying these costs;

(d) the manner in which instructions from the client and messages from the investment firm will be issued and administered;

(e) the manner in which funds or financial instruments of the client's will be settled, deposited and administered;

(f) the manner in which the client's accounts can be used;

(g) arrangements concerning the liability of the investment firm and the client respectively under the agreement;

(h) a statement from the client that he has taken note of the information which the investment firm must supply to him by virtue of the Decree, and that he is aware of the risks attached to the investment;

(i) the applicable law and the manner in which disputes will be resolved; and

(j) the circumstances under which the agreement between the investment firm and the client will come to an end, the circumstances under which

---

109. Art. 4:89(2) WFT and Art. 168 Conduct of Business Decree.

the agreement can be dissolved and the manner in which transactions in progress on or after the date of termination will be settled.

If the agreement relates to individual asset management, it shall also contain the following information:

(a) a breakdown of the managed assets into types of financial instruments and the value of the assets to be managed at the time when the agreement is concluded;

(b) the client's objectives with regard to the asset management;

(c) a specification of any qualitative and quantitative restrictions in respect of the financial instruments or categories of financial instruments in which investments may be made;

(d) the manner in which the management is conducted as well as the client's involvement in the management activities, including arrangements regarding the authorisation granted to the investment firm; and

(e) the frequency with which reports are issued to the client.

In addition, before providing any investment services, the investment firm must provide certain minimum information about its services and the relevant financial instruments.[110] Investment firms must supply their clients with accurate, clear, understandable and not misleading information about the financial instruments that they sell and the services they provide insofar as this is reasonably relevant for an adequate assessment of that service or financial instrument. This information must be provided prior to sale and the investment firm must during the term of a contract inform the client with regard to material changes in the information provided.

For financial instruments which qualify as "complex products" certain additional information must be provided in the form of a financial information leaflet. See 6.3 of Chapter 1 for further details.

4.1.6   *Exemptions*

The WFT and the Exemption Regulation provide for several general exceptions and for exemptions from the prohibition on the rendering of investment services or engaging in investment activities. General exceptions and exemptions from the licence requirement are available to, *inter alia*:

---

110.   Art. 4:20 WFT.

(a) registered credit and financial institutions (which include institutions situated in another EEA Member State using the European passport provided under the Recast Banking Directive insofar as the offering or rendering of securities services is permitted under the WFT. Credit and financial institutions established in the Netherlands falling under this exemption are nonetheless required to comply with certain of the continuing obligations of licence holders. This concerns the obligation to meet requirements for the administrative organisation of the investment firm, to comply with the conduct of business rules, to have a written agreement with clients etc. (see Chapter 1). This also applies to credit and financial institutions established in another EEA Member State;[111]

(b) private participation companies insofar as it concerns the shares in the company itself;[112]

(c) own account dealers (other than market-makers);[113]

(d) insurance companies;[114]

(e) investment firms which are subject to supervision in one of the third countries mentioned in Article 10 of the Exemption Regulation, which comprise the U.S., Australia and Switzerland;

(f) investment services which are provided to other group companies (i.e. intra-group investment services).[115]

In some cases the applicability of a general exemption may nonetheless result in the obligation to satisfy some of the continuing obligations. Furthermore, some of the general exemptions have additional conditions attached which have to be taken into account if they are intended to be used. In some cases, the investment firm falling within an exemption must notify the AFM before rendering its first service and at the same time submit certain information to it as specified in the Exemption Regulation. The AFM has published standard forms for this purpose which are available in Dutch and English.

4.1.7   *European Passport*

An investment firm established in the Netherlands, licensed by the AFM, intending to provide investment services (including ancillary services) or engage in investment activities through a branch in another Member State, can benefit from the so-

---

111. Art. 2:98 WFT.
112. Art. 13 WFT Exemption Regulation.
113. Art. 1:18(h) WFT.
114. Art. 1:18(d) WFT.
115. Art. 1:18(a) WFT.

called "European passport". The procedure is as follows. In order for an investment firm to commence its activities through a branch, DNB must have approved of this intention. The application for approval must contain *inter alia* the following data:[116]

    (a) the Member State where the investment firm plans to set up the branch;

    (b) a statement of the investment services which the investment firm intends to provide from the branch;

    (c) the name of the persons who shall determine the day-to-day policy of the branch, i.e. the branch managers.

Within three months after receipt of the application and the information required, the AFM shall decide on the application. The AFM shall approve of the intention, unless the investment firm's operations or financial position are inadequate to meet in view of its intention. Within two months of the notification having been sent to the host regulator, DNB shall inform the investment firm of any conditions which the host regulator attaches to the performance of the activities in the Member State concerned.

The European passport is also available to a Dutch licensed investment firm which intends to conduct its business as a cross-border services provider (i.e. not through a branch) to another Member State. In order to commence its activities, the investment firm must notify the AFM in writing of its intention. The notification to DNB must indicate to which Member State the investment firm intends to provide services and describe the proposed investment services or activities. Within one month after receipt of the notification and the information required, the AFM will notify the host regulator. The AFM sends a copy of the notification to the investment firm.

Investment firms holding a licence granted in another EEA Member State which have followed the notification procedure contained in the MiFID, as set out above, through the competent authorities in their home state, are also allowed to set up a branch office or to provide services in the Netherlands. The relevant investment firm continues to be supervised in its home country only but if it is a branch office it becomes subject to the conduct of business rules in the Netherlands.[117]

4.1.8   *Tied Agents*

A tied agent is a person who, under the full and unconditional responsibility of only one investment firm for whose account he acts, provides investment services and recommends these services or ancillary services to clients.

---

116. Art. 58 Financial Enterprises Market Access Decree.
117. Arts. 2:101 and 102 WFT.

4.2   Qualifying Holdings in an Investment Firm

The WFT defines a qualifying holding (*gekwalificeerde deelneming*) as a direct or indirect interest (in terms of shares or voting rights or similar rights) of at least 10 % in the capital of, *inter alia*, an investment firm holding a licence.[118]

The WFT prohibits the holding, acquiring or increasing of a qualifying holding or the exercising of the voting or similar rights attached thereto, unless a previous declaration of no objection (*verklaring van geen bezwaar*) has been obtained from DNB.[119] This declaration will be issued unless DNB is of the view that this would lead to a situation in which the shareholder might negatively affect the sound and prudent management of the investment firm concerned.[120] In practice, DNB will pay particular attention to and judge the trustworthiness of the shareholder or, if a company, its managing directors.

DNB can attach conditions to and impose restrictions on the declaration of no objection, for instance to ensure that the prudent management of the investment firm will not be affected.[121] The investment firm itself is obliged to inform DNB on a yearly basis with regard to the identity of persons holding a substantial interest in this firm, insofar as it is aware of the identity of these persons.[122] For a more detailed description of the application procedure, see paragraph 7.1.3 of Chapter 1.

4.3   Securities Exchanges

4.3.1   *General*

Pursuant to the WFT, operating a securities exchange is not permitted until a licence has been obtained from the Minister of Finance.[123] The prohibition on operating without a licence shall not apply to the operation or on management of a securities exchange with its registered office in another Member State that has been licenced by the supervisory authority of that other Member State, insofar as the market operator has taken appropriate measures in the Netherlands to better enable the long-distance members or participants based in the Netherlands to gain access to and to trade on this market.[124] On application, the Minister of Finance may grant a full

---

118.   Art. 1:1 WFT.
119.   Art. 3:95(1)(c) WFT.
120.   Art. 3:100 WFT.
121.   Art. 3:104(1) WFT.
122.   Art. 3:103(2) WFT.
123.   Art. 5:26(1) WFT.
124.   Art. 5:26(2) WFT.

or partial dispensation from the licence requirements if the applicant demonstrates that the objectives which the WFT is seeking to achieve (proper functioning of the financial markets and protection of investors) can beachieved in other ways.[125]

Euronext Amsterdam operates two regulated markets: one securities market (Euronext Amsterdam by NYSE Euronext) and one derivatives market (Euronext Amsterdam Derivatives Market, i.e. the Amsterdam market of NYSE Liffe Futures and Options).

Euronext Amsterdam as market operator also operates an unregulated market for small and mid size companies (SMEs) which seek a stock exchange listing, Alternext Amsterdam (which is part of NYSE Alternext). This market is regulated by Euronext Amsterdam and is subject to a lighter regulatory regime than the regulated stock market. Euronext Amsterdam also operates a number of Multilateral Trading Facilities (MTFs), including NYSE Arca Europe. NYSE Arca Europe is a pan-European MTF created by NYSE Euronext and approved and regulated by the AFM on which a number of European equities can be traded which are listed outside the Euronext zone.

Euronext Amsterdam is authorised to adopt and enforce rules for the conduct of the members admitted to the exchanges and has the responsibility to ensure members, participants and other relevant parties comply with these rules.

4.3.2   Admission

NYSE Euronext regulations comprise the rules issued by Euronext as market operator to regulate the European markets of NYSE Euronext. The Euronext Rulebooks for the regulated markets currently consist of two books (latest versions are available on www.euronext.com):

(i) Rule Book I contains the harmonised rules (cash and derivatives), including rules of conduct and enforcement rules that are designed to protect the markets, as well as rules on listing, trading and membership;

(ii) Rule Book II contains all rules of the individual markets that have not been harmonised (General Rules for the Euronext Amsterdam Stock Market).

The Euronext Rulebooks specify the various capacities in which an investment firm may be admitted to one or more of the securities exchanges operated by Euronext Amsterdam and NYSE Euronext. Members are divided into separate categories, such as trading members, clearing members and liquidity providers (who act as market makers).

---

125. Art. 5:26(3) WFT.

To become a member, a prospective firm must be licensed as an investment firm under the WFT (see paragraph 4.1) and enter into an admission agreement with Euronext Amsterdam.

Complaints from clients of banks or investment firms can be submitted to the independent Netherlands Financial Services Complaints Tribunal (*Klachteninstituut Financiële Dienstverlening or Kifid*). The Kifid decides on such complaints by rendering a "binding advice" (*bindend advies*) which a client must undertake to observe (subject to appeal) when his complaint is filed.

4.3.3 *Euronext Amsterdam by NYSE Euronext*

4.3.3.1 General

The Amsterdam Stock Exchange (AEX) is the former name of the stock exchange based in Amsterdam and it is the world's oldest regular stock market, which commenced operations early in the 17th century. In September 2000 the first pan-European exchange named Euronext was created by the merger of the Amsterdam, Brussels and Paris exchanges. In April 2007 the New York Stock Exchange Group merged with Euronext to form the first global equities exchange. In its current form, the Amsterdam stock exchange is being operated by Euronext Amsterdam, part of NYSE Euronext.

4.3.3.2 Markets and Securities

The types of securities which can be traded on Euronext Amsterdam include domestic and foreign stocks and depository receipts for shares, participation rights, bonds, Eurobonds, original foreign securities, claim rights and warrants.

4.3.3.3 Trading

The trade system applied at Euronext Amsterdam was traditionally based on trade through specialist firms or jobbers. The jobber's function has meanwhile been abolished and trade is now conducted through a centralised order book.

Companies are divided into one of two groups – auction or continuous quotation – depending on liquidity. Those with sufficient natural liquidity, defined as more than 2,500 trades per year, are automatically quoted on a continuous basis while those with lower liquidity are traded by auction. Auctions are organised twice daily, helping to focus liquidity at specific points in time. Companies in both trading groups can make their stock more liquid by using the services of a liquidity provider. What is more, a company with a liquidity provider can, if it wishes, be quoted continuously even if it does not reach the threshold of 2,500 trades annually.

The types of order a client can place with an investment firm include limited orders, orders at market price, stop-loss orders and pegged orders.[126]

Prices of the securities listed on Euronext Amsterdam are published daily in the electronic Official Price List (*Officiële Prijscourant*).

4.3.3.4　　　Clearing and Settlement

As a general rule, all transactions in officially listed securities are cleared and settled via LCH Clearnet S.A., the Securities Clearing Corporation of Euronext Amsterdam. Clearing is done through Clearing Members which effectively take over the rights and obligations for delivery and payment of securities from the buyer or seller concerned. Each member on Euronext Amsterdam which does not have a clearing function itself must have a clearing contract with a Clearing Member. Settlement of all transactions takes place three business days after the trade date ("T+3"). On the settlement date, the securities are delivered by means of a book entry by Necigef/Euroclear Netherlands, the Central Securities Depository (CSD), or another recognised CSD on the basis of "delivery versus payment".

4.3.3.5　　　Necigef/Euroclear Netherlands

The Securities Giro Act of 1977[127] introduced a generally applicable system for the transferring and safekeeping of securities. Under the WGE, Necigef[128] is designated as the Central Securities Depository in the Netherlands. Necigef is a "B.V." whose shares are held by Euroclear plc. Necigef acts as depository for all securities it designates. Bearer securities are eligible for admission either in temporary or permanent global or definitive form. Registered securities can also be kept by Necigef.

Almost all of the trade in securities listed on Euronext Amsterdam is effected through giro (book-entry) transfer of the securities as opposed to physical delivery.

Necigef's member institutions, which are mainly banks, have securities accounts with Necigef showing their entitlement to a certain number of securities kept by Necigef in giro depositories (*giro-depots*). These giro depositories represent the securities deposited with Necigef. Necigef's members themselves also

---

126. Rulebook I, 4203.
127. *Wet giraal effectenverkeer* [WGE] (Securities Giro Act), 1977 Stb. 333, art. 12(1).
128. *Nederlands Centraal Instituut voor Giraal Effectenverkeer B.V.*, also using the trade name "Euroclear Nederland".

keep securities in safekeeping in central depositories (*verzameldepots*). There are separate giro and central depositories for each kind of security (*e.g.*, Unilever and AkzoNobel shares are kept in separate depositories). The member's share in a giro depository also forms part of the corresponding central depository.

Investors which are not members of Necigef (*e.g.*, a client of a bank) hold their securities in securities accounts with a member institution. The investors are not owners of the "physical" securities. They are, in effect, co-owners of an undivided interest in the central depository and of the right to demand delivery of the physical securities. The records of the members indicate and evidence the individual entitlement of each investor.

The transfer of securities kept in Necigef is effected in book-entry form only and not by means of delivery of the underlying bearer or registered instruments. They remain either in the central depository or in the giro depository. Unless an investor indicates otherwise, securities in Necigef are transferred and held in safe-keeping on the basis of the WGE. Unless this right has been explicitly excluded, the investor is, however, entitled to demand delivery of "his" securities if he prefers the securities to be kept in a form of safekeeping not governed by the WGE.

The most essential element of the WGE, which in fact was one of the main reasons it was introduced in 1977, is that it provides an investor with a direct pro-prietary right to the securities kept on his behalf in the relevant member's central depository (which includes the latter's share in Necigef's giro depository). Each of the investors holds an interest in the securities which are in the central depository that is proportional to his holding as represented by his securities account with the member.

The above can be illustrated in a very simple diagram:

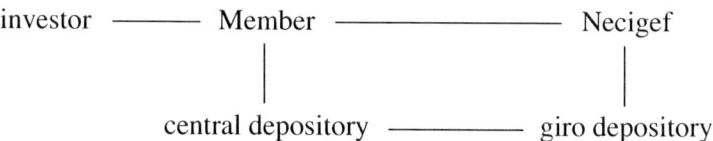

Giving securities to a member for safekeeping results in those to whom the se-curities belonged at the time they were taken into safekeeping by the member-institution, in addition to those who were already entitled thereto at that date,[129] becoming entitled to an interest in the central depository.

---

129. Art. 12(1) WGE.

4.3.4   *Euronext Amsterdam's Derivatives Market*

The European Options Exchange or EOE was established in 1978 at the initiative of the Amsterdam Stock Exchange Association (Euronext Amsterdam's predecessor). At a later stage, the EOE also set up the Amsterdam Financial Futures Market. This options and futures exchange is now operated by the Euronext Amsterdam Derivatives Market which is part of NYSE Liffe Futures and Options.

4.3.5   *The Dutch Government Bonds Market*

The Dutch government is an active borrower in the international and domestic bond markets. The issue and trade of Dutch government bonds takes place through regulated markets or MTFs. There are two methods of issuing government bonds: by direct auction and by tap auction, whereby potential investors can submit bids for particular bonds. Under a tap issue, potential investors can order bonds from the Agency of the Ministry of Finance, which fixes the bond prices daily. Orders must be placed through primary dealers appointed each year by the Dutch State Treasury agency (www.dsta.nl).

5.   REGULATION OF INVESTMENT UNDERTAKINGS

5.1   Introduction

The wish to subject investment undertakings to a separate regulatory regime dates back to the seventies. A bill for the Investment Undertakings Act (*Wet beleggings-instellingen*) was prepared and submitted to Parliament in 1977.[130] The preparatory process for this Act was, however, interrupted by the preparation of an EC Directive dealing with Undertakings for Collective Investment in Transferable Securities or UCITS. When this directive was adopted in 1985, a new legislative proposal was put before Parliament and adopted in 1990. The Investment Undertakings Supervision Act (*Wet toezicht beleggingsinstellingen* or WTB) entered into force on 15 April 1991. This act was replaced by the WFT as of 1 January 2007.

5.2   Types of Investment Undertakings

Under the WFT, an investment undertaking is defined as an investment corporation or investment fund which raises or has raised moneys or other goods for collective

---

130. *Handelingen Tweede Kamer* (Proceedings in parliament), 1977, 14.664.

investment with a view to sharing the proceeds of such investments among its participants (*i.e.*, in the case of an investment corporation, its shareholders).[131] In the Dutch context, an investment corporation is usually organised in the form of an "N.V." corporation. An investment fund is not a legal entity (*e.g.*, a partnership) but is based on a contractual arrangement between the investors or participants, the fund manager who manages and invests the moneys raised, and the depositary or custodian which is entrusted with the safekeeping of the fund's assets. Commonly used contractual arrangements are limited partnership agreements entered into by the investors as limited partners and the fund manager as general partner or a contract between the fund manager and the depositary, constituting a fund for the joint account of the participants (*fonds voor gemene rekening*).

The WFT covers both "open-end" and "closed-end" undertakings. "Open-end" undertakings generally offer participation rights (*i.e.*, stock or units) on a continuous basis and redeem shares at the participant's request, often at net asset value or at a price related to it. In the case of N.V.s, the issue and redemption of shares are restricted by the capital protection provisions of Book 2 of the Dutch Civil Code. The redemption possibilities for investment corporations with variable capital (*beleggingsmaatschappijen met veranderlijk kapitaal*)[132] are considerably broader than those for ordinary corporations. "Closed-end" undertakings will have a fixed number of shares which are generally traded at prices which reflect supply and demand rather than net asset value.

The UCITS Directive only applies to open-end investment undertakings located in the Netherlands, the sole object of which is the collective investment in transferable securities or other liquid financial assets of capital raised from the public and which operate on the principle of risk spreading. The Dutch legislature specifically did not want to limit its regulations to UCITS type undertakings and therefore introduced a much broader definition of investment undertakings. Within the WFT, a special regime was created for investment undertakings of the UCITS type in conformity with the provisions of the UCITS Directive.

5.3   Prohibition

Under the WFT, it is prohibited to raise money or other goods in the Netherlands for participation in an unlicensed investment undertaking, or to offer participation rights in an unlicensed investment undertaking.[133] The prohibition extends to

---

131. Art. 1:1 WFT.
132. Art. 2:76a BW.
133. Art. 2:65 WFT.

investment undertakings as well as to any offerors of shares or participation rights in investment undertakings.

The term "in the Netherlands" covers both an offer or an approach from outside the Netherlands to Dutch residents and from a Dutch resident to other persons in or outside the Netherlands. An offer of shares in an investment undertaking established in the Netherlands is automatically deemed an offer "in the Netherlands" which could be considered an application of the "home country control" principle.

The prohibition does not apply to:

(a) investment undertakings established in other EEA Member States which hold a UCITS licence (see paragraph 5.4.1.2); or to

(b) individuals who offer shares in an investment undertaking other than in the conduct of their profession or business.

5.4   Licence

5.4.1   *Licence Requirements*

5.4.1.1   General

The requirements which an applicant for a licence must meet are largely based on the same principles as the licence requirements for investment firms under the WFT (see paragraph 4.1.3.2). A licence must be applied for by the fund manager or, if the investment undertaking does not have a fund manager, by the investment corporation. In case of a Dutch UCITS investment corporation, the fund manager must apply for a licence (i) in its own name and (ii) on behalf of the UCITS investment corporation. The applicant must meet requirements regarding, *inter alia*:[134]

(a) the expertise and trustworthiness of the daily management (which must consist of at least two persons on the basis of the "four eyes" principle);

(b) capital adequacy (according to the Prudential Supervision Decree,[135] an investment undertaking must have net equity of at least EUR 125,000-300,000 – depending on the type of investment undertakings – and a depositary net equity of at least EUR 112,500);

(c) the conduct of its business; and

(d) information to be supplied to shareholders and to the public in a prospectus.

---

134. Arts. 2:67 and 68 WFT.
135. Art. 48 Prudential Supervision Decree.

In addition, a fund manager managing an investment fund has to demonstrate that:[136]

(a) the fund's assets are entrusted to a depositary which must be an entity separate from the fund manager; and

(b) the depositary can only dispose of the fund's assets with the cooperation of the fund manager.

The application must be submitted to the AFM which is the authority primarily in charge of the supervision of investment undertakings. The AFM can also grant a licence if the applicant for a licence can demonstrate that the objectives of the WFT are adequately achieved in a different manner.[137] Investment undertakings applying for a licence must pay a registration fee to the AFM as well as an annual fee. The latter fee is determined on the basis of the investment undertaking's balance sheet total.[138]

5.4.1.2 UCITS Type Investment Undertakings

The main advantage of obtaining a UCITS licence under the WFT is that this licence will be recognised by other EEA Member States on the basis of the mutual recognition rule laid down in the UCITS Directive. It will effectively give the licence holder a "European passport", enabling it to market its shares in other EEA Member States after having followed a relatively simple recognition procedure. A UCITS licence is given to the fund manager on behalf of the investment undertaking itself.

The following additional requirements are imposed on an investment undertaking which is of the UCITS type:[139]

(a) the principal office of the fund manager must be located in the Netherlands;

(b) the activities of the fund manager must, be limited to the management of the investment undertakings individual asset management;

(c) the assets of the investment corporation must be entrusted to a depositary independent from the investment corporation;

(d) the depositary of the investment undertaking must have its registered seat in an EEA Member State and at least a branch office in the Netherlands.

---

136. Art. 4:43 WFT.
137. Art. 2:65(3) WFT.
138. Decree on Funding Financial Supervision (*Besluit bekostiging financieel toezicht*, 2006, *Stb. 407*).
139. Arts. 2:67(2) and 2:69 WFT.

If an investment undertaking which has obtained a licence intends to market its participation rights in another EEA Member State, it must first notify the AFM and the competent authority in the relevant Member State.[140]

5.4.2.2 Foreign Investment Undertakings

The AFM will attach conditions to the licence granted to investment undertakings which do not qualify as UCITS and are not established in a jurisdiction where there is adequate supervision.[141] In this respect, the AFM requires, *inter alia*, that:[142]

   (i) the investment undertaking is organisationally or economically linked to a financial enterprise established in the Netherlands which is supervised by the AFM or DNB;
   (ii) at least two of the managing directors of the management of the investment undertaking reside in and are approachable by the AFM in the Netherlands and these managing directors will review the implementation of the investment undertakings policies and determine whether the implementation occurs within the agreed policies; and
   (iii) the external auditor must be available and approachable in the Netherlands.

5.4.2 *Continuing Obligations*

An investment undertaking holding a licence and the depositary, if attached to the investment undertaking, must continue to comply with a set of rules detailed in the WFT regarding their expertise and trustworthiness, capital adequacy, conduct of business and the provision of information[143] (see paragraph 4.1.5. of Chapter 1). These rules include the requirement to periodically update the registration document and prospectus which the fund manager must publish about itself and the fund(s) it manages. Also, since participations in an open-end investment undertaking qualify as complex products within the meaning of the WFT, a financial information leaflet must be published (see paragraph 6.3 of Chapter 1),[144] save UCITS, which need to publish a simplified prospectus. Acquiring a qualifying interest in the fund manager of a UCITS is subject to approval in the form a declaration of no objection from DNB. The application procedure for such approval is similar to the procedure for investment firms – see paragraph 4.2 of Chapter 1 for further details.

---

140. Arts. 2:122 and 123 WFT.
141. Art. 1:102 (2) WFT.
142. AFM Policy Financial Supervision Act 06-12 of 12 December 2006.
143. WFT Sections 4.2 and 4.3.1.4.
144. Art. 65 Conduct of Business Decree.

5.5   Exemptions

The WFT's licence requirements do not apply to the investment undertakings located in certain jurisdictions where there is adequate supervision.[145] The WFT also provides a few general exceptions and exemptions from its prohibition on the offering of participation rights and the raising or obtaining of funds by or through investment undertakings. Exemptions and exceptions are available, inter alia:[146]

    (a) in the event that participation rights in investment undertakings are offered to qualified investors only;

    (b) for an offer to fewer than 100 investors who are not qualified investors;

    (c) for participation rights which have a nominal value, or are offered for an aggregate consideration, of at least EUR 50,000.[147]

In some cases the applicability of a general exemption or exception may nonetheless result in an obligation to satisfy some of the continuing obligations. Furthermore, some of the general exemptions have additional conditions attached which have to be taken into account if they are intended to be used.

5.6   Voluntary supervision

A new regime, which has not yet entered into force, allows an investment manager or the investment institution itself to opt for voluntary supervision if the participation rights are offered only to qualified investors. This regime makes it possible that investment institutions come under supervision voluntarily even if they only aim at qualified investors. As a result these investment institutions can also offer their participation rights to institutional investors which are only allowed to invest in investment institutions that are supervised by a financial market supervisory authority.

Voluntary supervision will not require the investment institution to:

– publish annual accounts;

– value the non liquid assets by an independent expert annually;

– restrict the disposal of assets to a joint disposal by the manager and custodian in the case of an investment fund having no legal personality;

---

145. Art. 2:66 WFT. Such jurisdictions include the US (provided it relates to investment corporations registered with the SEC), Luxembourg, Malta, the UK, Guernsey, Jersey, Ireland, France and Malta.

146. Art. 1:12 WFT.

147. Art. 4 Exemption Regulation WFT.

– appoint an independent custodian if and to the extent the investment policy of the investment fund concerned poses a real risk to the assets of other investment institutions for which the custodian acts as a custodian.

5.7 Recognition of UCITS

The WFT's provisions apply equally to foreign investment undertakings seeking to market their participation rights in the Netherlands. However, an exception is made in this respect for investment undertakings which are established in another EEA Member State and which fall within the UCITS Directive and are authorised as such in their home state. If an investment undertaking in this category wishes to be able to offer its participation rights in the Netherlands publicly on a cross-border basis, it should submit written notification to the AFM.[148] This notification should include:

(a) a certificate, issued by the competent authority of the EEA Member State in which the investment undertaking is established, confirming that the investment undertaking meets the requirements set by the UCITS Directive;
(b) its articles of association or equivalent internal regulations;
(c) its visa-stamped prospectus and visa-stamped simplified prospectus (including a Dutch translation of the latter);
(d) information concerning the intended method of supplying information and the manner in which the trade in, distribution on and repurchase or redemption of the participation rights in the Netherlands will be effected;
(e) its most recent annual and semi-annual accounts, if available; and
(f) the English language texts of all information and documents which it must make public in accordance with the regulations issued by the relevant EEA Member State.

Two months after the submission of the notification and accompanying documents, the investment undertaking may commence the marketing of its participation rights, unless the AFM has notified the investment undertaking that the intention to offer the participation rights is not in conformity with applicable provisions of Dutch law or that the intended method of trading the participation rights violates statutory provisions outside the scope of the UCITS Directive.[149]

---

148. Art. 2:72 WFT.
149. Art. 2:72(3) WFT.

An investment undertaking which follows this recognition procedure must pay a registration fee to the Dutch Central Bank as well as an annual fee.[150]

If a UCITS type investment undertaking wishes to set up a branch office in the Netherlands, it has to notify its home regulator of its intention. Such home regulator will then inform the AFM of such intention and the AFM can impose certain conditions on the relevant fund manager with respect to its intended activities in the Netherlands.[151]

UCITS IV will enhance opportunities to market across the EU by introducing a full manager passport, UCITS merger procedures (domestically and on a cross-border basis), UCITS master feeder structures and an electronic regulator to regulator notification procedure.

5.8   Sanctions

Violation of the prohibition on offers of participation rights in investment undertakings and of certain other provisions of the WFT constitutes an economic offence under the Economic Offences Act.[152] In the offence is committed intentionally, the offender can be sentenced to a maximum of two years imprisonment and/or community service and/or a fine of up to EUR 25,000 for natural persons and EUR 100,000 for legal persons.[153]

Alternatively, the AFM can impose administrative fines for violation of the prohibition (see paragraph 9.3.4 of Chapter 1).

6.   ANTIFRAUD PROVISIONS

6.1   Market Abuse

6.1.1   *Introduction*

In October 2005 the Market Abuse Directive[154] was implemented in Dutch legislation (see paragraph 1.5.5).[155] In addition to this Directive the European Commission

---

150. Decree on Funding Financial Supervision.
151. Art. 2:70 and 71 WFT.
152. Art. 1 (2) WED.
153. Art. 6 (1)(2) WED.
154. Directive 2003/6/EC.
155. Market Abuse Act, 2005 (*Wet marktmisbruik*) Stb. 346.

introduced several Regulations[156] and CESR published several documents regarding this Directive.[157] The objective of the Directive is to establish an integrated and efficient financial market with market integrity: *'The smooth functioning of securities markets and public confidence in markets are prerequisites for economic growth and wealth. Market abuse harms the integrity of the financial markets and public confidence in securities and derivatives'.*

In 2005, this Directive was implemented in the Securities Transactions Supervision Act (see paragraph 1.4). In January 2007 the rules regarding market abuse were transferred to the WFT and are now found in Chapter 5.4 thereof.

The market abuse rules cover three prohibitions: the prohibition on (i) insider trading, (ii) tipping and (iii) market manipulation. In addition to these prohibitions the rules cover several obligations such as the obligation for issuers (companies of which financial instruments are admitted to trading) to publish price sensitive information, the obligation to notify transactions, and rules regarding investment recommendations. The prohibitions also apply to financial instruments that are admitted to trading on a multilateral trading facility. Below, these various prohibitions and obligations will be discussed further.

6.1.2   *Inside Information*

For the prohibition on insider trading and tipping and for the obligation to publish price sensitive information, the definition of inside information (*voorwetenschap*) is of major importance.[158] Inside information is defined as: *'awareness of specific information that relates directly or indirectly to an issuer' (...) 'to which the financial instruments pertain, or to the trade in those financial instruments, which information has not been publicly disclosed and whose disclosure might have a significant effect on the price of the financial instruments or on the price of derivative financial instruments'.*

This definition consists of four main elements: (a) specific information; (b) an issuer/trade in financial instruments; (c) no public disclosure; and (d) significant influence. These elements are further specified by the Second set of CESR Guidance.[159]

---

156. Regulation (EU) nr. 2273/2003, Regulation (EU) nr. 2003/124, Regulation (EU) nr.2003/125 and Regulation (EU) nr. 2004/72.
157. Documents can be found on the CESR-website (www.cesr-eu.org).
158. Art. 5:53 WFT.
159. Second set of CESR Guidance on the Operation of the Market Abuse Directive, Ref. CESR/06-562b.

(a) Specific information

Information shall be deemed to be specific information if it indicates a set of circumstances which exists or may reasonably be expected to come into existence or an event which has occurred or which may reasonably be expected to occur and if it is specific enough to enable a conclusion to be drawn as to the possible effect of that set of circumstances or event on the prices of financial instruments or related financial instruments.[160] It is not necessary that the information concerns one specific event; a set of circumstances may result in inside information.[161]

(b) Issuer/trade in financial instruments

An issuer is a legal entity or company whose financial instruments are listed (or likely to be listed shortly) on a regulated market or on a multilateral trading facility. Inside information does not always have to derive from the issuer itself. For example a change of legislation or a governmental financial contribution that is (un) profitable for the issuer could be inside infomation. Inside information regarding the trade in financial instruments could for instance arise if a substantial holding in an issuer is acquired or sold (prevention of 'front running').

(c) No public disclosure

Information is publicly disclosed if it is disclosed to the public without restrictions and therefore known to investors.[162] Distinction must be made between the information made publicly available by the issuer in the way the Transparency Directive[163] prescribes (see paragraphs 3.3.5 and 6.1.6) and information that was not made available in this specific manner, but of which the public nevertheless is aware.

(d) Significant influence

The explanatory notes regarding market abuse legislation state that this information must be meaningful.[164] From objective standards it should be expected that publication of this information will lead to a movement in the price of the financial

---

160. Section 1 (1) of Regulation 2003/124/EC.
161. Judgement of 31 May 2005, HR, JOR 185 (Flexovit) and Judgement of 11 February 2005, District Court (*Rechtbank*) Amsterdam, JOR 75 (Veer Palthe Voûte).
162. *Kamerstukken* II (Parliamentary Papers) [TK] 1996-1997, 25 095, nr 8, p. 6.
163. 2004/109/EC, pbEG L 390.
164. TK, 2004-2005, 29 827, nr. 3, p.8.

instrument.[165] This is information a reasonable investor would be likely to use as part of the basis of his investment decision. It is not necessary to know the direction of the price movement of the financial instrument.[166]

6.1.3   *Insider Trading*

6.1.3.1   Prohibition

The prohibition on insider trading is contained in Article 5:56 WFT. This article prohibits any person having inside information from entering into or bringing about any transaction:

- in or from the Netherlands or a non-Member State in financial instruments admitted to trading (or in which trading is requested) on a regulated market or a multilateral trading facility with a Dutch licence;
- in or from the Netherlands in financial instruments admitted to trading (or in which trading is requested) on a regulated market or multilateral trading facility with a licence from another Member State or admitted to trading on a trading system similar to a regulated market or multilateral trading facility in a non-Member State;
- in or from the Netherlands or a non-Member State in financial instruments (admitted to trading or not) whose value depends on the financial instruments referred to above; or
- in or from another Member State in financial instruments admitted to trading on a Dutch multilateral trading facility.

One's own intentions or resolutions do not qualify as a prohibited insider trading transaction.[167] For example, when a company decides to take over another (listed) company and starts building up an interest in the target company by acquiring securities in this target company, this would not qualify as insider trading.[168] However a prohibited insider trading transaction may arise if a company becomes aware of inside information in the course of a due diligence investigation.[169]

In Article 5:56 WFT a distinction is made between two different groups of insiders: (i) primary insiders and (ii) secondary insiders. A secondary insider is

---

165. TK, 2004-2005, 29 827, nr. 7, p.7, in which reference is made to the Netherlands Supreme Court ruling in the HCS-case, Judgement of Supreme Court of 27 June 1995, NJ 1995 No. 662.
166. TK, 2004-2005, 29 827, nr. 3, p.8.
167. Judgement of Supreme Court of 6 February 2007, NJ 2008 No. 467.
168. TK 1997-1998, 25 095, nr 8, p. 8.
169. TK II 1997-1998, 25 095, nr 8, p. 4.

a person that is (or should be) aware that he or she is in the possession of inside information, but who is not a primary insider. A primary insider is deemed to be aware of inside information because of his function or capacity related to the company. It is irrelevant if that person is actually aware of the fact that he or she is in the possession of inside information. The following persons (or entities) qualify as primary insiders:

- managers or directors of the company that determine the day to day policy;
- persons or entities that supervise the category above;
- persons or entities that hold a qualifying holding (shareholding or voting rights of 10% or more);
- persons or legal entities that possess inside information due to their work or profession, such as accountants and lawyers;
- persons or legal entities that possess inside information due to criminal activities.

6.1.3.2   Exemptions

Article 5:56 (5) WFT provides for exemptions on the prohibition on insider trading. The prohibition does not apply to conducting or effecting transactions in financial instruments:

(a) in compliance with an enforceable obligation that already existed at the time when the trading party became aware of the inside information;
(b) in the context of monetary policy, foreign exchange policy or public debt management;
(c) in the context of a buy-back programme;[170] or
(d) in the context of stabilisation.

In Article 5:56 (6) WFT a possibility is created to exempt other categories of transactions to which the prohibition does not apply. In the Market Abuse Decree the following transactions are exempt from the prohibition on insider trading:

- assigning financial instruments as part of a personnel scheme to directors, board members or employees, if in so doing a constant course of action is followed as regards the conditions and periodicity of the scheme;[171]

---

170. Commission Regulation (EC) No. 2273/2003 of 22 December 2003 implementing Directive 2003/6/EC of the European Parliament and of the European Council as regards exemptions for buy-back programmes and stabilisation of financial instruments (OJEU L336).
171. See also Judgment of 4 April 2006, HR, JOR 2006/133 and NJ 2007/144.

- exercising rights to shares as part of a personnel scheme on the expiry date of the right concerned or within a period of five working days preceding that date, and selling, within this period, the shares or depositary receipts for shares acquired by exercising these rights, if in the latter case the entitled party notified the issuing institution, at least four months before the expiry date and in writing, of its intention to sell, or granted the issuing institution an irrevocable authorisation to sell;
- a transaction that must be conducted or effected in order to be able to fulfil an obligation to transfer shares or depositary receipts for shares;
- concluding an agreement by which a party entitled to financial instruments commits itself irrevocably towards an offeror, in the context of a public offer that is proposed or being prepared, to offer financial instruments to which the public offer relates to the offeror;
- concluding an agreement by which a party entitled to financial instruments or a party potentially entitled to financial instruments commits itself irrevocably, prior to the issuing or secondary offering of those financial instruments, to buy one or more of those financial instruments;
- issuing or acquiring shares by way of dividend distribution, other than in the form of dividend with stock option;
- acting in good faith to serve clients via an intermediary, while only possessing inside information in respect of the trade;
- the conducting or effecting of a transaction by employees of a legal person where inside information is available, if these employees themselves only possess price-sensitive information in respect of the trade;
- the conducting or effecting of transactions in financial instruments in the context of a buy-back programme or stabilisation in a market in financial instruments, not being a regulated market;
- the sale of shares granted in connection with an employee share plan as referred to above, immediately after sale is first permitted pursuant to the conditions of grant, with the party concerned immediately utilising the proceeds from the sale to pay a tax obligation arising in connection with the grant.

6.1.3.3   Sanctions

The principal sanctions on any violation of the prohibition of Article 5:56 WFT are imprisonment for up to two years and/or a fine of up to EUR 19,000 and up to EUR 76,000 if a legal entity is found guilty. The maximum fine of EUR 19,000 may be increased to EUR 76,000 if the benefit that was generated from the insider trading exceeds EUR 4,750 (being one fourth of the maximum fine). The same applies to the maximum fine of EUR 76,000 if the legal entity concerned has derived benefit in excess of EUR 19,000 from the insider trading in which event a maximum fine of EUR 760,000 may be imposed on the legal entity.[172]

A person who is convicted of insider trading under the WFT may be ordered by the criminal court to pay to the Dutch State such amount of money as is estimated will prevent him from reaping the benefits of his criminal act.[173]

For administrative fines which the AFM can impose for violation of the prohibition reference is made to 9.3.4 of Chapter 1.

6.1.4 Tipping-off

6.1.4.1 Prohibition

Persons who have inside information are prohibited from (i) disclosing this information to third parties and (ii) recommending or inducing third parties to enter into or complete transactions in financial instruments to which the inside information pertains.[174]

6.1.4.2 Exemptions

The tipping-off prohibition does not apply to an entity or institution whose employees did not have inside information when they recommended third parties to enter into certain transactions. Furthermore, the prohibition does not apply to persons who disclose such information in the normal course of their employment, profession or function.[175] Article 3 of the Market Abuse Decree states two situations in which the prohibition does not apply:

(a) in case of 'sounding' for a public bid on financial instruments; or
(b) in case of 'sounding' for a public offer of financial instruments.

6.1.4.3 Sanctions

The principal sanctions on any violation of the prohibition of Article 5:57 WFT are similar to the sanctions applicable to violations of Article 5:56 WFT.

---

172. Art. 6(1) WED and Art. 23 *Wetboek van strafrecht* [Sr.], Criminal Code.
173. Art. 36e Sr.
174. Art. 5:57 WFT.
175. See for a restrictive interpretation of this exemption EC Court of Justice 22 November 2005, JOR 2006/49, with annotation by Kristen (Grøngaard).

6.1.5   *Market Manipulation*

6.1.5.1   Prohibition

The prohibition on market manipulation can be divided in transaction manipulation and information manipulation. Article 5:58 WFT contains the prohibition on both. Information manipulation means the dissemination of information which gives (or is likely to give) false or misleading signals as to the offer, the demand or the rate of financial instruments, while the person who disseminates the information knows (or should know) that this information is false or misleading.[176] Transaction manipulation may arise if:

(i)   a transaction or trade order is conducted or effected which sends or may send an incorrect or misleading signal with regard to the supply of, or demand for, or the price in, financial instruments (unless the party that conducted or effected the transaction or trade order had a justified reason);

(ii) a transaction or trade order is conducted or effected in order to maintain the price of the financial instrument at an artificial level (unless the party that conducted or effected the transaction or trade order had a justified reason); or

(iii) a transaction or trade order is conducted or effected involving deception or misrepresentation.

As a matter of guidance an enumerative description of examples of market manipulation can be found in CESR guidance and information on the common operation of the Market Abuse Directive (level 3).[177] For example 'wash trades', sales and purchases of financial instruments where there is no beneficial interest or market risk, and 'marking the close', buying or selling securities at the close of the market in an effort to alter the closing price, are considered transactions that constitute market manipulation.

6.1.5.2   Exemptions

The prohibition does not apply to a transactions or trade orders conducted or effected as part of:

---

176. Judgment of 16 August 2007, Rb. Amsterdam, JOR 245 (Nelemans regarding the publication of a false press release).
177. Ref: CESR/04-505b.

- monetary policy, foreign exchange policy or public debt management;
- a buy-back programme;
- stabilisation; or
- the dissemination of information by journalists acting in their normal professional capacity, unless these journalists obtain benefit or profit by disseminating the information.

In Article 5:58 (3) WFT a possibility is created to exempt other categories of transactions to which the prohibition on market manipulation does not apply, the 'accepted market practices'.[178] In the Netherlands no exemption for accepted market practices is acknowledged yet.

6.1.5.3   Sanctions

The principal sanctions on any violation of the prohibition on market manipulation of Article 5:58 WFT are similar to the sanctions applicable to violations of insider trading of Article 5:56 and tipping-off of Article 5:57 WFT.

6.1.6   Disclosure Obligations

6.1.6.1   Obligation

Based on Article 5:25i WFT, an issuer must, without delay, make inside information as referred to above which directly pertains to itself ('price sensitive information') generally available. The information must be made generally available in a non-discriminatory manner. The issuer shall make use of media that may reasonably be assumed to guarantee a fast and effective distribution of the information in all Member States. Publication shall take place by means of a press release that is issued simultaneously in the Netherlands as well as in each other Member State where the issuer's financial instruments are admitted to trading on a regulated market. The information should also be posted on the website of the issuer without delay and must be kept accessible on the website for a minimum period of one year. Furthermore, the issuer must send the information simultaneously with the general availability to the AFM. At the AFM website[179] brochures are available with examples of information or situations that qualify as price sensitive information.

---

178. Reference is made to the CESR website (www.cesr-eu.org) for accepted market practices of member states.
179. www.afm.nl.

6.1.6.2   Exemptions

For the obligation to publish price sensitive information without delay there is not a real exemption available. However the publication of this information can be postponed. The issuer may delay the publication of the information if the following three requirements are met:

(i)   the delay serves a legitimate interest of the issuer;
(ii) the delay is unlikely to deceive the public; and
(iii) the issuer can guarantee the confidentiality of this information.[180]

For instance, a legitimate interest as mentioned above is available if publication may influence the outcome or development of negotiations or if a decision of the board of the issuer is still subject to approval.[181]

6.1.6.3   Sanctions

Violation of the obligation to publish price sensitive information does not constitute a criminal offence. Violation can however lead to an administrative fine by the AFM, for which reference is made to 9.3.4 of Chapter 1.

6.1.7   *Insider List*

6.1.7.1   Obligation

Article 5:59 WFT requires issuers to draw up an insider list (and to keep this list up to date). The list should include persons who are in the possession of inside information on a regular or occasional basis. The issuer should also inform these persons of the prohibitions and the level of the sanctions entailed by any violation. The list must be updated regularly and without delay if changes occur. The list and its alterations must be preserved for five years.
        The insider list must at least contain the following information:

– the name of the person that is in the possession of inside information on a regular or occasional basis;
– the reason for putting this person on the list; and

---

180. Art. 5:25i (3) WFT.
181. Art. 4 (1) Decree implementing directive transparency of issuers (*Besluit uitvoeringsrichtlijn transparantie uitgevende instellingen*).

– the date that the list was drawn up and when it was last updated.

6.1.7.2 Exemptions

There are no exemptions available for this obligation.

6.1.7.3 Sanctions

The violation of the obligation of Article 5:59 WFT to draw up insider lists constitutes a criminal offence. If intentionally committed the principal sanction on a violation is imprisonment of up to two years (if unintentionally committed imprisonment of six months) and/or a fine of up to EUR 19,000 and up to EUR 76,000 if a legal entity is found guilty. The maximum fine of EUR 19,000 may be increased to EUR 76,000 if the benefit that was generated from the insider trading exceeds EUR 4,750 (being one fourth of the maximum fine). The same applies to the maximum fine of EUR 76,000 if the legal entity concerned has derived benefit in excess of EUR 19,000 from the insider trading in which event a maximum fine of EUR 760,000 may be imposed on the legal entity.[182]

For administrative fines the AFM can enforce for violation of the prohibition reference is made to 9.3.4. of Chapter 1.

6.1.8 *Transaction Notification*

6.1.8.1 Obligation to Notify Transactions[183]

Persons who (co-)determine the day-to-day policy of an issuer (such as directors), persons who supervise the policy[184] and certain managers who have the power to take decisions affecting the future developments and business prospects of an issuer, must report their transaction in the shares of the issuer (or in financial instruments whose value partly depends on the value of those shares). This also applies to persons who are closely associated with these persons, such as spouses, registered partners, children or other family and legal entities controlled by one of these persons.

Notification should be made to the AFM and should take place no later than on the fifth working day following the transaction date.

The notification must contain the following details:

---

182. Art. 6(1) WED and art. 23 Sr.
183. Art. 5:60 WFT.
184. Judgment of May 2003, Rb. Amsterdam, JOR 2003/149.

- name;
- address;
- issuing institution involved;
- reason for the notification;
- description of the financial instruments;
- nature of the transaction;
- date and place of completion of the transaction;
- price and scope of the transaction

On the AFM website notification forms are available to submit the notification. The notifications regarding the transactions are publicly available in the register on the website of the AFM.

6.1.8.2   Exemptions

Two exemptions are available for this notification requirement. The first exemption applies to transactions pursuant to a written mandate by a financial enterprise allowed to provide individual capital management services, if that mandate stipulates that the principal cannot exert influence on transactions by the financial enterprise. The second exemption applies to transactions in the context of monetary policy, foreign exchange policy or public debt management.

In addition to these exemptions the notification requirement is deemed to be fulfilled[185] if the AFM is already notified because of the notification requirement regarding a threshold[186] or a notification requirement regarding a director.[187]

6.1.8.3   Sanctions

The principal sanctions on the violation of this notification obligation are similar to the sanctions above regarding the violation of the obligation to draw up an insider list.

In addition, the AFM can instruct a person that made an incorrect transaction to adjust the notification.[188]

---

185. Based on Art. 7 of the Market Abuse Decree.
186. See paragraph 3.4 regarding notification requirement for holdings of certain thresholds and art. 5:38 (1) (2) WFT.
187. Directors and supervisory directors of listed companies must also report their holdings in the relevant listed company and any affiliated listed company pursuant to Art. 5:48(6) and (7) WFT.
188. Art. 5:61 (1) WFT.

6.1.9   Notification Requirement of Suspicious Transactions

6.1.9.1   Obligation

An investment firm which has a reasonable suspicion[189] that a transaction or a transaction order may be contrary to the prohibition on insider trading or market manipulation is required to notify the AFM of this suspicion, without delay.[190] Notification shall be submitted by ordinary mail, electronic mail, fax or telephone, on the understanding that in the latter case the notification shall be confirmed in writing if the AFM so requests. The notification must contain the following information:

- a description of the transaction or the instruction, the type of order and the type of trading platform;
- the reasons for the reasonable suspicion;
- details revealing the identity of the persons on whose behalf the transaction was carried out or who gave the instruction for the transaction, and the identity of the other persons involved in this transaction or instruction;
- the capacity in which the investment firm is acting; and
- other details that may reasonably be considered relevant to the investigation by the AFM.

The investment firm which made a notification pursuant to this requirement in good faith is not liable for damage sustained by a third party as a result. The investment firm is obliged to observe confidentiality that it has made such notification.

6.1.9.2   Exemptions

There are no exemptions available for this obligation.

6.1.9.3   Sanctions

If the investment firm does not observe confidentiality of such notification the principal sanctions on the violation are similar to the sanctions above regarding violation of the obligation to draw up an insider list and the notification requirement.

---

189. For guidance regarding possible signals of insider dealing or market manipulation, see CESR guidance and information on the common operation of the Market Abuse Directive (level 3), ref. CESR/04/505b, under V.
190. Art. 5:63 WFT.

For the administrative fines the AFM can impose for violation of the obligation, reference is made to 9.3.4 of Chapter 1.

6.1.10   *Insider Regulation*

6.1.10.1   Obligation

Certain issuers[191] are under the obligation to implement regulations containing rules with regard to the holdings of and transactions in shares of the company (or in financial instruments whose value partly depends on the value of those shares) by its employees, persons who (co-) determine the day-to-day policy of the issuer and persons who supervise the policy. The regulations must comply with the following rules of the Market Abuse Decree.[192] The regulation shall contain rules in respect of:

- the duties and powers of the compliance officer, if the issuing institution has decided to appoint such a person;
- the obligations of employees and persons who (co-)determine the day-to-day policy of the issuer and persons who supervise the policy of the latter persons with regard to the ownership of and transactions in financial instruments pertaining to the issuing institution; and
- where applicable, the period during which the persons referred to above and the managers who have the power to take decisions affecting the future development and business prospects of an issuer are not allowed to conduct or effect transactions in financial instruments pertaining to the issuing institution ('closed period'). On the AFM website a model for this insider regulation is available.[193]

6.1.10.2   Sanctions

The principal sanctions on the violation of this notification obligation are similar to the sanctions above regarding the violation of the obligation to draw up an insider list.

---

191. Issuers having their registered office in the Netherlands and of which financial instruments are admitted to trading on a regulated market or multilateral trading facility in the Netherlands, a regulated market in another Member State or on a similar system in a non-Member State or issuers in a non-Member State of which securities are admitted to trading on a regulated market or a multilateral trading facility in the Netherlands.
192. Art. 11 Market Abuse Decree.
193. www.afm.nl.

6.1.11 Investment Recommendations

6.1.11.1 Obligation

For the purpose of this obligation an investment recommendation (*beleggingsaanbeveling*)[194] is understood to be information addressed to the public in which an investment strategy is, either explicitly or implicitly, recommended or proposed concerning financial instruments of an issuer.[195] Extensive rules are implemented regarding the publishing of investment recommendations. An investment recommendation must include the publisher of the recommendation and the person (or entity) which has drawn up the recommendation. Further it has to state that the AFM is the supervising regulator. With regard to the accuracy of the information in the recommendations, rules apply regarding the source of the information, methods of assessment and the disclosure of the date of the first publication of the recommendation. Also the investment recommendation should disclose conflicts of interest, remunerations and financial interests regarding the investment recommendation.

6.1.11.2 Exemptions

There are no exemptions available for the publication of investment recommendations.

6.1.11.3 Sanctions

The principal sanctions on the violation of this notification obligation are similar to the sanctions above regarding the violation of the obligation to draw up an insider list (see above).

6.1.12 Civil Liability

The question arises of whether a person could institute a civil law claim against another person who has used inside information. Three positions ought to be distinguished here. The first is that of the contractual counterparty of the person using inside information. The second is that of other shareholders. The third relates to the position of the company which is the object of the inside information concerned. In addition, one must distinguish between cases where transactions are effected on the

---

194. Art. 5:64 WFT.
195. Art. 5:53 (5) WFT.

exchange, and cases where transactions are effected off-exchange. In the former, it will be difficult, if not impossible, to determine who the ultimate contractual counterparty is. In other words, the person who wishes to institute the civil law claim does not know whether the person who has used the inside information is his contractual counterparty or not. This leads to the conclusion that in this instance, a civil law claim must be based on tort rather than on breach of contract. In the case Bot v. Datex Holding N.V., Smit and Kippersluis,[196] the Amsterdam District Court held as a matter of principle that a claim based on the concept of tort may succeed. The Amsterdam District Court, however, applied a restrictive concept of tort and ruled that no act of tort had been committed in the case submitted to it.

If the transaction concerned is effected off-exchange, then it will be clear who the contractual counterparty is, and the civil law claim may have a contractual basis: the fact that the person abusing inside information did not disclose the information to his counterparty may allow for a claim based on fraud (*bedrog*) or on error of facts (*dwaling*); this, however, generally assumes that the contractual (or indeed pre-contractual) relationship between the parties includes a legal duty to disclose inside information. Such legal duty may not always exist.

6.2 Savings Certificates Act[197]

The Savings Certificates Act[198] regulates the trade in savings certificates (*spaarbewijzen*) and is aimed principally at preventing tax evasion. Savings certificates are defined as bearer securities which constitute a claim against the issuer for a fixed amount and do not pay interest during their term. As a result of this rather broad definition, the Act covers all kinds of zero-coupon debt instruments such as commercial paper, certificates of deposit and zero-coupon bonds or notes. Under the Act, a code of conduct has been established which deals with the way in which savings certificates are traded.[199]

The Savings Certificates Act provides that a transfer of savings certificates may only be effected:

---

196. Judgment of April 18, 1990, Rb Amsterdam, docket number H 88.1233.
197. See also F. Graaf, Issues of Euromarket Securities and Syndicated Eurocurrency Loans, § 2(j) (1991).
198. *Wet inzake spaarbewijzen*, 1985 Stb. 293, as amended.
199. Agreement of Feb. 2, 1987 between DNB, Nederlandse Vereniging van Banken (the Dutch Banking Association) and Postbank N.V., which was declared generally binding by royal decree [KB] of 11 March 1987 Stb. 129.

(a) through the intermediary of the issuer itself or a member of Euronext Amsterdam; or

(b) by and between individuals not acting in the conducting of a profession or business.[200]

The code of conduct further provides that a registration note must be issued by any company or institution which enters into a transaction involving savings certificates.[201] This note must state the name, address and domicile of the counterparty, the nature of the transaction and a description of the number, type and serial numbers of the savings certificates concerned. Unless the certificates are listed on Euronext Amsterdam, a legend must be printed on the certificates which refers to the registration requirement.[202] Transactions in commercial paper and certificates of deposit are explicitly exempted from the requirements in the code of conduct to the extent that the transactions are entered into by professional lenders and borrowers.[203] The Savings Certificates Act itself also contains certain identification requirements, which need to be complied with upon the issuance, transfer or redemption of savings certificates. Violation of the requirements of the Savings Certificates Act constitutes a criminal offence.[204]

---

200. Art. 3 *Wet inzake spaarbewijzen.*
201. Art. 2 KB.
202. Art. 4 KB.
203. Art. 1 KB. Such transactions remain, however, subject to the transfer restriction of Art. 3 Savings Certificates Act.
204. Art. 4 Savings Certificates Act.

Allen & Overy's Global Presence

AUSTRALIA
Sydney
Allen & Overy LLP
Level 7, Gold Fields House
1 Alfred Street
Sydney
NSW 2000
Tel. +61 (0)2 9373 7700
Fax. +61 (0)2 9373 7710

Perth
Allen & Overy
Level 27
Exchange Plaza
2 The Esplanade
Perth
WA 6000
Tel. +61 8 6315 5900
Fax +61 8 6315 5999

BELGIUM
Antwerp
Allen & Overy LLP
Uitbreidingstraat 80
B-2600 Antwerp
Belgium
Tel. +32 (0)3 287 7222
Fax +32 (0)3 287 7244

Brussels
Allen & Overy LLP
Avenue de Tervueren 268 A
B-1150 Brussels
Belgium
Tel. +32 (0)2 780 2222
Fax +32 (0)2 780 2244

CHINA
Beijing
Allen & Overy LLP, Beijing office
Suite 522
China World Tower 2
No. 1 Jian Guo Men Wai Avenue
Beijing 100004
PRC
Tel. +86 (0)10 6505 8800
Fax +86 (0)10 6505 6677

Hong Kong
Allen & Overy LLP
9th Floor
Three Exchange Square
Central Hong Kong
SAR
Tel. +852 2974 7000
Fax +852 2974 6999

Shanghai
Allen & Overy LLP, Shanghai office
18F Bank of Shanghai Tower
168 Yin Cheng Middle Road
Pudong, Shanghai 200120
PRC
Tel. +86 21 3896 5000
Fax +86 21 3896 5050

CZECH REPUBLIC
Prague
Allen & Overy (Czech Republic)
organizační složka
V Celnici 4
110 00 Prague 1
Czech Republic
Tel: +420 222 107 111
Fax: +420 222 107 107

FRANCE
Paris
Allen & Overy LLP
Edouard VII
26, Boulevard des Capucines
75009 Paris
France
Tel. +33 (0)1 40 06 54 00
Fax +33 (0)1 40 06 54 54

GERMANY
Düsseldorf
Allen & Overy LLP
Breite Straße 27
40213 Düsseldorf
Germany
Tel. +49 211 2806 7000
Fax +49 211 2806 7800

Frankfurt
Allen & Overy LLP
Taunustor 2
60311 Frankfurt am Main
Germany
Tel. +49 (0)69 2648 5000
Fax +49 (0)69 2648 5800

Hamburg
Allen & Overy LLP
Kehrwieder 12
20457 Hamburg
Germany
Tel. +49 (0)40 82 221 20
Fax +49 (0)40 82 221 2200

Mannheim
Allen & Overy LLP
Am Viktoria Turm 2
68163 Mannheim
Germany
Tel: +49 (0)621 3285 631
Fax: +49 (0)621 3285 6541

Munich
Allen & Overy LLP
Maximilianstraße 35
80539 München
Germany
Tel: +49 (0)89 71043 3000
Fax: +49 (0)89 71043 3800

GREECE
Athens
Allen & Overy (Greece) LLP
2 Navarchou Nikodimou
105 57 Athens
Greece
Tel: +30 (0)210 3256030-4
Fax:+30 (0)210 3256036

HUNGARY
Budapest
Morley Allen & Overy Iroda
Madách Trade Center
Madách Imre út 13-14
H-1075 Budapest
Hungary
Tel. +36 1 483 2200
Fax +36 1 268 1515

INDONESIA
Jakarta
Daniel Ginting Law Firm
in association with Allen & Overy LLP
The Energy Building
15th Floor
Sudirman Centre Business District
Ji Jend Sudirman Cav
52-53 Jakarta 12190
Indonesia
Tel. +62 21 2995 1700
Fax +62 21 2995 1779

ITALY
Milan
Allen & Overy
Studio Legale Associato
Via Manzoni, 41
20121 Milan
Italy
Tel. +39 02 290 491
Fax +39 02 290 49333

Rome
Allen & Overy
Studio Legale Associato
Corso Vittorio Emanuele II, 284
00186 Rome
Italy
Tel. +39 06 684 271
Fax +39 06 684 27333

Turin
Pavesio e Associati
*An independent law firm
in association with Allen & Overy
Corso Vittorio Emanuele II, 68
10121 Turin
Italy
Tel. +39 011 511 21
Fax +39 011 511 2333

JAPAN
Tokyo
Allen & Overy Gaikokuho Kyodo
Jigyo Horitsu Jimusho
38F Roppongi Hills Mori Tower
6-10-1 Roppongi, Minato-ku
Tokyo 106-6034
Japan
Tel. +81 (0)3 5114 1600
Fax +81 (0)3 5114 1690

LUXEMBOURG
Luxembourg
Allen & Overy Luxembourg
33 avenue J.F. Kennedy
L-1855 Luxembourg
PO Box 5017
L-1050 Luxembourg
Tel. +352 44 44 55 1
Fax +352 44 44 55 222

NETHERLANDS
Amsterdam
Allen & Overy LLP
Apollolaan 15
1077 AB Amsterdam
PO Box 75440
1070 AK Amsterdam
The Netherlands
Tel. +31 (0)20 674 1000
Fax +31 (0)20 674 1111

POLAND
Warsaw
Allen & Overy, A. Pędzich sp. k.
Rondo ONZ 1
34 floor
00-124 Warsaw
Poland
Tel. +48 (0)22 820 6100
Fax +48 (0)22 820 6199

QATAR
Doha
Allen & Overy
Level 8 Regus Offices
Al Fardan Tower
61 Al Funduq Street
West Bay, PO Box 24205
Doha, Qatar
Tel: 00 974 410 1676
Fax: 00 974 410 1500

ROMANIA
Bucharest
Radu Tărăcilă Pădurari Retevoescu
SCA
in association with Allen & Overy LLP
60 Dacia Boulevard
020061 Bucharest 2
Romania
Tel. +40 31 405 7777
Fax +40 31 405 7778

RUSSIA
Moscow
Allen & Overy Legal Services
Dmitrovsky pereulok 9
107031 Moscow
Russian Federation
Tel. +7 495 725 7900
Fax +7 495 725 7949

SAUDI ARABIA
Saudi Arabia
Abdulaziz AlGasim Law Firm
in association with Allen & Overy LLP
7758-King Fahad Road
Olaya-Unit No. 3
4th floor, Al-Mada
Riyadh
12333-4187
Kingdom of Saudi Arabia
Tel. +966 (0)1 218 2900
Fax +966 (0)1460 0602

SINGAPORE
Singapore
Clifford Centre
Allen & Overy LLP
24 Raffles Place
#22-00 Clifford Centre
Singapore 048621
Tel. +65 6435 7400
Fax +65 6435 7474

SLOVAK REPUBLIC
Bratislava
Allen & Overy Bratislava, s.r.o.
Carlton Savoy Building
Mostová 2, 5th Floor
811 02 Bratislava
Slovak Republic
Tel. +421 2 5920 2400
Fax +421 2 5920 2424

SPAIN
Madrid
Allen & Overy
Pedro de Valdivia 10
28006 Madrid
Spain
Tel. +34 91 782 98 00
Fax +34 91 782 98 99

THAILAND
Bangkok
Allen & Overy (Thailand) Co., Ltd.
22nd Floor, Sindhorn Tower 3
130-132 Wireless Road
Lumpini, Pathumwan
Bangkok 10330
Thailand
Tel. +66 (0)2 263 7600
Fax +66 (0)2 263 7699

UNITED ARAB EMIRATES
Abu Dhabi
Allen & Overy LLP
5th Floor
Al Mamoura Building B
Muroor Road
PO Box 7907
Abu Dhabi
United Arab Emirates
Tel. +971 (0)2 418 0400
Fax +971 (0)2 418 0499

Dubai
Allen & Overy LLP
Level 2
The Gate Village Building No. 8
Dubai International Financial Centre
PO Box 506678
Dubai
United Arab Emirates
Tel. +971 (0)4 426 7100
Fax +971 (0)4 426 7199

UNITED KINGDOM
London
Bishops Square
Allen & Overy LLP
One Bishops Square
London
E1 6AD
United Kingdom
Tel. +44 (0)20 3088 0000
Fax +44 (0)20 3088 0088

London
Canary Wharf
Allen & Overy LLP
40 Bank Street
London
E14 5DU
United Kingdom
Tel. +44 (0)20 3088 0000
Fax +44 (0)20 3088 0088

UNITED STATES OF AMERICA
New York
Allen & Overy LLP
1221 Avenue of the Americas
New York, NY 10020
United States of America
Tel. +1 212 610 6300
Fax +1 212 610 6399

DUTCH BUSINESS LAW SERIES

1. Marieke van Hooijdonk and Peter Eijsvoogel, *Litigation in the Netherlands: Civil Procedure, Arbitration and Administrative Litigation*, 2009 (ISBN 978-90-411-2855-3)

2. Ferdinand B.J. Grapperhaus and Leonard G. Verburg, *Employment Law and Works Councils of the Netherlands*, 2009 (ISBN 978-90-411-2858-4)

3. Bas Jennen and Niels van de Vijver, *Banking and Securities Regulation in the Netherlands*, 2010 (ISBN 978-90-411-2863-8)